THE PROFESSOR GAME

By Richard D. Mandell

ISBN: 0-385-11156-8
Library of Congress Catalog Card Number 76–23780
Copyright © 1977 by Richard D. Mandell
Printed in the United States of America
First Edition

to
E.E.K.M.

Contents

THE PROFESSOR GAME

Introduction

In 1900 there were about 250,000 American university students. Today, the City University of New York alone has more than that number of students. And the CUNY system, the third largest university system in America, is but one—although the biggest—casualty of America's recently and badly eroded faith in higher education. This institution of more than 260,000 students and more than 15,000 professors on nineteen campuses is enduring massive retrenchments. Besides the slovenliness of New York's financial management these past twenty years, a critical error, it appears, was the succumbing of CUNY's professors and administrators to the expansive euphoria that affected all planning of higher education in the 1960s. City College, New York's "Harvard of the Proletariat" and the other colleges of the system opened their doors to much larger numbers of applicants in order to provide blacks, Puerto Ricans, and others with free tuition and a try for a college degree. The great university would no longer have a student body made up overwhelmingly of the energetic, well-prepared descendants of East European Jews. Like colleges and universities all over North America, CUNY expanded old campuses, constructed new ones, and hired lots of professors to staff them.

Now CUNY is contracting. Construction of the new facilities has ceased. A combination of traditionally lavish benefits (CUNY's professors on the job are still among the nation's best paid) and New York's expected persistent financial problems will assure that CUNY's troubles will resist any but drastic measures. The recent merging of some facilities, the shifting of part of the university's financing to the state and national fiscs, the imposition of tuition of almost a thousand dollars a year and the ending of "open admissions"—all of these necessary retreats are evidence that CUNY, like many American universities, had very quickly become too large and too costly. And it seems clear that CUNY, like most other American colleges and universities, still has too many professors.

In the spring of 1976 the history department at Queens College had forty-two members. In the fall of 1976 it had thirty members. Of the twelve laid off, none had tenure; three were women; one was black; most were in their twenties and thirties. Of those who remain, all have tenure; all but one is white; all but one is male; nearly all are in their forties and fifties. Barbara Malamet, a thirty-three-year-old historian, a native of New York with a B.A. from Vassar and a Ph.D. from Yale, who was on the Yale faculty for five years before coming to City College, is furious. "I'm indignant, because I came here because I wanted . . . to work with people who grew up in New York. I had just gotten a new contract at Yale. Now, to be kicked out without an academic judgment—by a computer or something tantamount to that—is outrageous."

Even those who have kept their jobs at one of CUNY's many campuses are demoralized due to insecurities. Many are unable to concentrate on their research. Some pour out their unhappiness with CUNY in the classroom. Most are fearful of enrollment drops in their classes—for these statistics are readily available figures that administrators are likely to employ for the next round of cuts.

For a while the delicious gossip was confined to a rather narrow group of New England academics. Then Nora Ephron published the detailed story in the September 1976 issue of *Esquire*. The clean-cut young president (she took the job in 1972 when she was twenty-nine years old) of Bennington College (a little over six hundred students; seventy-three professors) in Vermont was, while continuing to live with her husband, who was also vice-president of the college, shacking with a fifty-two-year-old English professor. She also ran about braless and in short skirts. While all this was going on, Gail Thain Parker was lecturing her faculty on the need for austerity and correct professorial behavior. Later many professors who resent any kind of female academics and many who fear college administrators of any sort, smacked their lips with relish when they read in the newspapers that Gail Parker and her husband, Tom, had been fired. Nora Ephron, however, revealed later that the fall of the Parkers was softened by a $110,000 settlement with Bennington's trustees.

So fine was the gossip and Nora Ephron's confirmation of it that it became possible to overlook that at little, tolerant Bennington the end of the Parker regime was not brought about by such pecadillos (in addition to those mentioned above) as Ms. Parker's didactically intended reading from satirical academic novels before faculty meetings, an imperious carriage, frequent speaking tours (a long article in *Ms.* had given her marketable visibility), the parking of the car of the English professor in question in front of the president's house overnight, her serving at parties of bad lasagna and unthawed Sara Lee banana cake. At most of the best little American colleges, eccentricity is expected. Though Gail Parker committed a large number of well-observed *faux pas,* what brought the Parkers down was their effort to impose a plan on the college that would be in keeping with the college's reputation as a fine, innovating school and in harmony with expected enrollment and financing in the years ahead. Most specifically, the Parkers sought to increase the student-faculty ratio from about eight to one to about nine to one, reducing the faculty by ten or so, to a little over sixty. To do this required some tampering with Bennington's regulations regarding tenure. The professors on the job raised a ruckus (in the course of which the minor eccentricities of Gail Parker suddenly took on weight) against which the trustees were unable to hold fast. The Parkers had to go.

Another series of unpleasant shocks in the newspapers about the same time were revelations about the extent of cheating at West Point. In 1922 General Douglas MacArthur, then the institution's superintendent, formalized West Point's honor code and charged the cadets with enforcing it: "A cadet will not lie, cheat, or tolerate those who do." In 1951 a cheating scandal involving thirty-seven football players and fifty-three other cadets shook the academy to its foundations. Then, in 1976, 149 of the war college's cadets admitted their guilt as cheaters, but some of these claimed that 700, perhaps more, of the students now enrolled had cheated on exams at West Point. A questionnaire distributed among the cadets revealed widespread cynicism. Many cadets claimed that the honor code "inhibited personal growth and development." In the course of the testimony regarding cheating, Cadet Kenneth Curley revealed that West Point officials had very likely falsified his entrance scores so that Curley, a good athlete, could join West Point's lacrosse team. Comparable irregularities were common in order to assure that athletes or the sons of generals or of prominent politicians could enroll at West Point.

Many cadets blamed the breakdown in the honor code on the Army's own dishonesty: the My Lai massacre, falsified body counts in Viet Nam. Some mentioned Watergate.

These setbacks or revelations were all national news. A fearful apprehension, itself a manifestation of a more fundamental change in the way that most Americans regard their future, has already affected our colleges and universities. This same pervasive skepticism threatens to transform all of American higher education in the years ahead. Among the losers will be many of the 400,000 American professors to whom America has been so kind.

Irving Howe, himself a most productive and distinguished professor of English at Hunter College, remarked in a speech, ". . . the major residue of these contentious years seems disastrous: a rupture of ties, a breakdown of talk, a loss of coherence. The present moment is one of weariness, holding on to defenses, warding off attack from administrators and budget cutters; a moment perhaps unavoidably of marking time. There does not seem to be much sense of intellectual connection or purpose."

Evidence of deep insecurity can already be seen. One hard piece of depressing evidence is the abandoned deep hole in Manhattan at 68th Street and Lexington Avenue which was to house an $84-million project to unite the scattered, rented space of Hunter College. But $102 million in construction was also halted at City College and a $43-million project stopped at Herbert H. Lehman College in Brooklyn. Also at CUNY, professors in the department of educational psychology at the Queens campus are preoccupied with forecasting who will be the next of their number to be told (Barbara Malamet, the historian at Queens, got thirty days' notice) that his job has ended. Research has almost ceased. The younger professors of physical education at Brooklyn College draw up lists predicting the order of layoff and even lay little wagers on the results. The state of Georgia has ceased hiring new professors or giving those on hand any raises. Layoffs may be imminent. A cleaning woman who has worked at the Athens campus of the University of Georgia told a young professor of sociology that Gelusil wrappers and Pepto-Bismol bottles are regular items in the trash of the faculty bathrooms. She first began seeing such things about three years ago.

Whereas professors ten years ago could feel gratified that at last American society was giving them the recognition and rewards they deserved as the discoverers, preservers, and communicators of culture, professors now on the job endure a disintegrating confidence in the future. A formerly affable tenured historian of a large campus of the State University of New York system now avoids the younger members of his department. He reports that they are no longer capable of talking about the writing or the teaching of history. All they are concerned about is who will be chopped when the chopping comes—as it very likely must. "They give me nervous headaches," he says; "I keep my office door closed."

The faculty of the Irvine campus of the University of California is typical in that they notice there are now fewer and smaller parties. A professor of biology reports, "After the duty parties we used to separate in high spirits. Now, several may get drunk and abusive, or not even drunk, but still generally abusive. Their indignation or resentment comes out. It used to be easier to ignore bad manners. People carry grudges longer now."

The collapse of the academic job market has produced despair among those bright and energetic new Ph.D.'s who began preparing for professorial careers five or ten years ago. With wistful nostalgia, professors now on the job recall tales from the annual conventions of their various disciplines of 1965 or 1966. When one of those conventions ended, an almost Ph.D. from Berkeley or UCLA might complain, "Only three decent offers—one in Connecticut and two in the Midwest. I'm going to the Chicago Circle campus because the money's good and they're giving me a year of almost no teaching so I can finish the dissertation. But dammit, I wanted to stay on the coast!" A memorable quote from a still jobless participator in the Modern Language Association's meeting of December 1975 was from a new Ph.D. without hope who moaned, "I can read classical Greek. Doesn't anyone care?"

Many Americans are now questioning the worth of the professors who were hired during the happy years. Academic administrators at all levels are being forced to come up with some measures of accountability regarding professorial work in order to explain to the various constituencies of American professors just what the product of professorial work might be. Everyone agrees that professors are supposed to teach. They probably should teach energetically and well. But what else are they supposed to do? Are they supposed to do research? Don Harrell, a former English professor at the University of Arkansas, got editorial-page space—"Publish or Perish: I'm Glad

I'm Out"—in the New York *Times* in August 1976. Harrell wrote, "The bulk of what passes for scholarship in the big leagues does not need to be written, underwritten, published or read. Many of those [researching or publishing] will admit they're involved not out of commitment to the topic, but because of the dean's policy of up or out." Yet in a recent statistical survey of the work and life styles of American professors, Seymour Lipset and Everett C. Ladd, Jr., determined that even in the famous research universities long committed to "publish or perish" most professors publish little, and among the American professoriate as a whole, only 4 per cent are "heavily committed" to research. "American academics constitute a teaching profession, not a scholarly one," Lipset and Ladd reveal. But how much or how well do the professors teach? No one knows, because teaching until now has not lent itself to even the faulty and biased measurements that research does. We do know, however, that during the higher-education boom of the 1960s, as the salaries of professors almost doubled, teaching "loads" (that is, the numbers of hours professors teach per week) fell by half.

Professorial work remains inaccessible to examination. But for how much longer? It has been the case and remains so that almost all the statistical information we have about professorial work is based on questionnaires for which the sampled professors alone provide the answers. And these answers are never checked. Significantly, the efforts of some states to look closely into the work of public professorial employees arouses defensive pride and paranoia among the professors. In the state of Alabama, where Governor George Wallace (despite his antiprofessorial pose) has, until very recently, lavishly financed higher education of every sort, groups of professors obtained a court injunction against snoops. "We really felt bad about that," said Melvin G. Cooper, Executive Director of the State Ethics Commission, "because we thought that of all the groups our professors should be the first to step forward and encourage honesty in government."

Here and there universities come into the news because of consumer cases against irresponsible teachers and administrators. Ilene Ianniello, a senior, filed a suit against the University of Bridgeport for a return of $150 in tuition, the cost of her books, and legal fees. A required course in secondary education was "worthless." All Ms. Ianniello was taught was how to use an overhead projector. The only requirement was to write a book report, and all the students got A's.

Washington University in St. Louis agreed to return Veronika Nicolas's tuition when she took the university to court after she dropped out of a landscape-architecture course that was "pure junk."

Representative John Gower, a legislator in Wisconsin, has introduced a bill to increase teaching loads at the state's public colleges and universities. His "teach or perish" bill would require that during their eight-month work year, professors at the "doctoral" campuses teach eleven hours. At the two-year campuses the minimum would be fourteen hours. Several Wisconsin legislators have also suggested an audit of certain academic programs to determine how well they are meeting their goals.

College teaching in America is not likely to lend itself to specific examination. By growing agreement, the staggering outlays in the past twenty years on higher education have probably not produced a raising in the level of public taste. It does seem certain that the great increase in the number of college degrees awarded has led to a decrease in their usefulness or, more specifically, their use in obtaining a very good job. In a study written for the Carnegie Commission on Higher Education, an organization well known for its yea-saying, regarding colleges and universities, Paul Taubman and Terance Wales have concluded that, though college-educated persons earn more than their less-educated counterparts, their training has accounted for but little of the difference in earnings. About half of the difference is due to the fact that employers controlling access to high-paying jobs use educational credentials as a cheap screening device. Analyzing higher education as an investment, the authors conclude also that ability is a more important determinant of income and that the effect of ability grows over time.

The conclusions of Caroline Bird in her provocatively titled *The Case Against College* are less gently put. She uses the fictive example of a student who considers alternatives to attendance at a good college for four years where a B.A. would cost $22,256 for tuition, room and board, and personal expenses. After suggesting other uses for so much time and so much money, she concludes that "college is the dumbest investment you can make." At the end of an article-length adaption from her book published in *Esquire* in September 1974, "Joe," the student, goes to Princeton anyway, because it "sounds like a nice place to be for the next four years."

That is not a solid justification for such an outlay and for such a long time. Elsewhere the criticisms of higher education are increasing in number and in intensity. Such somber appraisals have rarely appeared before and were inconceivable during the era of high euphoria which was so brief and which ended just a few short years ago—though to the professors the golden years now seem far more distant in time than that.

The chapters that follow are mostly about American academic life now—that is, well away from the great campus boom of the 1960s. The total number of American professors is now close to 400,000, if one includes the more than 50,000 teachers in our two-year "junior" or "community" colleges. This book is about all of them. So far, serious American writing and almost all journalism on American academic life has concentrated on the small number of professors with newsy profiles at a few high-quality institutions where working conditions and the intellectual atmosphere are exceptional. The few thousand professors at Yale, Columbia, Chicago, Vassar, Swarthmore, and places like them will be subjects of this book mostly in the historical chapters and as they are objects of envy for those beneath them.

The lives of college professors have been greatly altered in the past fifteen years or so. The great campus boom that began in the late 1950s gave us more and larger campuses to accommodate the tripling of college enrollments. For a while there was an unprecedented demand for additional college teachers. Professorial morale was high. As the higher education boom went on in the late 1960s, the statutory demands for professorial work decreased steadily, wages doubled, and other perquisites improved also. Professorial work became more delightful than ever, and there were many more professors to enjoy it.

The greater attractiveness of professorial work was a consequence of the complete and uncritical adoption by almost all Americans of certain myths regarding the usefulness of the various degrees received when one finished at a college or university. People in and out of academia accepted a common explanation for our injustice, inefficiency, and vulgarity: only a few of America's youths were exposed to a humane, well-rounded education. Americans of any sort have scarcely ever doubted that more education, particularly more education of the most expensive kind, would lead those young adults offered it to work better, live better, and vote better, thus improving the lives of all of us.

For professors on the job or on the make, the great campus boom was glorious while it lasted. By the middle and later seventies almost half of the Americans of college age were getting to put in a few years at some (usually lovely) campus or other. But despite the lavish financing and staffing given to the American colleges and universities, the support seems to have improved little aside from the colleges and universities themselves. When they were much less common, bachelor's degrees may have brought with them promises of a leg up in the various white-collar and professional job markets. Now the mediocre bachelor's degree is an all too common commodity. It seems clear to many people, professors included, that we might have come up with several other means of occupying the time of many of our youths. The kinds of service the professors are trained to offer are not suitable for everyone.

The professors themselves share the general cultural disillusionment. They resent the pressure to approve by means of good course grades the badly prepared, lazy, and insensitive students who appear in large numbers before them. But the professors know very well that they depend upon those students and a steady supply of students in the years ahead in order to preserve their perquisites, their security, and their numbers.

This book, while being sympathetic with the disappointments and apprehensions of the American professors, will also be (I weighed the next word long and carefully) disrespectful. Though the failures of the colleges and universities can hardly be attributed to the professors alone, many of them are lazy and arrogant. Most professors continue to deceive their various constituencies and themselves regarding their performance as teachers, as researchers, as colleagues, and as servants of the larger society. The whole academic community has long and successfully maintained curtains of misinformation that hide what professors actually accomplish in order to pick up their (usually substantial) checks. The profession is remarkably free of standards or strictures to determine or enforce merit.

A great deal has already been written by professors about professors, and I have employed a lot of it in this book. However, this book about professors is exceptional in that the intended audience is not composed of professors themselves. Parents about to subsidize their eighteen-year-olds for four years may be eager to have some notions as to what they are about to receive for their outlays for tuition and the payment of other expenses. College students might be able to use some of the information in this book in order to get something closer to their money's worth in the way of personal attention, grades, and, conceivably, instruction and inspiration. A legitimate question for taxpayers and legislators to pose is whether a professor at a state university ought to earn from fifty to a hundred dollars or more (sometimes much more) for each hour he teaches.

An audience that I particularly have in mind is composed of ambitious people who are now graduate students or who may be considering work for the advanced academic degrees that for a few happy years in the sixties were admission tickets to professorial employment. In these unsettled times, ever greater numbers of intelligent malcontents plan to forsake the routine of life in the customary working and consuming world to submit themselves to years of discipline in graduate school. They envy the incumbent professors to whom America has been so kind. Many, many more than could conceivably be accommodated yearn for a career allowing the life of the mind to be so nicely integrated into a daily routine in such pleasant, stimulating surroundings. For, when compared with other choices of career, professoring is still so appealing as to be virtually above the contest with alternative kinds of employment. However, many (indeed very many) professor-aspirants have already failed in their struggle to get the Ph.D. and/or consequent job in our parklike campuses. They may feel that their disappointments were due not to faults of their own but to others. And they have received only mystifications from their professors as to what went wrong.

Everyone in academic life today is certain that graduate training in the years ahead will become yet more rigorous and studded with pitfalls. Prospects of respectable employment for impeccably degreed and eager-to-please Ph.D.'s have never been more bleak. The great boom of the 1960s carried with it the seeds of the present disillusionment. The reasons for grim prospects for academic employment will be exposed in the course of the narrative. I will also describe the apprehensions of the apparently lucky ones now working as professors. They are less happy in their jobs than they may seem to be.

If the main object of the book is to describe professorial work and life, objects along the way are to explain what is meant and what is revealed by insiders' terms that occasionally reach the newspapers or the ears of the wider public. So I will use parentheses containing a brief definition after the first appearance of such terms as "tenure," "teaching load," "seminar," and "publish or perish."

Besides dwelling on the professors' ambitions and fears, the book will also describe some aspects of professors' daily lives which are closely integrated with and, indeed, difficult to separate abruptly from their work. I will tell secrets, cite some rarely published statistics, describe some privileged rituals, and expose the occupational hazards of professoring to curious outsiders.

The book is most unusual in that, though on a topic that must be classified as nonfiction, it incorporates fictional sketches of five professors—each of whom lives a typical day in his or her different occupational surroundings. I have incorporated these "illustrations" or "days-in-the-life-of" because I could come up with no other way to be both sympathetic and pitilessly revealing. If these characters existed (and, of course, they do not!), they could not have exposed their attitudes toward their students, their research, and their communities without destroying the economic and social bases of their existences. The five character sketches are included as inserts to be considered as illustrations in prose. They might as well have been included as appendixes or as a supplement. These professorial days might be separately read before, after, or during the reading of the nonfictional bulk of the book. However, the text provides a universe for the characters, and the characters are intended to illustrate the text. I have also incorporated some fictional sketches in the later chapters of the book.

I

A Little Bit of History

Education has always been a precious acquisition, and those who offer it have always had a privileged place in society.

The modern reader should be reminded that large schools and the great *systems* of education are new under the sun. Education has almost always been offered and absorbed in small, isolated groups. The group could be as small as a tutor and a pupil, or smaller—a seeker of knowledge and a book. The schemes devised by the Greek philosophers called for a teacher with a few youths seated about him. Medieval universities were independent of secular governing authorities and rarely had a faculty of more than a few dozen. Even in early twentieth century America, which produced the first very large primary, secondary, and postsecondary schools, a university with more than a hundred professors was unknown before 1900.

Thus, until very recently, there was not much distinction between teachers and administrators and little difference between the teachers and the taught. The rector of a medieval university or the president of an old-time American college was the first among equals and his function was to maintain authority, not to co-ordinate specialties. At universities in premodern times the pupils were very young, and it was expected that their teachers would provide, in addition to knowledge, discipline and moral guidance when serving as proxies for the absent parents.

The rather popular notion that educational communities exist solely to impart knowledge may be due to the durable prestige of some educational experiments that took place in ancient Athens. The educational theorists of antiquity *did* pursue knowledge as an end in itself. And long after it was a dusty, ruined city, Athens lived on in the myth-making minds of teachers as a sweet paradise where the masters and scholars were priests and acolytes of investigative thought. Plato's shaded site for talking and teaching was called the "Academy," from which we have made other words to distinguish modern college and university life.

The word "university" comes from the Latin *universitas,* which in the Middle Ages was applied to many groups that had special purposes. The ancestors of our great institutions were first called *universitates magistorum et scholorum,* meaning guilds or unions of "masters" and of "scholars." The teachers and scholars often were strangers in the city to which they moved to pursue their studies. They banded together for protection against gouging merchants and disrespectful townies. A famous university drew students from afar; some from a distant area might live together in guarded, self-contained residences called "colleges." In the University of Bologna there would be "colleges" for Spaniards, for Englishmen, and for other groups.

What the masters in the universities offered to those who applied, paid the fees, stayed a few years, and passed various tests was, then as now, difficult to specify, but very valuable to those who acquired it. For centuries all formal education in Europe was ostensibly religious education. The Church needed disciplined, lettered men to explain the scripture. The great Church, being a bureaucracy, also needed letter-writers, chroniclers, managers, and accountants. As European society became wealthier and more politically organized, governments and businessmen also needed disciplined, lettered men and recruited them from the universities.

It has always been the case, even in the rigid society of ancient China, that the educational system provided a means by which lowly born, clever men could rise outside of the caste system. Warrior aristocrats have typically scorned learning, preferring instead the more accessible pleasures of seduction, drink, the tournament, and the hunt. That ambitious rulers gave special privileges to the teachers at their universities indicated not only their piety but also that they expected as products of the universities loyal, dependent technicians and administrators, who were unavailable from the titled and gilded nobility.

As always, the vast majority of those who devoted their lives to imparting higher education did so not only out of respect for their subject matter but also in order to raise their station in life. Then as now, just what the service *is* that one delivers in a university is difficult to display or demonstrate in any vivid, concrete fashion. So scholars, and especially teachers, devised titles, ceremonies, and distinguished badges in order to establish their status and to equate their position with those of the priests and the well-born. These distinctions were comparable to the rituals and visible symbols that all societies use to distinguish the privileged from the herd. Very early in the history of the university, teachers and scholars struggled for and obtained exemptions from the laws governing the common people and even the nobility and the clergy. As early as 1158 the emperor Frederick Barbarossa offered scholars protection on their journeys and certain compensations for injuries. In the medieval towns scholars were guaranteed good housing at fair prices, redress for exorbitant charges, and even protection against disturbing noises and smells. Members of the university community have always been rather free to devise their own curricula and rites of passage.

An overarching task of the university has always been to regenerate itself by turning out more teachers, who were called "masters." A master's status was arrived at by passing a series of examinations, by enduring a ceremony, and, finally, by receiving a certificate. A "bachelor" was merely a candidate for the teaching degree. To get a master's degree or the later doctor's degree (which evolved to become in English usage the "Master of Arts" and the "Doctor of Philosophy"—"M.A." and "Ph.D.," respectively), one had to give an inaugural lecture and otherwise demonstrate to properly titled and degreed superiors the absorption of a body of knowledge and the assumption of competence. There were always ceremonies, as there were among the priests, to indicate the change in status. A degree was called a *facultas ubique docenti* ("the ability to teach anywhere"). The phrase evolved into "faculty," which is now applied to the teaching staff of a particular university.

Long before there was an American college or university, there were dozens of universities from Sweden to Sicily, and from Warsaw to Ireland. They discovered, preserved, and advanced knowledge. The teachers at these places were alike in that they were men of God who had an academic vocation that was obviously and legally different from an occupation that was simply clerical. They corresponded with one another and conversed in Latin, everywhere the language of instruction until the sixteenth century. Though in most cases the monetary rewards for the academic profession were meager, the masters were granted compensatory prestige and recognition.

Once a man had adapted the rhythms of his life to the discipline of long study and had survived the horror of the examinations and the search for a teaching job, his position was usually secure and the work was interesting and healthy.

The wealth, vigor, and status of the universities were different in various parts of Europe. In Italy, where the first universities flourished in the eleventh and twelfth centuries, they later languished and the Renaissance occurred apart from them. In France the universities stultified under powerful state rulers in the fourteenth and later centuries. In politically fragmented Germany the many universities prospered, but were often subject to the whims of the local secular rulers who subsidized them. The two great English universities were unique in many ways. They were located far from the centers of political power in the lovely countryside. Since their sumptuous wealth was based largely on private benefactions, they were able to maintain quasi-independent roles despite political and religious upheavals. For centuries they furnished education and certain common experiences to the elite who were to run the nation. It was their earlier educations at Oxford and Cambridge which led some English Puritans to establish the first American college in the woods near Boston. The legislative act providing for the charter of Harvard College was passed on October 28, 1636.

Though living far from the mother country, the founders of Harvard and the subsequent colonial colleges were not merely re-creating a bit of English life. As was to be the case with the dutiful founders of hundreds of American colleges, they were preparing for the future. The land before them would need competent rulers and, of course, a learned clergy. The subtle and uncompromisable sectarian differences between the immigrants to America meant that there would be a variety of mutually exclusive ways to produce learned clergymen. The second American college, Anglican William and Mary, was founded in 1693 in Williamsburg. Yale was chartered in 1701 and settled in New Haven in 1716. Presbyterian Princeton was chartered in 1746. By 1776 there were nine American colleges. All, except for their supporting denominations, followed English models. The colleges were all essential to reinforce the proper moral precepts in the American elite and to demonstrate the separation of the American upper class from raw nature and barbarism.

The curriculum and the general tone of the American college were not much different in 1776 than they had been a century before or would be a century later. The beginning students were always male, anywhere from twelve to twenty years of age, and were expected to have some Latin and Greek—though from the very beginning most American colleges offered remedial work for deficiencies. The teaching method was rote memorization, the recitation of classical literary texts, and a passionate defense of the appropriate theological doctrines. Chapel attendance was compulsory twice daily. Training was ethical, not intellectual. The colleges were small. A large enrollment was a hundred—most had much less. Naturally the administrative structure was simple. The president, who was customarily a minister of the college's denomination, usually taught the senior class a yearlong course in moral philosophy. His wife was often expected to cook or otherwise manage the domestic affairs of the college. The teachers were called tutors.

A tutor's existence was not comfortable. The tutors lived with and endured the mischievousness and contempt of the pupils, who were usually of a higher station in life. The drill that teaching consisted of was of a most elemental sort. The tutors in the early colleges were the earliest victims of an enduring principle of American higher education—that the teachers themselves should be philanthropists.[1] It was expected not only that the teachers should force upon the students restriction and instruction, but also that they must, by their own low pay, subsidize the students' four-year reprieve from the necessity of earning a living.

Americans were the most wholehearted embracers of eighteenth-century rational philosophy and have always been irrationally optimistic about the products of an educational environment. On the other hand, they have always planned for education badly. Though there were only nine colonial colleges, by the beginning of the Civil War as many as 700 colleges had been founded, of which about 250 survived in 1861 and 180 survive still. It is significant that the little settlements surrounding the colleges were often named "Athens." As early as 1795, the trustees of Princeton, in applying for aid from the state legislature, declared that they wished to make New Jersey the Athens of America. The University of Georgia is still in "Athens." It was pointed out in 1880 that England, with a population of 23 million, was getting along with four universities, while Ohio, with a population of 3 million, had thirty-seven institutions of higher learning.[2]

Nearly always there have been more waiting places in the American colleges than there were students to occupy them, a condition that has rarely been the case elsewhere in the world. Those colleges survived which were consistently successful in attracting and holding students. One result of this quest for students has been that in America admissions requirements and academic demands are expected to be sufficiently lax not to frighten the wavering. But this has not been enough. In order to achieve the enrollment that justified their existence, the competing colleges could not possibly charge the students what the education actually cost. In America it has long been assumed that the various religious organizations and government bodies would by grants, tax exemptions, and in other ways support a minimally prepared late adolescent of the middle class through four years at a college or university. The role of private philanthrophy has been, in the aggregate, small and has been decreasing steadily since about 1900. Even when they were very low, faculty salaries have been the major expense for a college or university. The chief philanthropists of American higher education have been the teachers who were and are not expected to aspire to the living standards enjoyed by other professionals.

In most of the nineteenth century high academic salaries ranged from $1,500 to $3,000 per year, but much more usual salaries in the 1850s and 1860s at second-ranked schools were from $600 to $800 per year. Colleges struggling to stay solvent (a usual, not an unusual plight) cut salaries or held pay in arrears with promises for eventual redemption in order to hold on to the faculty.

This nasty situation was often defended by trustees or governing boards who claimed that luxury and learning were odd bedfellows. However, it has always been true that American academic life offered substantial, nonpecuniary income. Though they were considered passive employees by the businessmen who came increasingly to dominate governing boards, the nearly sacerdotal status of college teachers accorded them outward measures of respect. The academic year customarily lasted roughly thirty weeks, and the professor (a title that college teachers gradually assumed late in the nineteenth century) could enjoy the verdure and oxygenation that customarily surrounded the college site. Perhaps professors and students have always enjoyed one another despite the discipline from one side, the pranks from the other. In any case, there has almost never been a shortage of applicants for college teaching jobs. Indeed, enduring characteristics of American college and university life have been that students were undercharged and professors were underpaid and that, despite these facts, there have not been enough of the former and have been too many of the latter. The brief exception to these historic principles is the topic of the next chapter.

Though hundreds of American colleges followed the railroads and speckled the continent, they were often little more than places of incarceration for young men aspiring to membership in the elite class. The resident students learned gentility and rudiments of Greek and Latin literature, and were indoctrinated into some variety of Protestant factionalism. In 1870 roughly 50,000 young men (and a very few young women) between the ages of eighteen and twenty-two were enrolled in American institutions. This number was roughly 1.7 per cent of the Americans of that age group—a large percentage by European standards.

However, since such undertakings were not their object in the first place, the old-time colleges were far from satisfying the technical or professional needs of the larger American society. And at the same time the colleges fell dismally short of the demands for scholarly rigor and originality that certain American intellectuals had been asking for. The founding years of the great American universities began shortly after the end of the Civil War. However, little of the impetus for change came from the professors themselves.

Some impulses for reform had been around in the form of aborted proposals for decades. Many of the changes (similar to the expansion following the return of the GIs after 1945) were due to the sharp increase in critical and motivated students after the war of 1860–65 ended. The most far-reaching changes reflected the expanding wealth, confidence, and complexity of American cultural life in what has been called the "gilded age."

Until the later nineteenth century the American college resisted the pressure to become open and more responsive. In the 1820s Thomas Jefferson would have his new University of Virginia be nonsectarian and offer modern languages, mathematics, and the sciences. Students would be allowed to elect their course of study. The Jeffersonian university would award the M.A. for additional academic work beyond the four-year course. Significantly, when Jefferson recruited four Englishmen and a German for his faculty, he aroused the hostility of the press for insulting the American people. A few of the reforms that Jefferson had envisioned were put into effect at Virginia, but they were not imitated elsewhere.

By the later nineteenth century botany, chemistry, French, German, modern history, and English literature had worked their way into the curricula of most colleges, but they were considered distinctly inferior to rote learning of the classics and the ethical instruction that were assumed under the broad heading of "moral philosophy." The colleges were expected to turn out statesmen, lawyers, clergymen, physicians, and college teachers. Until long after the Civil War it was expected that engineers, financiers, scientific farmers, architects, public-school teachers, and editors would get all their training on the job. Yet America's enormous and potential wealth and energy required more and better-trained specialists than either the little colleges or informal training could provide.

The so-called Morrill acts of 1862 and 1890 were attempts on the part of the federal government to incite the states to found institutions that would meet more urgent practical needs. Each state received public lands the income from which was to be used to establish at least one college "where the leading object shall be, without excluding other scientific or classical studies, to teach such branches of learning as are related to agriculture and the mechanic arts." But the states procrastinated. Curiously, the models for making the new state institutions responsive came from wealthy private institutions. The inspiration for flexibility and service came largely from two great educators: Charles W. Eliot (1834–1926) of Harvard and Andrew Dickson White (1832–1918) of Cornell.

Eliot's permanent impact on the American university was immense and complex, but much can be attributed to his insistence upon the elective principle. During his forty-year presidency of Harvard, which he assumed in 1869, course offerings at Harvard were continuously expanded and graduation requirements relaxed. The sciences and other new disciplines were made equal in status to the old subjects. The results were extraordinary. By 1909 Harvard's faculty had expanded from sixty to six hundred and the endowment from $2 million to $20 million. One of Eliot's first acts as president was to increase salaries from $3,000 (already double a decent academic salary at the time) to $4,000. He was able quickly to assemble a galaxy of great teachers and scholars, who attracted still more of their kind. The new, freer, richer, and very much bigger Harvard also provided a joyous atmosphere for professorial work. The stimulating intellectual atmosphere was one result of improved working conditions which also included provisions for sabbatical leave and for exchange professorships with France and Germany. That great institution inspired changes in other American universities, and Harvard quickly reached a pre-eminence in American academic life which has never since been threatened.

The American university which most inspired the developing service schools in the Middle West and the West was Andrew White's Cornell University. Cornell was chartered in 1865 and opened in 1868 as a result of the gift of Ezra Cornell of $500,000 and two hundred acres of land in Ithaca, New York. Cornell University also used funds supplied by the Morrill Act. Like Eliot, White sought out lively teachers and, to hold them, provided freedom, dignity, and perquisites. He ignored religious affiliations in awarding professorships. He traveled to Europe to hire famous scholars and to purchase the scientific equipment they needed for their instruction and research. He started the first programs in American history, electrical engineering, and sociology. That last subject included lectures on topics such as crime, poverty, alcoholism, and insanity. The nonsectarianism, the looseness of student behavior (White once allowed dancing at a Founders' Day celebration), and the easy absorption of new disciplines made White's Cornell a target for vituperative conservatives. However, the notorious growth of Cornell, and then later the expansion of the Universities of Michigan, Wisconsin, and Minnesota along similar lines, suggested that there were intimate, mutually reinforcing relationships between freedom and distinction that a devotion to training useful specialists also attracted private benefactions, regular state subsidies, and, of course, that without-which-nothing of modern academic life, ever larger yearly installments of freshmen students.

Besides the purposes of preparing national and local elites and a devotion to service, a third great endeavor of the modern American university, that of research, was inspired by traveling American intellectuals who had been impressed with the prestige and independence of the German university professors.

After about 1840 small and then growing numbers of Americans interested in advanced training in philology, history, and, most especially, the sciences had gone to sojourn at the well-subsidized, revived universities in Germany. They returned enchanted with what they believed was "pure" learning and very often the phrase "scientific research" tumbled from their lips.[3] Many of these men subsequently entered American academic life and were able to suggest worthy projects for benefactors eager to monumentalize them-

selves by university endowments. Johns Hopkins of Baltimore died
in 1873 and left his $7-million fortune to a group of men who
wished to establish a university devoted mostly to study on German
models, that is graduate study beyond the B.A. degree and advanced
research. The fame of this innovating institution would be much
greater today if its early notoriety had not caused it to be so widely
and quickly imitated. Eliot's Harvard, as well as Yale, Chicago, the
University of California, and, subsequently, any place that wished to
dignify itself with the term "university," had to devote much of its
energies to graduate training and the publication of its novel findings.

Many Hopkins firsts passed quickly into respectable American
practice. The faculty expected good wages. Ever more after about
1900 the basis of a university's prestige was not to be rough esti-
mates of the moral impact the professors had on the many children
in their care but the research they were to publish on their own or
what they were able to inspire in those fledgling scholars and scientists in their care. Hopkins simplified the customary methods of subsidizing students by offering the first graduate fellowships. At the
same time that the lecture was becoming the usual method of undergraduate instruction in the reformed university, Hopkins pioneered
in the "seminar," wherein the professor met with small groups, usually numbering five to ten, of advanced students, who would criticize
each other's research and the published research of distant scholars.
To disseminate the findings of the research departments and to raise
yet further the university's prestige, Hopkins began publication of the
first American scholarly periodicals, the *American Chemical Journal,*
which began in 1879, and *The American Journal of Philology,* which
started in 1880. These pioneer efforts (modeled after the already
venerable journals published by the various European royal academies) led to dozens more subsidized journals and series of research
reports published not only by Hopkins but by institutions that
thereby demonstrated their enthusiasm for a salient object of the
universities on a new American model. The very high value placed
on original research meant, of course, that professors, in order to
demonstrate that they were indeed professors on the new model, had
to prove they were producing research results by publishing them.
And to accommodate the ambitious professors who had now to publish to earn respect and more tangible rewards, scholarly journals and
university presses proliferated steadily, until in America in 1975

there were more than two hundred journals and scholarly series and seventy-seven university presses.

The rapid elevation of research to be considered the noblest pursuit of a university and of the professors in it was complete in the leading American universities by about 1914. The epoch of American ebullience lasting from about 1890 to about 1914 was also a great period of university boosterism. Colleges in order to assume the name "university" not only had to attract students but had to give hard evidence that they favored research. Several new universities, including Clark, Chicago, and Stanford, were established on the new model. After 1890 the leading universities were run by men resembling the equally dynamic captains of industry, and university presidents watched one another in order to keep up. Besides those thousands of large and small scholarly and scientific publications that were only the most obvious evidence of profound changes for the professors, there were changes in their titles of address, new notions of what proper teaching should be, and much greater professional pride.

There were only six endowed professorships in America before 1776. For decades afterward, only that distinguished person who enjoyed the income from an endowment set up to subsidize just that special "chair" might legitimately be called a professor. Then, in the leading universities, it was learned that the title "professor" was easy to bestow and provided satisfaction in an occupation that draws psychic income from insubstantialities. By 1900 Harvard, Columbia, Cornell, Chicago, Michigan, and Wisconsin had more or less established the patterns to be followed by others for many decades. Lecturer or instructor was a beginning rank. There were three ranks of professor—assistant, associate, and full. The last adjective stays in lower case because it was not spoken or written in formal communication, the holder of the position being addressed simply as "Professor."

Until the reforms after the Civil War, the only earned American degree was the Bachelor of Arts (B.A.) which was awarded at a public ceremony marking the completion of a four-year course. Several American colleges awarded the "Master of Arts" to a gentleman who had previously earned the B.A., had stayed out of jail for three years or so, and paid a fee to cover the cost of the diploma. There were several attempts besides that of Jefferson to use the M.A. to certify advanced study. Yale awarded the first "Doctor of Philosophy" in 1861. By 1876, when Johns Hopkins was set up for advanced scholarly or scientific training on the German model, twenty-five institutions were offering the Ph.D. Soon the necessary initials for a proper professor of the very best kind were "Ph.D." after his name. Reforming university presidents purged undegreed professors to hire new Ph.D.s and thus tart up their catalog and their images. By its fiftieth anniversary in 1926 Johns Hopkins was a smaller Ph.D. factory than several other universities, but it could still locate 1,000 of its 1,400 graduates on college and university faculties.

Though in essence the Ph.D. was the recognition only of research proficiency and accomplishment, it was also a license to get a good university job that presumably required one to teach. Certain consequences have remained with us: an American drama repeated thousands of times every fall has been that of the newly hired university teacher dumped before expectant undergraduate students. These teachers may have only their own student memories to guide them. The new teachers were themselves students of a very different sort than the ones they are now paid to teach. The students with whom they may have had some contact as teaching assistants in the great graduate schools are very different from those they confront in the provinces. The certified researchers were probably enchanted by their specialties long ago, and submitted to three to ten years of precious training that has deepened and narrowed their professional interests. Inevitably there is a chasm between the professor's fascination with his research subject and the curiosity (if any) on the part of the youths he is presumably to instruct and inspire. The now solidly institutionalized nature of the training of the American professoriat has institutionalized the latent scorn and distrust between professors and the overwhelming majority of those they are paid to educate.

The offhand attitude toward pedagogy of those gainfully employed in the Ph.D. system had another and calamitous result. America in the late nineteenth century really needed an intelligent scheme for preparing public-school teachers far more than it needed monument-studded landscapes upon which privileged youths could amuse themselves while researchers called professors trained more researchers. The very low standards of the old-time American college were due to their superfluity and the prolonged weakness of American primary and secondary education. As the American university took its modern form, the university presidents, professors, and benefactors gave scant attention to teaching not only for undergraduates but, vastly more irresponsibly, to education for the masses. Yet local or state-wide educational systems were somehow being installed at the same time. Training for teachers and, more importantly, for teachers of teachers fell by default into the grip of of putative optimists and empire builders. The eighteenth-century orthodoxies of human improvability were shown to be wrong long before the still-prominent colleges of education were established. And the first generation of educationalists succeeded in establishing orthodoxies no one bothers to uproot. As pedagogy of any sort continued to be scorned as demeaning by professors who favored science and scholarship, the fast-moving teachers of teachers, who attached themselves to the growing universities, parodistically established their own elective system and standards of performance at the undergraduate and graduate levels. Graduate study in education, as in the humanities and sciences, requires a certain amount of credits, class attendance, examinations, and the qualificatory hurdle of a dissertation (as it was also called) and is capped by the award of a "Doctor of Education" (Ed.D.) degree. The fact that training in education remains a parody, and that professors in the scholarly and scientific disciplines know it, has kept the traditional professors steadfastly aloof from the enormous education-for-teachers industry. The educationalists still independently form their own orthodoxies and certain (and different) formal and informal requirements for *their* professors to be admitted to and advanced in that privileged community.

Some of the novelties in American colleges and universities during the gilded age can be attributed just to increases in their size. Until the middle 1970s American university enrollments increased at an average and rapid 5 per cent annual rate. Increasing American wealth and social mobility, the liberalization of the curricula, and devotion to service and research are all partial explanations of the growth. Another major explanation was the admission of women to higher education. Oberlin began coeducation when it admitted four women in 1837. There were several female "academies" before the opening of high-grade colleges at Vassar in 1865 and Smith and Wellesley in 1875. Cornell led in promoting coeducation. Then female enrollment increased very much more rapidly than that of males and by 1905 the percentage of women enrolled in colleges and universities was 40 per cent, a proportion that has varied little since that time.

A factor for growth that had complex causes but which can be stated rather starkly was that almost everyone knew that a college degree was valuable enough to pursue. The modern American university had absorbed areas of competence such as teacher training, engineering, business, dentistry, nursing, pharmacy, and librarianship which, before the adoption of the quasi-independent department as an administrative technique, had scarcely been professionalized at all. The bachelor's degree was on its way to being the admission credential for any occupation permitting a secure or bourgeois existence. And, of course, some B.A.'s were more valuable than others. A local B.A. was of value only locally. A B.A. from Princeton, Yale, or Columbia opened up grander economic and social vistas. Even before 1900 a youth could state frankly, "A degree from Harvard is worth money to me in Chicago."[4] Judicious, even cynical, selection of one's college and purposeful behavior once on the site became an American male's most effective means of jumping social barriers imposed by his birth. The era was also marked by the early admission of some ethnic Catholics, some Russian and Polish Jews, and a tiny number of Negroes to the socially prominent (and most useful) universities.

In 1905 about 240,000, or 4 per cent of the age group eighteen to twenty-two, were enrolled in American universities and colleges. By 1909 Columbia University had an enrollment of over 6,000; Harvard, Chicago, Michigan, Pennsylvania, and Cornell all had over 5,000. It may be noted that only one of these, Michigan, was a state university. Two thirds of the students were still in private institutions.

The splendor of a huge campus, enrollment in the thousands, and faculties numbering hundreds brought with them novelties. Friendly contacts between faculty and undergraduate students and, indeed, between faculty in one department and faculty in another department became exceptional. On an intellectual level, the various convenient compartments of knowledge that the university departments recognized and institutionalized had common origins with the grand encyclopedias, library classifications, and the great world's fairs. The departmental organization also made it facile for the university to graft on ever more areas for the discovery and diffusion of knowledge.

As in the ever-larger industrial empires that needed staffs of management specialists and white-collar bureaucrats, administrators were installed between those upon whom fell the responsibility for determining policy and the growing ranks of knowledge specialists and teachers. In academic life administrators were distinguished by academic titles: deans, provosts, chancellors, alumni affair officers. Each administrator had associates (a term taken from the professors), assistants, and clerical workers. As an organization, a university with an enrollment of 5,000 is very much different from one with 500 and really not much different from one with an enrollment of 50,000. The point is that universities have not changed much since 1914.

Professors are like other proud men in that they are apt to devise, in order to have an alternative to the crassness of actuality, a comfortable version of the good old days. According to many professors of the 1970s, academic standards have never been lower. This is not true. Few American students anywhere have ever been vitally interested in the subjects their professors researched and taught. In order to hold students from the attractions outside the classroom, the professors of the new university devised the technique which is the crudest acknowledgment of the barrier that subject matter sets up between professors and those they service professionally. This tactic, which is virtually unknown to English, French, and German universities (and is frowned upon in Canada as well), is the frequent, compulsory examination keyed to the rigid semester (now sometimes trimester) system and the credits of undergraduate accountancy. The snap quizzes, the midterm exams, and the final examinations which occur at least twice a year are habitual drills better suited to children (which the American student remains intellectually). However, they are absolutely necessary to reassure the professors that they are indeed always in command.

On the other hand, even if American universities were partially penal in character, the statutory requirements for evidence of sanctioned mental work were mild for faculty and students alike. We shall return to the faculty later. It seems clear that, until the 1950s, even at elite schools such as Harvard, Columbia, and Princeton, a diligent student studied from ten to fifteen hours a week. Most studied much less, if at all. All the standard means of cheating, including the purchased term paper, were invented at the same time that the reformed universities were becoming established. The honest "grind" was a social outcast. Among most students, those professors who were models of pedagogical conscientiousness were regarded on the campus with the notice one gave to large animals at a zoo. At the very time that the American professors were developing professional standards and their appropriate organizations, their students turned away from the professors and preferred the keen enjoyment of each other. There had been an elaborate extracurricular life in the old colleges that was manifested in debating clubs, religious revivals, secret societies, and informal sports. But these were merely cautious preparations for the maturing between 1890 and 1914 of Greek-letter fraternities, "class" (here meaning graduating class) spirit, intramural ("within the walls," or within the university) and intercollegiate sports.

For those students having the necessary social cachet and family money, membership in a Yale class between 1890 and 1920 meant admission to a deliriously happy caste, one of the most indulged groups of gilded youth that has ever graced the earth. The balls, football games, glee clubs, luxurious private dormitories, chorus girls, and open roadsters were only the more obvious manifestations of a four-year period of intense, ceremonialized friendship. Graduation, which, considering the academic standards of the time, was difficult to avoid, was not an accomplishment but a tragedy, for it meant the dismissal from paradise. One seeks in vain in the novels of F. Scott Fitzgerald for evidence that college life was in any way demanding in academic terms.

The professors and most university presidents (but not the alumni) opposed most of these extraneous developments, but since the terms of their employment depended on enrollments and benefactions, they had to consent to the rich growth of ancillary attractions. Nowhere was the powerlessness of the new professors more apparent than in the astonishing growth of intercollegiate sport. There has not yet been a satisfactory explanation why football grew so grandly and naturally out of American collegiate life.[5] In any case, football had already reached grotesque proportions when Harvard (with fewer than 5,000 students) opened a stadium holding 57,000 in 1903. There were twelve deaths on the gridiron in 1902. Many professors have been convinced that intercollegiate football is anti-intellectual and fundamentally dishonest but, over the years, have succeeded only in making the game less murderous. On every campus the students initiated the sports, but money-making spectator sports quickly fell to the absolute control of the alumni and the athletic departments. So satisfying are these extravaganzas to those who subsidize American universities that everywhere athletic programs became and remained parasitical separate states within academia.

There are some other aspects of the mature American university that must be mentioned here. One healthy idea was that most of the subsidization of the students (for American tuition, even at its highest, has always been low in proportion to the actual costs of what was provided) should be at the expense of other groups in addition to the professors. Early recognition of this was the donation of public lands for public universities in the Morrill Act. The period 1865–1914 also saw the rise of American industrial empires and the consequent foundation of private, untaxed fortunes that were literally too large to be spent on personal indulgence. The ruling ideology of social Darwinism condemned charity. The fund-raisers of the new universities cleverly appealed to the millionaires' yearnings for self-monumentalization and their guilty consciences—for an air of piety and good works still hung over higher education. To legitimize newness, the donated buildings were set in pretty landscapes like those of European country palaces and decorated in historical styles: Greek and Renaissance for the libraries and medical schools; Romanesque and Gothic for the sprouting chapels, schools of divinity, and law quadrangles. The new universities favored mullioned windows and massive furniture in durable oak. The University of Chicago, founded in 1892 and nurtured by a substantial fraction of the already vast Rockefeller fortune, was deliberately antiqued not only with Gothic architecture but by immense wrought-iron chandeliers with porcelain candles that held light bulbs.

The University of Chicago pioneered in faculty raiding. For his new university President William Rainey Harper collected among others, five professors from Yale and eighteen from Clark plus eight former college or seminary presidents to serve as administrators under him. Harper also pioneered in the devising of academic ranks, rituals, and traditions.

All over the United States newly large and rich universities legitimized themselves with ceremonial and symbolical trappings. With the rise of the first intercollegiate sport, which was rowing or crew, school colors had been assumed and had acquired some ability to inspire vociferous loyalty in the northeastern schools in the 1860s and '70s. Increasing contacts with the European universities and the ineradicable feelings of American inferiority inspired burlesques of ceremonies that had long since fallen into desuetude in European universities. Harvard, which already had considerable prestige at the time, used caps and gowns first in 1886 at the ceremonies marking its 250th anniversary. As would often be the case, Harvard provided a model, and the custom (if it was that) was grasped by college presidents eager to legitimize their novelties. By the late 1880s one Gardner Cotrell Leonard was publishing articles on academic heraldry that brought about some uniformity in ceremonial practice. Most of the first caps and gowns he designed and sold were, it turned out, manufactured by Cotrell and Leonard, his family's dry goods firm in Albany, New York. And, as might be expected, the brash, rich new institutions such as Chicago, Stanford, Michigan, and California raised symbolically reassuring bell towers, purchased ceremonial maces and chains of office, commissioned the composing of "Alma Mater" songs and the designing of official seals. The presidents paraded their robed scholars on anniversaries and awards days. Even the older places took on appropriate "new traditions" in order to keep up. Yale's great expansion of facilities was done in Gothic style. Princeton and other old American colleges ordered graduation robes and hoods that made their wearers look like reef fishes or jungle birds. At present the prescribed colors for the trimmings, edges, and tassels of some typical academic costumes are sage green, peacock blue, and salmon pink for physical education, public administration, and public health, respectively.

The successful, perhaps expedient absorption of bogus festivals, the necessity of imposing grounds and sentimental architecture, and most especially the integration of the highly visible athletic programs all show that the new American universities, whatever they might be, shelter educational and research functions that are either too complex or too insubstantial (or both) to maintain confident public support without more obvious indications that suggest (without proving) worthwhile activity.

As the American universities achieved their mature form (though not their mature size—as will be seen), the teaching members within them began to take on the characteristics of a separate professional class. The professors' feelings of distinction were naturally intensified by the wider social and intellectual chasm that separated them from the undergraduate students, who tended ever more to come from nonelite families. Professorial titles of address and the initials after their names demonstrated their separateness, and the society about them accorded professors the respect traditionally accorded to physicians and lawyers.

But not the income, alas. It was apparently accepted that study and teaching on all levels are quasi-sacred pursuits and that comfort and learning are odd bedfellows. In the period 1890–1910 raiding universities in the West were offering salaries of from $4,000 to $7,000 per year. Such salaries permitted a family to have a large house and Irish servants, to dress well, and to travel. However, these salaries were exceptionally high. At the old disciplinary colleges, which were cutting costs in order to survive, salaries were still $500 to $1,500 per year. A respectable salary in a state university for a thirty-year-old assistant professor was $2,000 per year. Thus academic yearly earnings were about the same as those for a highly skilled industrial worker. And it is just at this level that average academic wages tended to stay since that time.

The jobs had the nonpecuniary compensations that they were to keep: life with handsome young people, healthy surroundings, plenty of free time, the easy fusing of one's working hours and one's time off the job. Titles and outward respect could be considered substantial psychic income. From 1910 to about 1950 a professor at a famous university was required to teach ten to fifteen hours a week; one at a lesser place, up to twenty hours a week. Research and committee duties (the new universities subscribed to a revived medieval myth of self-governance) were as burdensome or as casual as one wished to make them. College professoring was a natural refuge for those who were reasonably intelligent and articulate, who hated the world's hurly-burly, and who had some extra income of their own or from the heiresses they had married. College professors were a remarkably contented lot. Their clothes were old-fashioned. As they aged, they tended to become caricatures of the odd young fellows they had been twenty or thirty years before. Then as now, isolation and leisure fertilized harmless eccentricity.

Professors were never quite as free as they usually seemed to be. As always would be the case, much conformity in intellectual behavior was due to the informal pressures among the professors themselves. Unlike the British and the Germans, the Americans have had few families that produced generations of professors. Still, for two centuries college teachers came from secure, northeastern Protestant families and kept the expected prejudices against Catholics and Jews. Since hiring criteria in academic life are excessively subjective, outsiders were discouraged from even applying for jobs. In proportion to the population, the professors were a tiny occupational group. There were perhaps 20,000 college and university teachers in 1900;

70,000 in 1930. Officially the new American university favored intellectual distinction and provided freedom for its exercise. Some professors published a lot and often in their special journals. Yet one must search hard for evidence that the professors of the period contributed much original or of lasting intellectual importance to American science, art, literature, philosophy, or social criticism.

The same rigid system of academic accounting with its credits and frequent compulsory examinations that stultified and made hostile the students may have atrophied the fantasy and long-range time perspective of the professors as well. Others have remarked that the few American geniuses who happened also to be college professors felt demeaned by the mediocrity and smug moralism of their academic and social atmosphere and were restless. Most either left or were forced out. The failed professorial careers of William James and George Santayana at Harvard, of Edward Macdowell at Columbia, and of Charles S. Peirce and Thorstein Veblen are all instructive here. Certainly the product of the American academic intellectuals in the years 1880–1940 was of far less originality and of far less enduring substance than the published work of a very much smaller number of English dons and of French or German professors over the same period.[6]

Most of the atmospheric factors leading to mediocrity and conformity were and have remained subtle. For a while, however, the strictures for doctrinal orthodoxy could be narrow and could operate with sudden force. The decisive authority of the new, big universities now lay with sovereign boards of trustees or governors, who acted through the university president. The more forceful trustees were also likely to be wavering benefactors who had become rich in the schools of hard knocks.[7] Though these men may not have been conventionally educated, all the same they had ideas. Their ideas as to the purposes of a university did not always harmonize with those of professors who had been inspired by the supposed *Lehrfreiheit* (teaching freedom) of the German universities. In America *Lehrfreiheit* came to be interpreted as "academic freedom" and was extended (as it was not in Germany) to what the professor said and did outside the university walls. But even in the university the prevailing American moral views required that up-to-date views of evolution be handled gingerly in the biology classes. A Southern professor dared not state anywhere that Negroes ought to be welcomed into American life. To speak in class or in public in favor of strikes, regulation of the railroads, boycotts, or bimetalism was to invite a trial before the trustees or a swift, unexplained dismissal. Business-men-trustees tended to look on the professors as hired hands. In the 1890s, a series of widely publicized firings, culminating the discharge by Leland Stanford's widow of the economist Edward A. Ross in 1900, led to a sharpened awareness by vulnerable professors of just how capricious their paymasters could be.

In the spring of 1913 eighteen full professors of Johns Hopkins (where, significantly, the ideal of *Lehrfreiheit* was strongest) sent a letter to colleagues of equal rank at nine other universities. They urged the formation of an association of professors. Later, six hundred professors accepted invitations to become charter members of the American Association of University Professors, which was formed in January 1915.

The AAUP is much more restrained in its activities than other professional or trade associations formed in order to raise the status and to promote the welfare of their members. The only organizational umbrella of the entire American professoriat was formed in response to threats to (the American view of) academic freedom, and since then the defense of academic freedom has been its salient purpose. Most of the later (and very modest) improvements in professorial life were brought about independently of any professors' organizations. Examples of changes in university life that professors scarcely influenced at all are the formation of college entrance examinations and accreditation standards for departments and professional schools. The desires of professors for better salaries and for nonsalary compensations such as health insurance and pensions have been advanced by the AAUP only by the regular publication in their *Bulletin* of statistics showing just how badly rewarded (compared with other professionals) the professors have been. But the cost of membership in the AAUP has been steep (thirty-six dollars for someone earning a salary of $16,000) in 1975, and membership has never approached more than one third of those in the profession. This lack of militancy or even common ground is further evidence of the essential and deeply based satisfaction of American professors.

Even the unique institution of tenure, which has been defended as a guarantee of academic freedom, is only partly attributable to the work of the AAUP. Tenure is a faculty member's right to hold his academic appointment until retirement, once competence has been demonstrated. The notion that teachers merit special privileges and special guarantees for their jobs has a history that reaches into medieval custom.[8] Tenure, which the AAUP has defended because it was good for the scholarly community (that is, job security assures the freedom of inquiry for academic intellectuals), is far more often used as a shield for indifference and the neglect of professional duties which harm the university. In any case, at the respectable universities following the new model which came increasingly to dominate higher education after 1915, tenure came typically to be awarded after a four- to six-year initial contract as an assistant professor. This is the usual up-or-out system in the academic profession.

The changes in academic life that took place between about 1915 and 1955 or so were due to growth in the numbers of colleges and universities and also to the assumption by ever more institutions of the missions of research and service. Part of the steady expansion might be attributable to increases in population and in national wealth. But also the proportion of the age group eighteen to twenty-two attending college increased steadily, rising from 4 per cent in 1900 to over 14 per cent in 1939 and over 30 per cent in 1960. Enrollment in American institutions above the high-school level was under 250,000 in 1900, a little over 1 million in 1930, almost 3 million in 1957, and rose very rapidly to be more than 9 million in 1976.

During the same period the American states and municipalities steadily strengthened or, in any case, expanded their primary- and secondary-school systems, thus producing a far larger population minimally prepared for the American conception of college-level work. Many colleges were freed for a long period from the task which is now called "remedial" work. If the new universities were devoted to teaching elites, research, and service to the larger community, it was the third category that received the most emphasis in the half century before 1955. The public universities in the Midwest and in California became larger than the great private institutions in the East. The fastest-growing institutions, both in their number and in their aggregate enrollment, were the new quasi-vocational "junior" or two-year colleges and municipal universities that were themselves outgrowths of the public-school systems and their devotion to democratic service.

An obsession for Americans as for no other people has always been to rise in the social and economic order. At least in America there have been more possibilities to rise. Money assists one's ascent, but another accepted way has been by credentials obtained through higher education. And ever more as the twentieth century marched on it became a dogma in the middle-class American family that a college degree was the essential prerequisite for employment that was not soiling and for a decent, reasonably secure life.

It continued to be the case that any American with a little family money or who could locate some opportunity for part-time employment on or near the campus would find an institution that would accept him or her. Even the problems caused by the massive influx of subsidized GIs in 1946–48 were solved by crowding. Usually students' tuition would pay one fourth to one third of the actual costs of their education. However, American colleges and universities, even if they were supposed to be devoted to democratic service, have never worked effectively as class levelers. On the contrary. Despite the linking in American myth of education and democracy, the colleges have tended to duplicate and preserve existing social distinctions. In 1960 one per cent of the undergraduate students at Stanford University came from blue-collar families. At Henry Ford Community College in Dearborn, Michigan, about 67 per cent did. It has long been undeniable that students from the lowest economic strata received the worst educations from the time of their entry into kindergarten until their graduation from low-profile colleges. A graduate from Princeton or Yale can set himself to do practically anything he wishes. One would hesitate to call the rural denominational colleges or the urban community colleges instruments for social mobility. Some graduates of Negro colleges can scarcely read or write. The hard truth is that colleges and universities are most often essential to *preserve* a family's position rather than to advance it.

Some other changes in college life affected the professors and their status in the thirties, forties, and fifties. One was the effulgent growth and variety of extracurricular activities which took place all over the United States. Long before the Second World War, fraternities and sororities, theater groups, student newspapers, and political organizations became expected parts of collegiate existence. This enrichment of the students' lives and the devotion of their sincere energies to them is surely evidence of the lack of satisfaction that lay in the curriculum to which the professors were devoted and which they scarcely ever questioned.

As the Great Depression caused American intellectuals to become more earnest and introspective, it also had corollary effects on the

universities. College degrees—and from particular colleges at that—
became critical means by which well-placed Americans made sure
that their children could keep their place in professional or bourgeois
society. A phrase of the time had it that "a college degree is like
money in the bank." It was only in the course of the Depression that
greatly increased demands for admission to the five or ten acknowledged great American universities permitted the professors at those
places to establish high standards for preparation and for undergraduate performance and to hold them. The New Deal also began
using the heretofore neglected experts and researchers of the better
universities in various "brain trusts" that sought to solve social problems. One of the stories of the 1930s went like this:

> How do you get to Washington?
> Go to Harvard and turn left.

The institutionalized co-operation between the federal government
and academic intellectuals produced its greatest coup with the Manhattan project—the research and development campaign that absorbed the well-subsidized physicists of Princeton, Chicago, and
Berkeley (as the main campus of the University of California is
called). The explosions of atomic bombs in 1945 were emphatic evidence that the work of university researchers had value of deadly intensity. Thus the horrors of Hiroshima and Nagasaki eased the way
in America for intellectuals to apply themselves to the causes of social problems, to disinterested research, and to instruments for war.
From that wartime period of slippery ease with which the atomic scientists co-operated to make holocaust weapons we can date the development of the large, publicly subsidized research university into a
sort of academic brothel, where any kind of accommodation could
be purchased from its exquisitely specialized experts, if the price was
right.

Another spur for the tendency toward giganticism of the American
university was the sudden and massive influx of veterans after 1945.
They were (harbinger of things to come) subsidized by the national
government and (most agreeably astonishing to the professors) were
much more serious and tenacious than their younger classmates. At
the University of Minnesota in 1947, only 35 of the 6,000 GIs
flunked out—an unprecedentedly low percentage.

What of the professors during these years when higher education
assumed ever greater earnestness, adaptability, and grandeur? After

all, they were the essential keepers of the gates between degree-centered education and the enormous numbers of people who were prepared to put in the time for it. Several studies have shown the remarkable inflexibility of professorial wages. In the inflations of 1921–22 (a 60 per cent increase in the price level) and 1946–48 (an increase of 50 per cent) professors' money wages remained just about constant. The losses in purchasing power were psychologically devastating. The professors were reminded that they had no recourse to those who authorized the payment of their checks and had no bargaining power whatsoever. On the other hand, their jobs were rather secure and, due to the inflexibility of their wages, their real incomes rose steadily during the long deflation of 1929–38. Most authorities agree, however, that real wages for a university professor in 1955 were lower than they were for a professor similarly employed in 1905.

The essential explanation for the continued low wages and one which almost no one has ever been courageous enough to state is that professorial employment was, as it always had been and would be, extremely satisfying work for certain people. The direct and conclusive evidence for this claim is that there have always been more job applicants than there were jobs for them to fill. For the first fifty years of its publication, the *AAUP Bulletin* is filled with statistically supported articles that demonstrate just how low (relative to other professions requiring as much formal preparation) salaries were. Only those with something extra coming in were able to carry off professorial existence on the bright side of shabbiness. Professors feared job seekers whose eagerness for employment could increase the work and lower the wages. Professors with jobs continually raised information screens or other obstacles before the young men and women seeking the essential credentials. Professors had to deter the young, capable, and energetic from clamoring for the few attractive positions (with their low salaries) that opened up.

Chapter VI will return to graduate work and professorial apprenticeship, but it is worth noting here that in fields in which there are relatively few occupational alternatives to professorial employment it requires a great deal more time to get a Ph.D. Since about half the doctored chemists are able to find employment in industry, their graduate training, including the finishing of their dissertation, has commonly taken three to four years. Until the past few years, one could make similar observations about physicists, psychologists, geologists, and biologists. On the other hand, philosophers, Egyptologists, and historians of feudalism have no professional alternatives to teaching. Ten years of graduate training has been and remains a low average for these and comparable fields.

When one reads of the mystification and misery of academic job seekers in 1905, 1937, or 1950, there is an almost spine-chilling immediacy and timeliness in all those stories. Here I must quote from a classic treatment of the college professor dating from 1958:

> The average salary of an assistant professor is approximately that of a bakery truck driver and his occupancy of a job is likely to be less permanent. Yet it may require a large part of the time of twenty highly-skilled men for a year to hire him.[9]

If the training of the professors and their working conditions changed little in a half century, the appearance of the campus around them changed more. The steady growth of the educational system increased the numbers of professors, even throughout the Depression, from about 70,000 in 1930 to about 100,000 in 1940 and 160,000 in 1950. Private philanthropy was inadequate to subsidize more than a small proportion of the education that ambitious American parents now required for their children. Increasingly, college professors were government employees. Large, multipurpose universities patterned on Cornell, Michigan, and Wisconsin became common all over the United States and were providing cheaper (since they were government subsidized) alternatives to the private schools. The inferior (read nonprestigious) private colleges continued to wither.

The proportion of the American gross national product that was devoted to higher education continued to rise from about one quarter of one per cent in 1900 to about one per cent in 1950. After the skimpy though eagerly grasped assistance for GIs, it became expected that the federal government might subsidize certain disadvantaged groups by tuition grants and that the government might increase its small role in subsidizing scientific research. By the mid-1950s there was also in existence a much-respected apparatus for the collection and projection of statistics upon which planners at all levels in government and in the universities could anticipate demand for degrees. The crystal balls of academic planners were therefore warning of the arrival at college age of the war and postwar baby booms. Therefore, academic planners had in hand projections for increases in the numbers of jobs for the familiar kinds of college professors when the projections of growth were thrown off by the announcement on October 7, 1957, that the Soviet Union had launched an artificial earth satellite that could be seen by the naked eye and that gave out radio beeps. Thus was launched also the sweet and short euphoria in the collective existence of American college professors.

II

The Glorious Years

The tiny beeping of Sputnik in space during October and November of 1957 was amplified on earth into a technological and political humiliation for the United States. American patriots were astonished and disappointed and began a panicky search for an understandable explanation that might lead to a ready solution. The education industry offered the best and simplest answer: American higher education was inferior to Soviet high education. The Soviets yearly turned out 80,000 engineers to our 30,000. There was a shortage of Americans trained in "disciplines" such as mathematics, the exact sciences, and foreign languages. There was even a shortage of teachers in these and other areas.

The solution was manageable for the richest country in the world, for, with a little proper planning, we could buy better education. Educational authorities said, "Give us enough money and we will give you citizens capable of maintaining American supremacy by means of space satellites or anything else."

Accordingly, the significantly named National Defense Education Act of 1958 provided for student fellowships and institutional subsidies to encourage study in the neglected areas. And the act of 1958 favored new programs in young universities rather than traditional ones in the established eastern colleges. Increased federal aid in the 1960s provided scientific equipment and dormitory construction for the colleges, as well as grants for students whose meager financial resources would have earlier prevented them from attending college. The enthusiasm for higher education was infectious and grew at the local level, too. Encouraged by several federal programs that offered matching grants, the states provided greatly increased financing for new buildings, for a higher level of maintenance of academic facilities, and for higher academic wages. These large injections of money from so many places brought about changes in the size, shape, and appearance of American campuses. There were also some changes in the working conditions of the American professor. His wages improved, but his morale improved a great deal more in the decade or so after Sputnik.

Sputnik serves best as historical punctuation—the means of dividing time for purposes of narrative clarity. Prior to 1957, American colleges and universities had grown at a steady pace. From 1870 to 1970 university enrollments doubled every fourteen years or so. The proportion of eighteen-to-twenty-two-year-olds attending college grew ever larger, and their numbers increased much faster than the rapidly growing American population. Consequently, higher education (like education on all levels) absorbed an ever larger proportion of the gross national product. At all times relatively more Americans went to college than the youth of any other nation. Even in 1950, 19.5 per cent of the Americans in the eligible age group were enrolled in a college or university, while other advanced nations could cite less than half that number: for example, the Netherlands, 7.6 per cent; Canada, 7.1 per cent; France 4.4 per cent; Great Britain, 3.5 per cent; the Federal Republic of Germany, 3.5 per cent. After 1960 university enrollments in other industrial nations grew even more rapidly than enrollment in the United States. At present, growth in higher education is most dramatic in the Eastern bloc countries. However, university enrollments as a percentage of the eligible age group, even in the Soviet Union, have never equaled half of the American percentage.[1]

Actually, pressure for public support to expand greatly the American colleges and universities predates Sputnik. The influx of GIs had already strained academic capacity in the period 1946–49. Various educational hustlers in the early 1950s sought out, treasured, and graphed statistics which projected past growth trends into the 1960s and 1970s and showed an upward swoop. Besides, the postwar service economy would surely require experts that the existing colleges and universities could not supply.

Popular and special magazines were critical of the output of American universities. In an article called "Coming Avalanche," published in March 1956 *Newsweek* warned that the number of students would double before 1970. Many other magazines supported recommendations by the economist Beardsley Ruml to improve college financing by raising tuition and to increase opportunity by providing federal subsidies for poor students. Ruml suggested raising student-faculty ratios from 12 to 1 to 20 to 1 and employing the best teachers more effectively by using techniques such as TV hookups.

Harmonizing with pleas that were already more than a quarter of a century old, Ruml suggested that professors' salaries be doubled in order to keep the good ones in the years ahead. Ruml was somewhat exceptional as a favorer of education in that he concentrated on the teachers as resources, rather than on inadequate physical facilities.[2] Similarly, the distinguished Harvard historian Henry Steele Commager wrote an article for the New York *Times Magazine* on January 29, 1956, entitled "The Problem Isn't Bricks; It's Brains."

No American politician has yet come up with an effective riposte for demands for more and better education. Daniel P. Moynihan has claimed that after Sputnik "the . . . 'school lobby' . . . became very possibly the most influential in Congress."[3] And the education lobbyists met little resistance after Sputnik. Proeducation statisticians responded deftly to the demands for their services and built certain assumptions into their forecasts. They demonstrated that heretofore casually treated, though precious national resources (in this case, Ph.D.'d college professors) would be almost used up in the years ahead.[4] In 1959 the National Educational Association predicted ever more "critical" shortages of college teachers with each coming year. Using the NEA's model, the U. S. Office of Education concluded that the nation would have a cumulative Ph.D. deficit of 125,000 by 1974. A presidential committee foresaw between four and five teacher openings for every Ph.D. "between now and 1970." The Ford Foundation predicted "frightening gaps" between national supplies and national needs for new doctorates. Obviously the old research universities would not be up to the job of supplying the professors the nation needed.

College presidents and trustees, speaking to local or national legislators, used phrases like "disastrous shortage," "virtually paralyzed before a national problem of fundamental significance," "a major national scandal." In 1963 a widely used and predominantly statistical report of the NEA gave added substance to fears of a shortage and warned, "The gradual improvement in our general standard of living seems to be conducive to a tolerant attitude, a widespread lack of readiness to recognize and respond to a drastically changed situation." Should colleges be faced with a demand for new staff, they would have to hire teachers without Ph.D.'s—*"In short this means second-rate education for a larger and larger number of our youth"*[5] (italicized in the original). Such expectations held well into the sixties and were reinforced even further in 1967 by the handy statistics in David G. Brown's *The Mobile Professors* (Washington, D.C., American Council on Education).

Sure enough, in the academic year 1962–63, there were about a thousand fewer doctorates available for teaching than the 7,400 or so required to maintain the "desired quality" (that is, the proportion of Ph.D.'s on universities' teaching staffs).[6] This brief shortage or "gap" was not to recur. Beginning in 1962 the graduate schools' output of doctorates expanded rapidly—in fact doubling in about seven years. The proportion of new Ph.D.'s prepared to enter teaching remained constant, at about half the total number. The expanded colleges and universities did indeed provide for lots of new jobs in order to accommodate increased enrollments and new tasks. However, many new teaching, research, and service positions were taken over by less impressively credentialed (and lower paid) professionals. There were new jobs for instructors and assistant professors, but "during the 'sixties, the fastest-growing academic groups were not the subaltern groups but marginal—teachers who were graduate students, researchers who did not teach."[7] In short, there were always enough Ph.D.'s to go around. The lavishly financed colleges of the fifteen years after 1957 were, by almost any sober judgments of our own day, far more than adequately responsive to demands for growth.

Without debating the philosophical underpinnings of the American nation, one can say that most Americans have uncritically embraced a particular and complex set of ideas about human nature, the functioning and purpose of the universe, and the worth of human action. These concepts were first vigorously stated in the seventeenth and eighteenth century by a series of European philosophers from John Locke to Jean-Jacques Rousseau. The philosophies of the Enlightenment also inspired the course of several political revolutions. The most enduring of these revolutions was the American one.

The historians of ideas now believe that, given the economic and social climate of the nineteenth century, several varieties of political liberalism were logical consequences of the debates of the *philosophes* over man's improvability and good government. Americans have always been traditionally and enthusiastically liberal. Indeed,

America's ideological-political history might be viewed as a contest between cautious liberals and impatient ones. Americans have never provided a stump or even a position as *éminence grise* to ideological pessimists or conservatives. Our radicals have been suppressed.

A foundation of liberal philosophy is that man as an individual and in the mass is and are essentially good; that his surroundings, depending on their quality, either foster or pervert that goodness. In an ideological atmosphere that is overwhelmingly liberal, the debates over social policy take the form of deciding what atmosphere or environment is best to release or channel man's desires in order to improve himself and his fellows. For about two centuries now it has been assumed that the state can and should provide a conducive atmosphere through the educational system.

Ever since the publication of Rousseau's *Emile,* an educational tract in the form of a long novel in 1762, many educators have proposed that students be placed in healthy, pleasant surroundings so that they can freely accept the knowledge offered by a kind teacher and by nature itself. Enthusiasm for education led to the founding of those seven hundred or so colleges before the Civil War. Only in America have students been offered lovely parks and other environmental encouragement (rather than stark compulsion, as is the case in most other societies) to accept the intellectual stuff that is offered to them. Liberals assume that learning should be pleasant, easy, and natural. Only since 1945 have there been established large systems of education elsewhere in the world which are as devoid of stated objects or as open to applicants having so little notion why they are on the scene.

Most South American countries, India, Indonesia, and many African countries now have new and enormous universities where education without object or requirements is there for those youths who can isolate themselves for a time from the necessity of gainful employment. This lessens the uniqueness of the American (as opposed to the traditional European systems) and also indicates that liberal-inspired regimes rule the natives where these "universities" (as the places are called) continue to grow, keeping those in residence off the job market for a few years.

American higher education (or, for that matter, higher education elsewhere) does not bring about equalization of opportunity or equalization of result. Higher education has, in effect, usually preserved the social status of those who use it. Indeed this is the explanation for the variety in the intellectual standards and in the social utility of American colleges and universities.[8] In our history, the chasms between inspirations and effects in higher education are as marked as they are in our policies toward race or foreign affairs.

For decades now, there have been no positions in the national or local educational lobbies for any but professed liberals. However, in the late 1950s and, particularly upon the assumption of office by John F. Kennedy in 1960, a lurking theme in American life became many-voiced and strident. *Excellence* became our holy grail and the impelling slogan for a decade. Arrogant liberals in positions of power became inspired to pursue "excellence" as no Americans had before them.

The Indochinese War, the space programs, the "wars" on poverty, and the expansion of the American universities are all of a piece and, as it has turned out, all disappointments. None of these Promethean projects encountered significant resistance until American critics (who were always on hand) eventually found their voices and touched larger numbers of Americans who could no longer be charmed by the rhetoric of "excellence." The ideological clashes, the revelations, and the disillusionments of the early seventies caused Americans of all sorts to make do with more modest positions in the cosmos.

But for a while the pursuers of excellence had their way. Some of them assumed that because education in the past had been inferior and inadequate, wholesale education had not yet transformed America into the paradise of the *philosophes* and the rationalists. Moreover, they felt that the American educational system should do much more than offer knowledge. If the American legal system and private enterprise had so far failed to bring about racial justice, then the schools should do it. Liberals in the federal government would help with money, guidelines for assistance, and penalties for non-compliance.

It goes without saying that it had long been hoped that the American elementary, secondary, and postsecondary school systems would all be responsive to the duties to inspire social discipline and to further social regeneration. But the little schools for little children were sunk in communities and have remained only marginally accessible for political or ideological use. And besides, children's schools have never attracted American philanthropists or politicians seeking monumentalization. On the other hand, colleges and universities were not subject to neighborhood control and might be refashioned by the large sums of money that academics have always yearned for.

More characteristic of the ideological climate of the great American decade was the assumption that intelligence should be applied to solve problems. Considerable respect was given to recognized possessors of knowledge. Beginning with the first liberal-inspired attempt to administer social justice, the New Deal, especially reputable professors were routinely used to inform and then to advise policy makers. By the 1960s professors were themselves determining policy. In early 1974 no less than five cabinet posts—State, Treasury, Defense, Justice, and Agriculture—were held by men who had earlier been professors at prestigious universities. Each of the presidents after Harry S. Truman was an "education" president. Dwight D. Eisenhower had himself been the president of Columbia University. John F. Kennedy and Lyndon B. Johnson accepted conventional notions of academic excellence and coupled these notions with their trust in academic experts.

The eager-to-spend federal government and the states had, as a model for the pursuit of excellence, the success of the University of California in its triumphant campaign for academic quality. Few persons outside the business of education paid much attention to the innovations in California until some time after they were put into effect. Yet very soon after the new university in the hills north of Oakland was chartered in 1868, the state legislature pioneered in the granting of construction subsidies, free tuition, and the admission of women. The University of California also founded research institutes in agriculture, mining, and engineering whose findings helped greatly to increase the state's wealth. Very early also, the state established a series of separate "normal" colleges (later loosely united into a system separate from the university) devoted to training teachers for the state's primary and secondary schools. Furthermore, California made it easy for communities to establish two-year "junior colleges." These last-mentioned institutions (besides performing mundane tasks) also served as sops to community leaders who objected to the lavish gifts and public financing that the first and greatest campus in Berkeley received.

The new population center in southern California soon demanded its own great university and in 1919 a normal college in Los Angeles became the "southern branch," which grew fast and became known by the initials UCLA. By 1923 the University of California (including its branches and research stations) had an enrollment of 14,061 students and was the largest university in the world. The biggest and most prestigious campus was at Berkeley, which continued to pioneer in student self-government, faculty self-government, and the establishment of groups of scholars to work in novel areas of study. Since about 1900 it has been expected that the state's governors, senators, and millionaires would be graduates of the great university, particularly of the Berkeley campus.

On the West Coast, where optimism was always rampant, new ideologies rooted quickest, and social experiments were most quickly started and abandoned. California became and remains an ideological battlefield for innovating right and innovating left liberals. However, until the coming of Ronald Reagan to power in the state, all parties agreed on the desirability of more education—particularly higher education, which is so expensive. For many decades all of the California systems of higher education—and that now means the many-branched great university, the nineteen state colleges, and the more than ninety community colleges—were supported by a more generous level of government support than those in any other state. State planning of higher education culminated in the provisions for even greater comprehensiveness, control, and outlays with the publication in 1958 of the *Master Plan for Higher Education in California, 1960–1975.*

The attention of the community of American professors has always focused most sharply on the very campus that the state's elite treasure most—that grandiose site on the slope just across the bay from San Francisco. The ruthless pursuit of excellence at the Berkeley campus might be best dated from the assumption in 1930 of the presidency of the university by Robert Gordon Sproul, the first Californian and the first Berkeley alumnus to take the job. Sproul resented the enormous and seemingly unassailable prestige of the great (though even then relatively smaller) institutions in the Northeast. In any case, the central theme of his twenty-eight-year reign was to convince the Sacramento legislators that his university could and should compete for and pay for top faculty members by offering them higher salaries and superior facilities for teaching and research. By 1929 Ernest O. Lawrence, the inventor of the cyclotron, had already become Berkeley's first Nobel Prize winner.

In the 1930s, the 1940s, and the early 1950s professors who had made reputations or appeared about to make them were not at all difficult for Sproul to pick up. Sometimes the mere visit to that exhilarating site was enough. However, for proven or promised excellence Sproul offered salaries that were 20 per cent higher, teaching burdens that were a little lower, and better equipment and surroundings. And Sproul had little competition—particularly when he went after brilliant Jews. Many American Jews were smarting because their careers had been arrested by subtle quota systems which limited the proportions of Jews in most of the departments at all of the other great universities. Jewish professors were liberated at Berkeley and came to be half or more than half of some departments as early as 1939. Since that time anti-Semitism has been an unendurable offense at Berkeley. Philo-Semitism has slowly spread to become *de rigueur* and almost a correlate of the quality of an American university.

Energetic Jews and energetic gentiles who valued intellectual liveliness attracted to Berkeley others who in turn attracted and created a lively student body. Around the campus a symbiotic society grew up that pioneered in marijuana smoking, athletic sexuality of every variety, movie cultism, and free political expression. Berkeley became a paradise for academic intellectuals and screwballs. Various crises— the worst being the oath controversy of 1948–51—passed over Berkeley and the place continued to attract energized faculty, appreciative students, and goofy hangers-on. State and then federal subsidies flowed in. And the signs of excellence poured forth unabated. Between 1958 and 1964 six more of the university system's scientists received the Nobel Prize, bringing the total to twelve. During the same period twenty-nine faculty members were elected to the National Academy of Sciences, bringing the total to eighty-seven, and members of the faculty won 299 Guggenheim fellowships.

During the same period, 1958–64, a lot of other university presidents meanwhile had obtained legislative laissez faires to seek out academic excellence in the form of glittering professors prepared to move for a price. But, alas, by this time most of the men, Jews as well as gentiles, with auras of excellence were more difficult to purchase with slightly boosted salaries, lowered teaching loads, and more luxurious surroundings. However, all hard-working professors enjoyed believing that they *might* be sought out, and there were grand years for some few hundred academics who could flash "excellence" and suggest they might be lured away.

If the pioneering in assuming new purposes and the responsiveness of the Californians provided models for growth in the 1960s, there were also modest, earlier models for the federal largesse that became so various and massive. There were grants of land in the nineteenth century, certain small subsidies for research between the wars, and the subsidies for enrollment (which we might consider the liberals' atonement for war) in the GI bills after 1945. Still, federal expenditures for higher education in 1954 were only $44 million. After Sputnik, federal aid grew very rapidly to total $700 million in 1960. But the great days were still ahead. Federal outlays for higher education including academic research were $1.993 billion in 1965; $4.363 billion in 1968; and $8.785 billion in 1975.[9] The subsidies take many forms: tuition grants to students and to institutions, subsidized loans and loan guarantees for students, subsidies for dormitory constructions, matching grants for the construction of libraries, laboratories, and other facilities, and, of course, vastly increased subsidies for research—particularly expensive scientific research.

It is noteworthy that outlays in 1975 for undergraduate student support alone were about $4.5 billion (estimated) or one hundred times the *total* federal expenditure for higher education in 1954. This expansion over twenty years occurred "almost without comment, with neither criticism from fiscal conservatives nor praise from fiscal liberals."[10] Over the same period of time, state aid to education, particularly financing for new buildings (much of which was an opportunistic snatching at matching federal grants) and compensation for new personnel, was also increasing rapidly, particularly in wealthy states such as California, New York, Wisconsin, and Massachusetts.

This influx of government money into the colleges and universities had effects beyond mere growth. Coupled with (and in essence inconsistent with) the democratic notion that higher education was to be not only encouraged but almost insisted upon was the previously discussed obsession with excellence. Significantly, subsidies for research often went for the setting up of new centers for highly specialized and expensive graduate training. In a 1963 message to Congress, President Kennedy said:

> We need more graduate centers and they should be better distributed geographically. Three-quarters of all doctoral degrees are granted by a handful of universities located in 12 states. The remaining states produce only one-fourth of the Ph.D.'s.[11]

The politics of excellence meant not so much a prejudice against the elitist schools (indeed the influence of Harvard in the federal government has grown steadily) as an attempt to set up additional sources of excellence, to spread it around, to make supremacy (paradoxically) general. As always, excellence in American academic life is not demonstrated by its instructional intensity, moral worth, or long-term practical value to the society as a whole. All these worthy objects simply cannot be guaranteed or otherwise concretized. A rather mundane, though vivid, type of excellence is demonstrated by bigger, tidier campuses, striking new offices, and classroom buildings of obviously expensive construction. Other criteria are accelerated enrollments and more books in the libraries (really *statistics* showing more books in the libraries).

However, the most "visible" signs of quality among the professors themselves were the ones long put forth by the established, incontrovertibly classy universities. The most visible or obvious demonstrations of supremacy in academic life are the production of new Ph.D.'s and the publications of researchers in residence. Doctors' degrees, journal articles, and scholarly books are the products of the labor-intensive graduate schools. That this labor is of a particularly expensive kind and that most of the products may be of dubious social utility was scarcely worth mentioning in the late fifties and the sixties. New journals rose to welcome the output of research findings, and there were jobs for the swelling number of Ph.D.'s. The jobs for the Ph.D.'s were there because of the continued expansion of higher education.

In addition to excellence and a mandate to make it visible, the universities accepted some other new tasks as they grew. During the period under discussion the executive and judicial branches of the government were sincerely eager to guarantee equality of opportunity. A tenet of the liberal creed is that all persons arrive equal in the world. Since their environment (read education) determines their success or failure, the educational system was commanded not only to expand but to seek out representatives of groups who had for various reasons been denied higher education in the past. Or, to employ a phrase favored by the educationalists themselves, the educational system or systems were expected to be more aggressive in their attempts to meet national and community "educational needs."

Crucial barriers to larger admissions to colleges and universities had been the obvious ones of tuition and expensive sustenance while the partakers enjoyed residence at them. Another more subtle but more effective barrier (because it affects students' performance) has been the irrelevance of the liberal arts curriculum to youths of the nonprofessional, unleisured classes. One solution to the problem was the American "community," "junior," or two-year college, which had already existed as a sort of post–high-school technical and (occasionally) academic training institution. The first junior college was created in Joliet, Illinois, in 1901. Later, as one might expect, California led in establishing these institutions and even now has one third of them. Community colleges continue to be more common in the Middle West and West. At present there are more than a thousand two-year colleges enrolling more than 3.5 million students. During the middle sixties they were opening at the rate of one a week.

One feels uneasy including the junior colleges in an American "academic" system. They are designed to support and ornament the communities they are in and have provided subsidized (the junior colleges are almost always financed by local revenues) vocational training for ambitious people nearby. More than half of the junior-college students have full-time or part-time jobs.

On the other hand, the American local college is almost never a technical school on the British, German, Scandinavian, or Japanese model. From the beginning almost all of them had academic pretensions. Though found most often in cities or towns, they were designed for landscaped "campus" settings. Besides responding to demands for a variety of technical, commercial, and remedial courses, they usually "required" courses, just as the four-year colleges did, in literature, the social sciences, and the laboratory sciences. Indeed, hundreds of two-year colleges in a predictable scenario of ambition inflation expanded to become the four-year colleges of the familiar type that offers creditable bachelor's degrees. Similarly, at the same time, older four-year colleges added departmental graduate training and professional schools in such subjects as law, medicine, dentistry, and others to merit the appellation "university." Another way in which the Californians led in educational progress was that their master plan provided for the smooth transfer of energetic and talented students from the grass-roots junior colleges to the state colleges and all the way up to Berkeley. However, as is the case with the partakers at any level of the American university system, whether one is a student or a teacher, one almost never begins in the boondocks and finishes in the great academic capitals. It is not at all unlikely that a biologist could get his B.S. at Stanford and his Ph.D. at UCLA, have his first teaching appointment at the University of

California at Riverside and his second at the State College in Chico, and settle finally at a community (two-year) college in Oakland. The reverse order is conceivable, but would be nearly miraculous.

The American colleges and universities were also required to expunge some of the guilt of the larger liberal society regarding America's enduring racial scandal. The northern schools, particularly the better ones, had long been at least tokenly integrated. Segregation in the grade and high schools, of course, had always been solidly institutionalized and preserved American racial separation. But the children's schools, being locally controlled, have proven themselves remarkably inflexible in the face of justice as defined by liberal morality and the courts. However, the liberals' domination of higher education and the particular defenselessness of the universities—especially those newly dependent upon federal aid—lent themselves to several efforts to legislate (academic) racial justice.

In Alabama and in a few other places there were well-publicized resistances (almost exclusively by politicians, let it be noted) to integration. A few hundred dark-skinned American heroes first braved the Southern all-white campuses. Now it seems as though desegregation in the colleges, at least, was carried off rather nicely. However, the integration of blacks accounted for little of the great expansion. Blacks accounted for a little less than 4 per cent of college and university enrollment in 1950; a little more than 9 per cent in 1974. The proportion of blacks attending predominantly white schools has increased slightly, and the increase is greatest in the South. The bulk of black enrollments are still in the predominantly black colleges or in community colleges in big cities. For purposes of the argument here, the modest absorption of black teenagers is really an indication of the acceptance by academics of new roles. In practical terms on the campuses this often means remedial work, the recruiting of minority groups, and the providing of programs in black studies (in the Southwest, Chicano studies as well).

The big universities also took on contract work for the Department of Defense under fat, loosely supervised research and development grants. Large amounts of federally provided money came to dominate the research programs of certain universities such as Harvard, the University of Michigan and Michigan State, Illinois, California, and, most particularly, the universities with solid research programs in the sciences, such as Massachusetts Institute of Technology and Cal Tech. That this work was often to devise effective means

of brainwashing, war "game" planning, death gases, various dooms-
day weapons, and other such diabolical projects has in the past
fifteen years evoked only hushed murmurs of objection from a few
academic scientists with social consciences. For some time it has
seemed as if the big research universities will take on anything if federal money comes along with it. It should not be surprising that a
study produced by a university in 1969 revealed that only 5 per cent
of the members of American graduate faculties believed in "direct
social involvement."[12]

During the 1960s the expansion of the several higher education
systems and their assumption of some new responsibilities led to
steady demands for properly credentialed staffs. As late as 1971 a
book on professors advised youths considering professorial employment that, "like many other professional occupations, that of the
college professors remains a career possibility for the many rather
than a monastic order for a few."[13] There was optimism in the
ranks of professors, too. In the early sixties tales of many jobs
offering high wages and few duties swept through convention hotels
at the annual meetings of biologists, language scholars, and anthropologists. Chairmen from new or rapidly growing "universities" in
New York or Wisconsin might be given wide latitude in hiring
new colleagues. A public college in Kansas or Alabama that had
never had a sociology department might hire a chairman in 1963
who at the annual sociologists' meeting of 1964 would seek out and
hire two full professors, three associates, three assistants, and two instructors and then hire seven more faculty members the next year. In
the early sixties the exquisitely complex hiring and job-shifting system described in 1958 by Theodore Caplow and Reece J. McGee in
their *Academic Marketplace* almost broke down.[14] A young historian
from Detroit who began graduate work at the University of California at Berkeley in 1958 had expected eventually to earn about
$8,000 a year as a tenured full professor in some college in
Kalamazoo or Ypsilanti. How agreeably astonished he was in the
spring of 1966 to be offered, among others, assistant professorships
paying $10,500 at the University of North Carolina, $11,000 at the
University of Hawaii, and $12,000 at the University of Sherbrook
near Montreal. Established personable professors with desirable credentials could weigh various job offers and move onward and even
upward, if their existing situation was in any way confining. Salaries
went up faster than the cost of living.[15] Statutory demands for

professorial work (most specifically, the hours required for actual teaching) were eased. High morale brought some professors perilously close to euphoric arrogance.

Words that infected academic rhetoric in the 1960s and that were close cousins to the national word, "excellence," were "exposure" and "visibility." In those halcyon days, growing enrollments, expensive-looking buildings, and frequent dedication ceremonies were not vivid or concrete enough for up-to-date universities to demonstrate their legitimacy. Formerly slumbering and newly ambitious colleges bid most frantically for proven, publishing scholars who might be induced to come down a notch or two. Even old universities competed for "names" who published prominently or otherwise got into the news.[16]

The technique of "raiding," which had first been practiced by Johns Hopkins University in the nineteenth century, by the University of Chicago after 1900, and most impressively by Berkeley in more recent times was then tried by everyone else. Berkeley itself was raided and then everyone raided one another. *Time* devoted some Timese to the topic on January 12, 1963:

Last week Brown [University] triumphantly made off with Berkeley's Historian Carl Bridenbaugh, president of the American Historical Association; Yale exults in such recent catches as Berkeley's Microbiologist Edward Adelberg and Stanford's husband-and-wife Historians (China) Arthur and Mary Wright (he got a new chair; she became the first woman tenure holder on Yale's liberal arts faculty). On the other hand, Stanford got Yale's Historian David Potter. To replace Potter Yale snagged Johns Hopkins' topflight Historian C. Vann Woodward, whose terms were a blue-ribbon chair and a year's leave of absence with pay before he even reaches New Haven.

Time, playing journalistic stool pigeon, further informed on the successful three-year plot of the University of Texas to "kidnap" the University of Illinois's William Bradley, an authority on the molecular structure of materials. Bradley admired a bright young scientist, Dr. Hugo Steinfink, whose work complemented his own. Texas "lured" Steinfink from an oil company in Houston "with the promise of unlimited freedom and such tools as a $30,000 refractometer. The presence of Steinfink hooked Bradley, and the deal was clinched by a new $4,000,000 eight story laboratory."

The quest for exposure took New York State's young and lavishly financed public university system down crazier paths. The days when

Berkeley could pick up academic gaints by showing them some scenery and giving them a 20 per cent raise were forever past in 1964 when the legislature in Albany established five Albert Einstein chairs in the sciences and five Albert Schweitzer chairs in the humanities—each of which paid $100,000 in salary and research assistance. Presumably these "Nobelists" (to employ a neologism of the time) and knowledge titans would establish new academic solar systems consisting of shining, though lesser, scholars plucked from universities with grand traditions of excellence. Among those attracted to the $100,000 jobs were the culture critic Marshall McLuhan and the historian Arthur Schlesinger, Jr. The workaday demands for holding the $100,000 chairs were small. At the City University of New York Schlesinger gave a few lectures a year to undergraduates and held a weekly two-hour seminar for graduate students. A *Time* (January 12, 1963) reporter who was on hand for one of these sessions noted that "what Schlesinger does, he does exceedingly well."

For decades before the education rage of the sixties, the state of New York was known for its measly financing for higher education. Then in the sixties the enthusiasm became unrestrained. The State University of New York system was set up to surpass in grandeur the older system in California. One vast university (among many) was planned for Buffalo and, as the Berkeley campus was known out west as "UCB," the Buffalo campus was to be known by the less graceful initials "SUNY AB"—State University of New York at Buffalo. Even before a projected totally new $650-million (the figure was printed once in *Time,* but in fact was never confirmed, or realized) campus was built, it touted itself in 1966 as the "Berkeley of the East." Warren Bennis, a provost and later a vice-president at SUNY AB, recalled that during these heady days he heard "that the University of California at Santa Cruz is being touted as the 'Buffalo of the West,' while the University of Maryland claims to be the 'Santa Cruz of the East.' "[17] Barbara Probst Solomon, a novelist who was hired in 1966 to teach courses in film in the English department there, said that Buffalo, "like all instant universities, in order to combat a physical environment that is hell, acquires faculty quickly by offering high pay and low teaching loads." She described SUNY AB as "filthy rich," saying, "It is buying up scholars and along with them supersalesmen who have no idea what they are selling or who the 'customer' is. There is so much money floating around as to create total chaos."

In order to hold her job as a "writer in residence" in Buffalo, Mrs. Solomon did not actually have to reside there. She observed, "I often gave my children breakfast in New York in the morning, saw them off to school, spent forty-five minutes in a jet to Buffalo, taught a few classes, and then came back to New York not long after they got home from school."[18]

The linking of some professors' names with large wads of money everyone assumed was honestly gained brought almost all professors a delicious public respect. Less desirable was the media puffery that focused on those professors, also few in number, who immersed themselves in the protest movements of the later 1960s.

Almost needless to say, it all began in Berkeley. The roots of the time of troubles lay in the academic years 1962–63 and 1963–64. The issues were almost quaint: free speech and a "peoples' park." Really, some pushy students wanted to employ university facilities for ideological proselytizing and some idle university land for democratic use. The regents of the university balked. A battle began. During those early months in Berkeley an effective rhetoric of "relevance" evolved to combat the conscienceless quests for "excellence." Protest tactics evolved in the same period. So did the means of attracting the media opportunists. A thin layer of clever and determined protesters well watched by the FBI and CIA and the television cameras then spread among the quality universities of both coasts. Some professors, almost invariably impeccably degreed, young, in the humanities, and far fewer in number than the scientists doing contract research for the Defense Department, contributed certain reasoned arguments to the rhetorical tool kit. As the 1960s progressed, the so-called radicals focused on the resonant issue of Viet Nam. American society appeared to be breaking apart as the decade ended and social cohesiveness appeared to be loosest in the big universities. A few jingoistic professors had their lectures interrupted or were attacked in the student newspapers.

Contemporaneously, some black students in a few colleges realized that the promised "equal opportunity" in the universities offered bleak prospects of producing equal results in the universities or away from them. Naturally, they were very disappointed and posed for the cameras as "Black Panthers." The campus protest movement climaxed with the demonstrations in April of 1970 against what appeared to be Richard Nixon's swashbuckling in Cambodia. At Kent

State and in a few other places some alarmed and irresponsibly armed security forces and some badly led cops killed young revelers who were no more dangerous than the members of the generation of panty raiders that preceded them or the streakers that followed them.

One should indeed skip rapidly over that peculiar period, now euphemistically referred to on the campuses as "the disturbances." These embarrassments passed quickly and completely—before the end of the war, before the fall of Richard Nixon, before the awaited installation of "relevance" in American higher education. The American professoriat came through the experience scarcely altered at all and on almost no campus did the disturbances leave in their wake durable scars on the facilities or achieve any significant reforms whatever. A survey in late 1969 of 60,447 faculty members showed that over 80 per cent of them felt that student demonstrators threatened academic freedom and over three fourths favored suspending students who disrupted the functioning of colleges and universities.[19] These overwhelming majorities in favor of calm have prevailed.

The campus disturbances that climaxed in 1970 were harbingers of the end of an era in American history that probably lacked any solid ideological bases in the first place. What most Americans realized as the seventies began was that aggressive liberalism was being tamed everywhere. The American empire was in retreat. The *natural* environment appeared to be in danger. The economic boom was being maintained by speculation. Racial and economic justice appeared to have been visions.

The professors shared somewhat in the general disillusionment, but their apprehension took on a certain special anxiety. As the early years of the seventies went on, it became clear that the brutal supply-demand relationships that had almost always held in the academic marketplace were becoming manifest again. There were more openings for students than there were students to fill them; there were more professor candidates than there were jobs to support them. And the politicians who had so richly subsidized students and professors during the apotheosis of liberalism began to share the general skepticism.

Though the earlier optimism on the campuses was evaporating, those professors who were established in their jobs still had for their use a vastly larger and nicer academic plant and held on (with a nervous grip, to be sure) to improved working conditions. The figures of growth cited below may be a little confusing because the statistics available do not cozily fit the historians' periodization of fifties, sixties, and seventies more or less assumed for this historical chapter. Nevertheless, they could make points. As noted earlier, federal aid to higher education was negligible before the war and is increased enormously after 1957. But federal outlays are only part of the story, for state aid to education (always the main source of subsidy for higher education) also increased sharply. In the academic year 1959–60 the states spent $1.4 billion on colleges and universities. By 1969–70 that annual figure had reached $6.123 billion. Within these figures are some rather dramatic changes for particular states. New York State increased its rate of expenditure over the decade by almost 700 per cent; Massachusetts by over 600 per cent; North Carolina by almost 500 per cent. Even California, which already spent twice as much as any other state in 1959–60, had increased its rate of expenditure by almost 300 per cent over the decade.[20]

What these figures indicate, besides their own grandeur, is the even greater assumption by the public fisc of the responsibility for higher education and the consequent continued decline of the private college and university. During the same period, however, the great private institutions, such as Harvard, Yale, Columbia, and Stanford, which in the course of their flourishing had turned out hundreds of nascent millionaires, launched successful drives to increase their endowments. They also nearly tripled their tuition and effectively sought out federal largesse, mostly for research support.

During the sixties student enrollments increased almost a half million a year. The expansion of the graduate schools was proportionally much greater and consequently led to a rapid growth in the number of doctorates awarded. This expanded capacity to produce Ph.D.'s was the reason for the more than adequate number of credentialed candidates for the newly made teaching and research positions. It is worth noting here that the increases in finances, enrollments, and staff were yet more dramatic in Canada, which also participated in the North American academic marketplace.

The cold figures above do not reveal certain dramatic short-term changes that were taken in even by casual observers of the campuses. All over in North America there were established education factories with a new standard of magnificence in their architecture, landscaping, amenities, and general maintenance. There were, of course, beautiful campuses before 1960. The sloped bay-view setting of Berkeley comes to mind, as do the campuses of the Universities of Colorado, Utah, and Michigan, Princeton, Duke, and several northeastern women's colleges. However, in the course of the 1960s old private colleges, shabby city universities, and forlorn rural colleges projected and accomplished the completion of hundreds of student unions, libraries, and performing-arts centers and allowed for them a level of financing that attracted daring architects, who applied their talents lavishly. Even little Wells College on Lake Cayuga got a new library of extraordinary proportions and dazzling originality. Sooty Wayne State University in Detroit decorated itself with a convention center of marble and crystal that is a jewel of modern design. University students came to expect—in addition to their lecture rooms and dormitories—ballrooms, movie houses that were well upholstered and free, basketball courts, and colossal swimming halls—all of which were kept at delightful temperatures the year-round and were maintained by phalanxes of janitors and cleaning women.

Whole new campuses, large enough to accommodate the staff and functions of America's two or three largest universities in 1910 grew quickly to completion and respectability. Cleveland State University and the Chicago Circle campus of the University of Illinois, both of which opened in 1965, as well as many other four-year colleges and even junior colleges that did not exist before 1960, have much larger undergraduate enrollments than Princeton, Yale, Columbia, or the University of Chicago. All of the academic functions of the State University of New York at Albany are housed in an immense structure of inspiring airiness that was erected on farmland in one fell swoop between 1965 and 1969. The new Santa Cruz campus of the University of California threads its way among a redwood forest overlooking the Pacific Ocean. When the facilities at Santa Cruz were being built, there was a ban on the cutting of a tree of more than twelve inches diameter without the president's permission. Architecture and nature produce an ambiance so splendid that while there one feels the effort was worth it.

Almost without exception the kinds of facilities and level of maintenance on the campuses all over North America improved. As American municipal parks declined to become trashy, the campus lawns, walks, and gardens were planted, watered, and trimmed.

Campuses in Oregon or Florida or Arizona became objects of pilgrimage for strollers, tourists, and parents shopping for the prettiest place to park their offspring for a few years. The teaching staffs of the pretty campuses enjoyed the psychic income earned while working in lovely surroundings. They also felt honored by the vogue for their professional product, however difficult it remained to specify just what that product might be.

There were, of course, more substantial sorts of income for the academics. For a while some energetic professors had the job mobility that was more characteristic of oil-well drillers or actors. The number of hours professors were required to teach at the better universities fell by almost half. Their salaries increased at rates faster than the cost of living, faster than wages in general and in 1970 were almost double what they had been in 1960. As the turbulent decade drew to a close, it was expected by optimistic professors that the projections of growth that had justified the great expansion of the graduate schools could be extended yet further. Things might be even better in the future than they had been in the recent past.

Or would they? After some of the big national conventions of scholars that took place according to tradition late in December of 1969 there were peculiar omens. At the meeting in Denver of the Modern Language Association the number of departments seeking new college teachers was half what it had been the year before. At the annual meeting of the American Historical Association thousands of old and new Ph.D.'s were there expecting interviews that were steps to new jobs, but only about two hundred employers were looking for an average of two new professors each. Observers at the meeting of the American Economic Association had no hard figures, but it appeared to be a buyer's market. One chairman said, "We're in the market for just one person this year compared to three last year. We've talked to thirty people already." A manpower specialist for the American Institute of Physics reported that 40 per cent of the 1969 crop of new Ph.D. physicists were still looking for jobs.

Professor Henry W. Sam, chairman of the English department at Pennsylvania State University, observed that during the previous year 626 people applied to him for a job, but that not one of them expressed an interest in teaching freshmen. A huge midwestern university revealed that it would be graduating seventy Ph.D.'s in June 1970, but it would be hiring just one new faculty member. A lot of job seekers felt that they might have been hoodwinked.

Illustration A:

JOHN LOSTEIN OF BALESTON

John Lostein's composure is shaken by even a brief encounter with Arthur Prescott, Jr., who is also a full professor in the economics department at Baleston University. And Prescott's ritualistically cheery "Hi, John!" is especially nettlesome on this cold December morning. Lostein has been constructing the three timely ad libs that will update his next lecture in his popular course "Intermediate Macroeconomic Theory." Lostein and Prescott crossed paths in front of the four-story Gothic-style building containing the lecture hall that would be the scene of John's performance.

Prescott had an amiable manner, but almost everyone conversed with him warily, since he was the department's gossipist. Prescott's only book was his revised dissertation, which he published twenty years ago. He had since managed to publish an occasional lucidly written theoretical article in order to maintain his marginal position in a department composed largely of big producers. Prescott seemed to bear up under the epithet "a one book man." How he did anything at all seemed miraculous to John. Arthur was always available for the swapping of stories with colleagues whose marriages were breaking up or with agonizing graduate students who needed catharsis. Over the years Prescott had learned from such sources that Lostein had been seen drunk and accompanied by a broad with a blond wig while leaving a sleazy Manhattan singles bar, that he drove forty miles to see blue movies and to go to a massage parlor, that in April of 1971 Lostein applied to the department for travel expenses for a speech given in Seattle for which the expenses were already provided by the bankers' association there, that Lostein in his office screamed, "Fuck off, Funderburk," to a graduate student who had whined that Lostein's C+ would mean the cancellation of his scholarship, that Lostein regularly referred to his dean as "Dumbo." Both economists were almost fifty. Prescott was sinewy and healthy, though he looked dusty in his orangish-brown suit with cuffs and narrow lapels. Each time he saw the energetic gossipist, Lostein compulsively gauged between forefinger and thumb his own heavy abdominal folds and touched the persistent little sore on the side of his nose.

Today John examines with care the pleats on his maroon double-knit slacks and the toggles on his narrow, black $42.50 loafers. He has never articulated the position to himself, but feels that when he lectures, he is the offerer of a sacred performance. He must be especially clean and must labor to inspire moods of deep respect and keen excitement for his special subject.

At precisely 9:00 A.M. John struts into the rectangular lecture hall which has three hundred wooden seats that creak and which, in other ways, looks like the interior of a very old movie house. Though it is a cold Monday late in the semester, only twenty seats are empty. For John Lostein lectures with great authority on the interaction of aggregate expectations and short-term interest rates—a hot topic in these troubled times. It is well known that he consults on contract with the Governors of the Federal Reserve Board and that in 1973 he sold a 6,000-word article to the New York *Times Magazine* which accurately predicted the very high interest rates of 1975. John is a lucid and colorful lecturer and his renown adds to the demand for places in his courses. And students at Baleston do not cut classes.

John lectures only on Mondays and Wednesdays. The remaining class meetings of the three-credit course are handled by his five graduate teaching assistants, each of whom meets weekly for an hour in seminar rooms with four groups of fifteen students to discuss the lectures and the items on a list John provides of outside readings on macroeconomic theory. The books and articles are on reserve in the undergraduate library. They also discuss some graphs that John Lostein has photocopied from recent government documents and bank newsletters.

Despite the badly timed encounter with Prescott, the lecture goes even better than usual today. John draws several impromptu graphs on the green "blackboard" demonstrating the steady correlations of bond prices in the utilities industries with disposable income for blue-collar workers. In fact, he confides to the 280 on hand, "I have been trying to impress this upon Andy [the first name of the man who, it is whispered about, will shortly be named the new Secretary of Treasury] for months."

As sometimes happens when John feels especially cocky, he talks fast and the lecture which had been planned to fill exactly the fifty-minute period is finished six minutes early. Opening the floor to questions (here he puts aside his lavalier microphone), John walks about the low stage. He deflects a question as to which of the many presidential candidates are most likely to be favored by the New York bankers, but dwells instead on their character faults, referring to two of them by their first names. When, forty-five seconds before the bell, one of the eleven coeds (Baleston had been sexually integrated in 1967) asks with a tongue-in-cheek air what the prime rate and thirty-year FHA mortgage rate will be one year hence, John snaps back, "Nine point five and ten point two five respectively," smiles grandly, gathers up his many note cards, and dismisses the class with a big wave. As he leaves by a back door to escape further pesky questions, John murmurs to himself with some pride, "Bitch, that little phrase would have cost the directors of the Bowery Savings Bank five hundred dollars minimum." In fact Professor Lostein (John uses his title only when he is away from Baleston; on campus he insists on "Mister") in ten days would impart—with some accompanying graphs and data, naturally—just these figures to just these gentlemen for a consulting fee of $750.

It is a twelve-minute walk from his lecture room to the offices of the economics department. On the way, John smiles in response to the "Hi's" of many. When possible he uses names: first names for professors in other departments whom he has met at parties or in the course of committee work, "Mister" so-and-so for those few of the graduate students and even fewer undergraduate students whose last names he has memorized and not yet forgotten. The "Hi" is a little more drawled and he smiles more in order to indicate cordiality to those whose names he should know but does not. He slows his pace going by the well-populated steps of the hall where most of the sociology lectures are. For here he surreptitiously stares at especially lovely, lolling bosoms and, in the summertime, occasionally a little beaver, for coeds flock to major in that department of the great university. If he were not so pressed for time, John might have taken a detour for more erotic looking through the long central hall of the department of fine arts or into the periodicals room of the undergraduate library.

Up three flights of steps (that skinny bastard Prescott took them two at a time) for a chuffing lunge at the bank of forty pigeonholes holding the professors' mail. As always there is a lot for Dr. Lostein. Today there is a request for a two-hundred-word biography to be inserted into a who's who John has never heard of called *Distinguished Social Scientists of the World,* published in Bristol, England. One pays forty pounds and gets a copy of the book when published. John crumples the richly printed brochure. A personage of his stature never pays for entries into biographical directories. There are ads for new texts in introductory economics, which John has not taught in twelve years, from Prentice-Hall and Scott, Foresman. He tosses these, but keeps a new paperback sample text called *Readings in Economic Theory,* for he can sell this some time later for 40 per cent of the retail price to a book dealer on the university's shopping street. He also tosses a fifteen-page mimeographed report on the Faculty Forward Planning Committee's "Suggestions for Reorganizing the Lower Division Curriculum," but keeps an out-of-print dealer's catalog for "Books of Economic History." John will put a check mark alongside those items that the university's research library may lack and need. He will send it on to the library's order department.

Alas, the yearned-for mail is not there. Six months ago John had been taken on by a classy New York literary agent who was hustling a ten-page proposal for a "popular" exposé of the Federal Reserve System for which both of them anticipated an advance "in the five figures." Of John's previous books, his first (really his reworked doctoral dissertation) had been published by the Baleston University Press. Another had been a collection of edited *Readings in Economic Thought,* and the last was a long report on *Recent Developments in Computer-based Income Forecasting* which he wrote jointly with an old buddy from graduate school who taught at Berkeley. There was a row over the royalty split (the sum in dispute was less than fifty dollars), and now they are enemies.

John searches in vain for a narrow letter from Sam Jacobs at the Cook Institute inviting him to sit out the next fall semester at full salary in Washington. Nor is there a handwritten letter from a secret lady with whom he had a rendezvous at long intervals in Boston.

So John ambles off to the office which he has hated all these years. Though large, the room is always overheated by the clanking steam radiators and still has a medium-brown linoleum floor. The psychologists just got red-carpeted (though smaller) offices in a new high-rise that John can see from his dirty window. Once seated behind his yellow oak desk, he quickly scans a Dutch journal and an English journal for articles or books on harbingers of interest rates, finds nothing, and inserts them at the ends of rows of pastel-colored magazines high up on one of his many bookcases. He spends more time on a little-known, remarkably prescient twelve-page weekly newsletter from Washington, D.C. In a little administrative coup, he convinced the library to send it to him first for immediate perusal before shelving it, even though its subscription costs $475 a year.

Then John pulls before him a pad of lined yellow paper to make anticipatory sketches for his income tax, which he always prepares well in advance of the filing dates. His gross income would be about $58,000. Of this figure, $32,500 is his salary for the nine-month year (John never teaches summer school). About $23,000 would be for consulting ("crystal-balling" he calls it) with treasury officials in Washington, bankers in New York and Boston, and insurance executives in Hartford. Only $2,500 would be income from investments and some dribbles from royalties and the sale of articles.

One would expect that a man in John Lostein's inside position would have an outstanding portfolio. He had, in fact, been building one when the first marriage broke up in 1967. Those holdings had almost tripled in value since. But Rhoda got it all, and she and the three boys still kept him on the line for child support.

Some of John's income never appears on his income tax form, since his paychecks are docked for maximum contributions to a tax-deferred retirement fund, T.I.A.A.–C.R.E.F., that the Carnegie Foundation implemented for college teachers in 1906. Also, he puts 15 per cent of his consulting or "moonlighting" money into another tax-deferred mutual fund allowed by the Keogh Plan, which was especially set up in 1974 to benefit the self-employed. John took the usual exemptions. He padded his travel expenses, listed subscriptions and memberships, claimed depreciation on his private library of 2,000 volumes and on some tape recorders, two typewriters, a pocket computer, and a Hasselblad camera. Still he would not be able to chisel any more to get his taxable income down below $31,500. It is only at times like these that John envies his brothers, the overworked optometrist in Jacksonville and the worried furrier in Brooklyn, who finally took over their ailing father's business in 1964.

John often wonders if he ought to work so hard to stay on top of interest rates. Much of his checking of trade balances in distant countries, his analyses of bankers' reports from Frankfurt, Geneva, and Hong Kong, and the testing of new equations on Baleston's computer had only tangential relevance to his graduate seminars. Due to his income tax bracket, of each $1,000 he picked up consulting, he kept only $610. However, he has to admit to himself that his consulting releases him for the danger (which is always exciting) of chasing when out of town, and ever more he needs unassailable excuses to get away from Marie, who (astonishing coincidence!) is becoming a shrew just like Rhoda was.

Sometimes John feels up to the ready camaraderie in Baleston's famed faculty club. But the place was a conversational trap, where drones like Prescott spent two-hour, three-martini, four-cigarette lunches. Today John takes the long walk to the college street, where he eats Chinese and, as hoped, encounters only nodding acquaintances.

Back at the office John's determination overcomes his laziness and he picks up the first draft of the third chapter of the book that the agent has not sold. He simply cannot get going, so he sticks the manila folder in his briefcase and attacks matters in the "in" box. For the three letters of recommendation for former students applying to teach at jerkwater colleges, he drafts encomiums that are nearly identical and puts them in the "out" box for the secretaries. In a letter that has been nagging John's conscience for two weeks, a professor in Calcutta wants more substantiation for a provocative statement that John made in a speech, later published, in Mexico City in 1971 about savings gaps in underdeveloped countries. Fan letters of this sort are the worst. John no longer quite believes (if he ever did) what he said in that speech, and to produce supporting data would require three days of work—something a five-hundred-dollar-a-day man is unlikely to do for a bozo in Calcutta. John drafts an evasive thank-you note.

As he had for three previous afternoons, John tries to get at two books for which reviews are already overdue. He had promised himself that he would not do the "sitting duck," which was a right-wing polemic against deficit financing until he had disposed of a 421-page report from a bold group of young economists in an institute in Stuttgart. There were novel aperçus in the work and it *had* to be publicized and even praised to Anglo-Saxon specialists, but the language of the German social scientists was becoming ever more jargonized at the same time that John's grip on even classical German was becoming weaker. Still this 1,500-word review had to be done for the *Journal of Econometric Projections,* whose editor is a major consultant for several foundations where John's reputation must be maintained.

Wretched language! Wretched work! And despite the fact that he has no posted office hours today, there are interruptions. One of the basketball-scholarship athletes disputes the grade a teaching assistant gave him on an essay examination. John will not speak with him unless he confers first with the T.A. (John invariably supports them, even when they are incompetent or heartless) who graded it. Two men in their late twenties merely stick their heads in the door to check whether John has read the chapters and verified the correlations in the tables of their seminar papers. He has not. They leave smiling politely and bitterly. Another graduate student "dropping by" has to be seated in a yellow oak straight chair as John explains carefully that he cannot accept his proposed topic for a twenty-page seminar paper unless the student first checks the *Internationale Bibliographie der Zeitschriftenliteratur* (which they refer to as the "I.B.Z.") for previous work on the topic in other languages. When the student complains that his German is only his third language and that this might be a three-day job, John replies, "So be it."

Before the student can close the door, young Hertskowitz nips in. Despite the pressure of urgent tasks, John beams at the twenty-nine-year-old assistant professor whom he had bullied the department's search committee into hiring last year. Though, like John himself, Ted Hertskowitz had his B.A. *summa cum laude* from Brooklyn College, the Ph.D. was unfortunately only from Maryland. That university had given Ted a fat fellowship, which he needed, since he was poor. But Hertskowitz was long on energy and wit. As John predicted, Ted was "coming along." Two solid articles accepted, a book prospectus viewed very warmly by the editor of the University of Chicago Press, invitations (arranged via the long-distance lines behind the scenes by John himself) to some classy conferences, and the prospect of doing a couple of chapters for a report on chronic unemployment by the Cook Foundation in Washington.

Unlike John, who started as an instructor at Indiana in 1956, Hertskowitz had never bothered to middle-westernize his rich New Yorkese. The young man was short and pudgy and confidently wore his flared, knit trousers too far above the ankle. He wore wide ties with expressionistic patterns. When relaxed, the older and the younger men traded dialect stories, bellowed with laughter, and, as unconscious demonstrations of their racial bond, slapped their own and each other's knees.

"Wish I could kibbitz today, Ted, but look at this desk." Both shrug and the younger leaves with a "See you later," not having been asked to sit down.

Then John makes phone calls. Reservations in New York for a single at the Roosevelt Hotel (which had a lower academic rate) and for a late supper for two at La Seine. He phones Washington to order some recent Senate documents on the new trade restrictions in Argentina. He calls the library three times to use his authority to speed the search process for some books that a dissertation student needs that were reported "missing." He scolds a high official in the payroll office for not yet correcting a mistake made in his with-holding five months ago. He calls a faculty wife in the business school to "regret" that due to his work in New York, he cannot come to her large cocktail party. Each time John makes a call, he crosses the appropriate item from today's "list of things to do" in a brown booklet he carries at all times in the right pocket of his sports jacket.

He pushes a button on the Pulsar, which flashes red numbers to tell him that the late-afternoon mail should be in. He dashes to the pigeonhole. Only book advertisements and intrauniversity mimeo-graphed news. Downcast, John stops for a long leak at the huge chlorine-stinking, high-ceilinged faculty men's bathroom and walks back to his office. He steps in, and as always he is disgusted by the smells of his own nervous sweat and nervous farts, the odorous leit-motifs of hard work since he began graduate work at Harvard in 1953.

He cannot face Buntfoot's dissertation chapters, though the poor boy has been calling him almost daily now. So John dallies by neat-ening some files and then at 5:30 sharp slams the yellow oak door with the frosted-glass window shut to lock it and begins the half-mile hike through sleet to parking lot K. He stamps his dirty loafers be-fore getting in the green "88" wagon with 15,532 miles on the odom-eter. The wretched weather makes the go-and-jolt drive along the sinuous campus road more irritating than usual. The traffic on the throughway is slow too. Happily the campus FM station is playing some Schubert piano music that he can hum along with.

When he enters the up-to-date kitchen of the three-year-old condominium, Marie is annoyed that he is twelve minutes late, but has the wisdom to keep eight-year-old Becky and six-year-old Naomi out of the way until John settles in the red-carpeted study with a large tumbler of iced dry California sherry. Two years ago Marie and John swore off hard stuff before eating, since they blamed the presupper martinis for detonating a couple of savage battles that terrified the little girls.

When John met Marie, she was a twenty-six-year-old graduate student in anthropology at a nearby (and inferior) university. At that time Rhoda's complaining, jealousy, and ever-shriller voice were becoming insupportable. The first encounter was in a students' bar that he hung around during the campus disturbances in 1968. Marie got pregnant two months before John's divorce was final. They agonized for several weeks and finally decided to have the kid. She then put off work on the dissertation in order to meet John's demands for bourgeois domestic life. Her bitching was about John's lack of interest in the little girls, his parsimoniousness, and his inability to account for large blocks of time at the university and when he was off consulting. But both knew that a basis for Marie's discontent was her abandonment of the old dissertation which was to have been based on data collected on the poor in a neighborhood just four miles away.

Today, the large meal proceeds without tumult. The girls have been adequately shushed beforehand, and John is so distracted by his failure to do justice to Buntfoot's chapters that he rises to none of Marie's subtle provocations. As Marie smacks the Melmac together in the efficient little kitchen, he reads some Beatrix Potter stories to the children. Father and daughters are seated at the formica-topped dining table which is still sticky since Marie wiped it so perfunctorily. John is enraged, but keeps still.

After Marie bathes the children, they knock on John's study door at 8:15 for the " 'night" kisses. John finally tackles Buntfoot's chapters at 9:00.

Young Buntfoot is the first person trained in advanced econometric techniques to examine with proper care the captured Nazi statistics on trade balances, domestic prices, retail prices, and interest rates for the period 1933–44. During this time the German economists were extraordinarily successful in promoting the nation's prosperity by manipulating banking and currency exchange rates. Buntfoot's results, which would certainly be prominently published, would cause a ripple among macroeconomists, among historians, and very likely among some Treasury Department laggards John has been trying to convince about the usefulness of managed currency and manipulated money markets. But the boy's writing is slovenly and obfuscating. It merits the slashes of John's wicked red pencil.

Once launched on this kind of work, he goes into an intellectual trance and abandons it with regret. But eventually John's eyes begin itching and watering uncontrollably, and at 1:15 A.M. he finally creeps in beside Marie, who does not stir. But the excitement does not die and John Lostein lies awake for hours due to the heart-thumping joys aroused by that kind of professorial creativity that makes his life so worthwhile.

III

Viewed Large

A good round figure to start with is 400,000. That is roughly the number of professionals who now teach full-time in American educational institutions above the level of high school. The round figure includes the instructional staff of medical schools (a little over 6,000) and about 50,000 teachers in technical schools and in some junior colleges which do not use the customary professorial ranks. This more than one third of a million excludes those who illegitimately assume the title of "professor" and who are so elevated by their positions in degree mills. A "degree mill" is a business set up to sell phony academic degrees and titles. The self-improvement magazines, of course, advertise mail-order houses from which one can, if he or she wishes, order nicely printed diplomas signed by people who call themselves "professor" and who place academic initials after their names.

Excluded from the large number that begins this chapter are a great many people who teach in respectable academic institutions. There are various part-time teachers—mostly younger people who are graduate students giving the less-specialized instruction. To use the most common abbreviation, these are called "T.A.'s" for "teaching assistants." Most big universities also employ whole phalanxes of laboratory assistants to supervise and instruct the science classes. Within the loose national brotherhood of college teachers there exist well-known levels of prestige. Any individual professor knows in his heart of hearts where he and his institution rank. Many outsiders will recognize the broad outlines of what follows.

Full-time teachers are usually about half of the full-time employees at a college or a university. Universities can be immense enterprises, demanding more complex and more flexible administrative networks than those of giant profit-making corporations or those of a small South American state. There are the presidents (who are supposed to interpret the will of the specialists below them to the trustees above them and vice versa), provosts (who customarily do the actual major work of administration), deans (who would be the equivalent of division heads in a large corporation). All have their appropriate associates and assistants. There are accountants, librarians, physicians and psychiatrists, computer programmers, coaches and trainers —all with their appropriate assistants and secretaries. A college with an enrollment of only 1,000 will have a fleet of sedans, station wagons, and buses. The football coach of a state university embarking on a campaign to end a losing streak expects as his perquisite a small jet airplane with a pilot who addresses him as "Sir." The state's bishop of sports will fly to and from provincial pep rallies and to small towns to woo seventeen-year-old hopefuls for the new winning teams. The University of California possesses several ocean-going vessels. So chauffeurs, car mechanics, jet pilots, and bosuns are on university payrolls. Still, on the college and university balance sheets, faculty salaries, which are usually from one third to one half of the total budget, are by far the largest item.

There are certain figures which are likely to correlate well with the quality of an institution of higher learning and the worth of its degrees. The usual bold figure is the student-faculty ratio. The second, a more refined figure than the above, is the amount of total faculty compensation divided by the number of students. Some rough figures are necessary here: If University A or College AA has ten or fewer students per faculty member or the faculty compensation per student is $1,500 or more, one can conclude that the purpose of the institution is to bring the students into rather frequent contact with the teaching staff. At Harvard and Princeton the student-faculty ratios are roughly 7 to 1 and the faculty compensation per student is about $2,500. Of course, other factors not lending themselves to statistical precision—reputation, the visual impression, upkeep of the facilities, and, most especially, the expectation of the students before they appear on the scene—contribute to making a good or a great school. Still the correlations of excellence and the ratios of students to faculty and, more so, of faculty compensation per student are very dependable.

If an institution has more than twenty students per faculty member and the assembled faculty members receive less than $750 per student on hand, one can assume that those who guide that university's destinies have a take-it-or-leave-it attitude toward the hordes who apply to them supposedly for humanistic, scientific, or professional training and inspiration. A loose, antitraditional atmosphere on the student-dominated campus will be infectious and difficult to combat. Most of the few who show up eager for a college education as sanguinely conceived will succumb to the atmosphere of torpid anti-intellectualism and physical indulgence. The students will sleep a lot. Rock music will be a pestilence in the dormitories. However, one ought not to assume that the professors at the lower rank institutions are overworked. One should assume the contrary. Energetic professors at the sloppy places are resented by their acclimated colleagues. It is easier for professors to win popularity and the deans' gratitude by being easygoing buffoons in the classroom and by failing only those who consciously or subconsciously wish the opprobrium. At most colleges and universities, if a professor sits on committee meetings several hours a week, he is left alone to live the nonprofessional three fourths of his life exactly as he chooses.

It has been clear to more than one entrepreneur that, if one could organize a "college" in which the student-faculty ratio was very high —say 30 to 1—and were free to charge high tuition—say $2,000—and high prices for room and board, one would have lots of money to play with. Indeed, though the organizational process was complex, the simple figure (or close to it) of $60,000 per professor arrived at by simple multiplication was sufficient to inspire many to take advantage of the seemingly boundless demand for college degrees in the 1960s.

The most notorious of the academic businesses was Parsons College in Fairfield, Iowa, which had its heyday during the presidency of Millard George Roberts from 1955 to 1967.[1]

Roberts had been the minister of a fashionable Presbyterian church in New York City. Before 1955 he had no previous college-teaching or administrative experience. Nevertheless the trustees of the little moribund college in Fairfield hired him, for he promised to increase sharply and steadily their supply of that without-which nothing of American higher education, students. One of Roberts' first acts as president was to spend $10,000 on his inauguration ceremony.

Sure enough, enrollments went from 357 in 1955 to 810 in 1959, then to 1,863 in 1961 and to a top of 5,141 in 1966. He advertised in *The Wall Street Journal* and other places for "second-chance" students and "late bloomers." He had as many as twelve recruiters who scouted the country for youths with poor high-school records or who had failed at other colleges. The recruiters were paid commissions by the head. Recruits were assured beforehand that they would not be axed and that A's and B's were easy to obtain. The critical characteristic of a potential student was his ability to pay.

Tuition approached that at Princeton and at Swarthmore. The school made a 40 per cent profit on its standard room and board charges. The summer school operated at 87 per cent capacity. The college and Fairfield, Iowa, boomed.

One of the specifications in Millard George Roberts' contract was that his basic salary be twice that of the highest-paid professor at Parsons. The college also provided his house, a white Imperial, and an Aero Commander, on which he logged 210,000 miles in 1966. He spoke on reform in higher education before groups of teachers and before chambers of commerce for fees of three to five hundred dollars.

One of the initial appeals and an advertising gimmick of the Parsons operation was that Roberts hired bright-eyed, impeccably degreed professors for Yale-like salaries of $15,000–$25,000 per year. (This is still the early sixties, note well.) However, between these professors and the students he installed uncredentialed "preceptors" and "tutors," who also taught much more and earned one fourth to one half as much. Roberts claimed a student-faculty ratio of 15 to 1, which is high and barely respectable. If only professors were counted (the usual practice), the ratio was closer to 50 to 1. The ratio at the University of Iowa was 10 to 1.

One might argue that professors who settled at such a place should have known what they were getting into. Parsons was much in the academic news in those days. There were (less lucrative, it is true) jobs elsewhere. Roberts demanded that the professors teach a lot and that they stay in their offices. He changed their grades if they were too low, spied on them, and treated them like ordinary employees. Some dissidents wrote and distributed exposés. They claimed the library was a farce, that their profession was being demeaned, that the place was being run like a business. They attracted reporters from *Time* and *Life* and, subsequently, the accreditation boards. Roberts was eventually caught in a tangle of lies—mostly about his disposal of large sums of discretionary money.

There were lawsuits, the withdrawal of accreditation by the North Central Association of Colleges and Secondary Schools, and climaxes of personal bitterness between the remaining professors, the college's administrators, and the businessmen in the town. The trustees fired Roberts in 1967 and Parsons College declined rapidly. The campus is now the home of the transcendental meditation movement and is called Maharishi International University.

The reason that the struggles and the collapse received so much publicity was Roberts' serious error of promising academic respectability (as well as above-scale wages) to people who had all the credentials one expected of very good, real professors. Many—perhaps a third—of the college students in the United States put in their time at places where the authenticity and intensity of education are more feeble than that at Parsons College. One can almost assume this of the black colleges, and the financially strapped private and (to a lesser extent) public colleges with local constituencies that admit and cherish anybody who might be called "a student." Besides the payment of tuition and attendance, these places require little and offer little and are therefore almost selling degrees. The trained attendants who staff these colleges are called professors, but they are usually demoralized opportunists incapable of doing other work at anything like the same pay. Most of the little quiet colleges are old and keep out of the news. Their circumspect presidents speak in platitudes only to the *local* chambers of commerce, and they drive somber Buicks or Mercuries.

In our time teachers, researchers, and colleagues distinguished by the title "professor" can be found all over North America. Still, the distribution of these personages is uneven, though far less so than it was even twenty years ago. Postsecondary education—often that of a faculty-intensive kind—has long been a major industry in New York City and, most especially, Boston. Well-landscaped universities have long provided acres of ornamental shrubbery as well as economic trees growing the essential green in large towns such as Berkeley, New Haven, Ann Arbor, Bloomington, and Columbus. As we observed in Chapter II, the need for technical experts, feelings of cultural inferiority, and evangelism (both pious and liberal) inspired the founding of the land-grant and denominational colleges of the nineteenth century. The steadiness of the economic impulses generated by a local college bootstraps idealism. After 1945 and again after Sputnik in 1957, almost any academic hustler found enthusiastic support from retailers or owners of acreage near a town that considered expanding its college. The stated reasons often went: "so our kids can live near home instead of in those dormitories in Lansing or Baton Rouge."

New or altered charters jumped the appropriate political hurdles in the capitol. The appropriate committees of the state house of representatives assured the initial financing. The federal government guaranteed federally subsidized loans made by local banks for construction. The functional, modular buildings went up, thus supplementing the slapdash "temporary" quarters in Quonset huts and a high school built in 1910.[2] New deans hired new department chairmen, who hired new professors—all of them at slightly above market-level wages. Sure enough, large numbers of students appeared as anticipated by the projected growth curves. The town boomed and the citizens were newly proud of their oasis of culture. A few townspeople may have objected to drunken students having acceleration contests with motorcycles on Main Street. However, the professors usually made acceptable neighbors, and almost everyone was pleased enough so that a new cycle of buildings, staff, and students began.

The schematic above took place all over North America between 1947 and 1970. That is why we have more than 400,000 professors. Few Americans who graduate from high school now live more than an hour's drive from some complex of parks and institutional buildings which is called a campus. Few American neighborhoods of houses in the $60,000 class are without their college professor.

The fragmentation of knowledge and, consequently, of learning that the American colleges have witnessed and advanced is mirrored in university organization charts. In the traditional undergraduate (that is, freshman, sophomore, junior, and senior years) college, the major divisions are usually humanities, social sciences, life sciences, and physical sciences. A dean for each supervises three to eight chairmen, who in turn take care of the professorial troops who number from five to forty per department. We need not dwell on the areas of specialization customarily supervised by appropriate deans except to mention again that a college, though nicely compartmentalized, is loosely managed. The laxness encourages all sorts of maneuvers and border disputes. Many thousands of committee hours have been spent by influential historians redefining themselves as humanists rather than social scientists (or vice versa) in order to come under the wing of a more manageable dean.

The great trick is for a professor to set himself afloat as the head of an "institute," of which the largest universities have dozens. Some of the more than thirty institutes of the University of Colorado are listed below:

> Bureau of Economic Research
> Bureau of Governmental Research and Services
> Business Research Division
> Clinical Research Center for Children
> Cystic Fibrosis Research Center
> Engineering Research Center
> Institute for Arctic and Alpine Research
> Institute for Behavioral Science
> Institute for Study of Intellectual Behavior
> Joint Institute for Laboratory Astrophysics
> Research Program on Personal and Social Problem Behavior
> Research Program on Social Processes

An institute is launched when an academic hustler with a few research publications to his credit nets a very large grant to be spent over a three-or-more-year period. The grant can be from a private or governmental foundation. This was easier in the late sixties than it is in the late seventies. If a university does not have its own all-purpose grant consultant, it can hire one at five hundred dollars a day. The professor with money is then wooed by equipment salesmen. He hires clerical and technical staff. By means of offering consult-antships, he pieces off his allies in his department (where he also holds on to his job), demands that the campus chief of facilities and grounds find him so and so many thousand square feet of air-conditioned space, and thus casts the operation adrift.

The Gerontological Research Institute, the Institute for Studies in Kansas History, or the Institute on Swamp Ecology may be under the titular supervision of some dean or other, but its director can (and sometimes does) give his academic boss a heave-ho if he comes snooping. A clever institute director may and often does hire himself out to consult three or four days a month to other distant institutes at the rate of $300–$750 a day. (Indeed the budget of his own institute has provision for reciprocity.) This money is in addition to his budgeted salary. This is why some professors can pay regular alimony to their Mark I wives and still buy Chris-Crafts to enjoy with their

Mark II wives. All the institute has to do to mollify the foundation directors who write the big checks is to be favorably described in occasional newspaper articles and from time to time to publish articles which are tiresome to read and have lots of statistical graphs. A nice job as long as the outside money lasts.

The big or "good" universities employ many professors in the "professional" schools of law, medicine, dentistry, or librarianship. These professors do not answer to deans in the traditional disciplines. For these schools the accreditation (the term refers to a stamp of approval by an organization, usually national, which has standards for correct facilities and the credentials for the staff) standards are precise; the admissions standards are rigid. The students in professional schools usually know what they want and how to work for it. The professors have stated objectives or pre-existing models upon which they shape their working lives. The hours they teach are usually longer and the wages are higher. Consequently, the professors in the professional schools are surer of themselves in the larger society and are less eccentric and less noticeable than professors in the academic disciplines. The same observations hold for the teaching staffs of those professional schools such as business administration, engineering, pharmacy, and nursing that include undergraduate teaching. An embarrassing exception among the professional schools (and an exception in many other ways as well) are the schools of education, which will receive more discussion later.

Before the great boom in colleges and universities that began in the late 1950s, prestige figured larger as an occupational reward awaiting the professor-in-training. Professors still have considerable prestige in the world outside the college, but now the professors have more agreeable working conditions and higher salaries besides. However, among the 400,000 prestige still matters (and varies) enormously—far more indeed than any other variable in the occupation.

In order best to set forth the subject matter of this book, it is necessary to offer a simplified and workable rating system for American colleges and universities. We can begin at the summit: For the professors themselves, there is but one "top" university, and all professors know what it is. The holder of an endowed chair (a "chair" is the name given to a gift to a university the yearly income from which provides a subsidy to the salary of an especially desirable professor; the "chair" takes the name of the donor of the gift and endowment, and its "holder" must sign academic correspondence with some title

such as "Sidney Babbitch Professor of Chemical Engineering") in
Ann Arbor, the "Distinguished" (some chair holders are required
thus to designate that they are enjoyers of subsidized professorships)
Professor of Slavic Linguistics in Austin, Texas, the ostensibly comfy
director of an institute for particle research in Stanford, the music
historian with five thick books to his credit and whose living-room
picture window in the Berkeley hills overlooks that stunning pan-
orama—all these personages know very well that they have not made
it to the top.

This writer recalls vividly a visit to chat about some matters of
mutual interest in a large, wood-paneled office at the top of a balus-
traded staircase in the Widener Library at Harvard. Though born
into a family which owned a small store in Queens, the man behind
the desk had these credentials: B.A., New York University; Ph.D.,
Princeton; teaching jobs at Illinois, Columbia, Chicago; and then, at
age forty-one, a full professorship at Harvard. The University of California published his unaltered Ph.D. dissertation. He founded an interdisciplinary journal, and then wrote two unusual books on traditional problems that were published in hardback respectively by the
Oxford University Press and by Knopf. The Knopf book was later a
Vintage paperback. While still in his early thirties he had wickedly
ironic epistolary arguments in some journals with scholars in Rome
and Madrid. He scorned anyone who knew but one extra language.
He had advanced steadily from scruffy apartments to, successively,
seven-, ten-, and fourteen-room houses and demanded that his
French wife keep a table that became justly famous. He was a sore
loser and cussed. Once when he was yet thirty years old and on the
faculty at the University of Illinois, some graduate students and other
assistant professors signed a petition claiming that they would quit
the departmental softball team unless he resigned from it. A few
years later when he left Chicago for Cambridge, Massachusetts, a
saying swept the corridors: "Harvard's loss is Chicago's gain!"

Anyway, he had been at Harvard for three years when the conversation inspiring this tale took place. He characterized former colleagues as tersely as ever: "that asshole prime," "Henny Penny,"
"hillbilly Pooh-Bah," "closet-queen schmuck," "double dummy,"
etc. Though he was still healthy and obviously pleased with his status, he was at the same time oddly wizened and defeated. Unlike
Harvard's economists and specialists in American foreign policy, his
discipline was not nor would ever be marketable in Washington. At

age forty-four he still had several decades of life to kill, and there was simply nothing worth doing after having made it, as he had, at Harvard.

There are about ten universities in the next and still the first rank. They include Yale, Princeton, Columbia, Stanford, and Chicago. The only public university that indisputably ranks with them is the University of California at Berkeley, which is always called just "Berkeley." At these places outsiders can assume that the similarity of instruction, the generally elitist atmosphere, the importance of innovations and discoveries, the relatively frequent mentioning in television broadcasts—all make them comparable (but only comparable) to Harvard. These institutions are indeed first class but in the occupation, the professors on the job do not rate with those at the top university.

Next are some twenty-five places we might also call "great" universities. They include all the "Big Ten" schools, a few more state universities such as the University of Texas, plus five or six well-heeled private universities such as Cornell and Duke.

Before moving on down, there are some points to establish. One can and many do become very well educated at the University of Youngstown and at Loretto Heights College in Denver. At these places the serious student must choose his or her friends carefully and demand attention from those professors who are not yet torpid. On the other hand, with less determination a young adult can fritter away his parent's money and four years of his time learning almost nothing traditionally considered academic at Ohio State or the University of Minnesota. It is worth emphasizing again that the discussion here is not about education, but about prestige as perceived by the professors. One might be reminded that the professors who labor in the big and glamorous campuses referred to above number less than one fifth of the total population discussed in this chapter.

Another fraction of the occupational class works in private, often small undergraduate colleges with very high tuition, a long history of selective admissions, and rigorous, intellectual demands. Some of these places are Swarthmore, Reed, Oberlin, Smith, Bryn Mawr, Williams, and Claremont. Professors at these colleges have considerable self-respect, but they are a little aside from the usual pyramid of prestige. Once accustomed to these pleasant places, the teacher tends to stay in the league, for the demands on one's time and a quiet prejudice *against* outside fame are such as to work against his or her establishment of a reputation (i.e. publication) in the discipline-oriented national mainstreams.

To return to the mainstream rankings: Below the enormous "multiversities" (whose readiness to take on new and possibly dubious functions and therefore to grow yet larger has led them to be called all-purpose academic whorehouses), beneath the "good little schools" and some specialized, primarily graduate institutions such as the Pratt Institute and the Peabody School of Music, there are about a hundred respectable colleges and universities. By "respectable" I mean that those on the teaching staff never have to explain when away from home where the place they are employed is located. Professors at respectable institutions wistfully model their professional behavior on what is believed to be the behavior of the professors better placed above them. The respectable institutions in their course offerings, equipment, student-faculty ratios, parklike appearance, and in the successive waves of fashion they embrace, resemble the great universities. But these lower-ranked institutions only *resemble* the better places. An absorbing task of the trained work force at these middling colleges and universities is to move up and away to where the football teams appear on national television, where latrine graffiti are generally funny, where the faculty clubs have waiter service, where the majority of the students are not anti-intellectual, where many of the buildings are reassuringly old-looking, where the main library has runs of scholarly periodicals of the 1930s, where the campus shopping street has a Chinese restaurant and a sprawling store where one can buy (sometimes on sale) the best Danish furniture and Marimekko prints.

A large number, perhaps a third, of the professors teach at respectable places. They include all but the few best public universities as well as second-place state universities such as Michigan State, most of the campuses of the State University of New York system, and the larger California campuses after Berkeley and UCLA. Here we must also include several private institutions such as Notre Dame, the University of Southern California, Fordham, and Washington (of Saint Louis) and a lot of municipal universities such as Wayne State (in Detroit) and the University of Missouri in St. Lous.

Beneath the respectable schools is a large group which has been described as "academic Siberia." A refiner of academic jargon has suggested that "academic Alaska" might be better usage since Siberia undoubtedly has many institutions of superior quality.[3] Another academic with much experience in such places has referred to his service as "down and out in academia."[4] Yet another ranked institutions as being in "Heaven," "Purgatory" or "Limbo"—the last being the lowest ranked.[5] The Siberian institutions have about one third of the professors and about half of the American students—which is another way of saying that the ratio of students to faculty is relatively high. These are the underrenowned church schools, the "regional," "branch," or "urban" campuses of many middle-ranked state universities, the black colleges specializing in social life. Here, too, are certain experimental schools and the private women's colleges that are really finishing schools. All of these places do indeed keep those enrolled off the crowded job market and offer some sort of education. But the teachers are demoralized and desperate to get out if competent, and demoralized and torpid if incompetent. There is almost no literature, factual, or fictional, about this major portion of the academic world.

Prestige, reputations, and prejudices vary among the disciplines and academic departments of a university. The intrauniversity rankings offered below apply throughout academic life. Beginning at the top, law and medicine teachers are somewhat above and apart from the rest. These professors are few in number and are almost administratively independent in a large university. They do not teach undergraduates, and the professionals they prepare enter quasi-unionized, highly paid trades. The professors' elevated position is substantiated by their own high wages. One could make similar observations about the somewhat lower ranked teachers of dentistry, pharmacy, optometry, and business. Librarianship and nursing, which offer useful training for women who will not earn well, naturally are much lower in prestige than those named above.

Historians and, just below them, the political scientists rank high. Though not always conservative, they dress with restraint. They are fluent talkers and effective persuaders. They intrigue with skill and often rise in university administration, where they bestow favors on former colleagues who flatter them. Philosophers also talk well and dress cleanly, but stay out of the power struggle—possibly as a result of reflection. Social scientists—for purposes of this book sociologists, psychologists, and anthropologists (henceforth S.P.A.'s) will be assumed to be one group—rank low. Their manners are coarse, for they are still sentimentally close to their East European progenitors.

They arrive at committee meetings late and smoke cigars. They are the only professors who screw undergraduates. They wear acrylic knits, sweat under the arms, play poker, and lunch only with their own kind in groups of four or five.

Of high to middling prestige are the high-strung English professors. The titles of their dissertations and serious articles are hilarious when read aloud at a party of S.P.A.'s, who thus demonstrate to each other that worthwhile discoveries are only possible in the newer disciplines. The scholars of our language and literature are apt to develop tics, to fight like sopranos, and to carry grudges for years. The professors in the foreign languages are likely to dress like tropical birds and are even whackier. Professors of foreign language have low internal prestige. Foreign-language departments are sometimes referred to as "zoos."

The mathematicians, biologists, chemists, physicists, and those related to them have high prestige but their rankings are somewhat aside from those listed above. Even ambitious scientists seldom maneuver domestically but rather among those personages in Washington and in the foundations who are able to finance the equipment they need to facilitate their curiosity. On their campuses, scientists are rarely able to sound convincing when they explain just what they teach or how they do research. Rarely do they take positions on principles important in the larger community. The aloofness of the giants of theoretical physics in Berkeley during the course of the California oath controversy of 1948–51 remains a scandal of recent academic history. The scientists have also had their prestige damaged by the eagerness of large numbers of them to do any kind of weapons research and their smug silence during the peace movement.

Though the great chic in American society for scientific novelty at any price may be waning, scientists still rank high in the nonacademic world. But within academia the scientists look and behave too much like other professors' bourgeois neighbors. Almost the only standardly conceived intellectual indulgence of the scientists is art music. The physicists are especially fond of Bach's and Mozart's compositions for solo instruments and pay large sums to possess the last word in stereo equipment.

Occupying a vast area far below the professors in any other category are the professors of that branch of study and training that we might wish to merit very great respect. The lowest of the low in academic life are the educationalists, the professors in the schools or departments of education, whose job is to prepare those who will teach in the nation's primary and secondary schools. These isolated and scorned souls are bewildered in committee meetings, where they tend quietly to grind their teeth and to blink their eyes slowly. When challenged or otherwise required to say something, their mouths go dry. They speak, as they write, in passive voice with added filler words of "situation," "process," "meaningful," and ceaseless "y'know's." English professors may call their obfuscating jargon "Educanto." There is no requirement that the educationalists even at Teachers College at Columbia or the education schools at Stanford and Berkeley learn a language other than their own kind of English. The educationalists never read anything except their own pious literature, which revolts all other academics.

The educationalists are hard fighters among themselves, but they are rarely given room to swashbuckle on the larger university scene. Should a professor of education try to have his way, the heretofore divided plant physiologist and teacher of mechanical drawing alike would close ranks to undermine him. The scorn for educationalists is justified among the professors in the standard disciplines by the assumption that the educationalists themselves invariably cleanse their fiefs of graduate students or professors who might wish to apply the critical or performance standards of the great world. These same observations also hold for schools or departments of physical education.

It is worth noting here that almost all research on colleges and universities is carried out by the more worldly professors of education at a few large universities such as Columbia, Berkeley, or Michigan. The resulting books and articles (a couple of presses flourish on this kind of commerce, which is regularly subsidized by the U. S. Department of Education, the National Education Association, and the Carnegie Foundation) are overburdened with moralistic "shoulds" and "oughts" and are almost always devoid of substance. Few were of any use whatever to the writer of the book in hand.

Before revealing how much academics earn, it is wise here to make some observations on academic titles and the prestige that goes with them. The title of "professor" was imported from Germany. Until about 1870 professors were rare in the United States, but shortly afterwards every college had to have them. In America, in order to have lots of professors and in order to differentiate between them, the Americans provided for assistant, associate, and "full" professors.

Usage has varied in America, but rank designations have held steadily for the past twenty-five years. The lowest academic rank is instructor and is now commonly applied to those recently out of graduate school who are seriously being considered for permanent employment and professorial title but who do not yet have the Ph.D. They very likely were hired on the assumption that their dissertation would soon be finished and that they would thereupon be promoted to assistant professorships.

The big jump in status, which occurs three to seven (most often five) years after the assistant professor has reached this rank (or never, whereupon the assistant is given a year's notice that his job will end), is to associate professor, which usually means that the professor's employment is permanent. In academic terms, he has tenure. He has a kind of job security enjoyed by no other profession in America, for the process necessary to discharge the tenured professor is so complicated and studded with dangers that few university administrators have been willing to see the process to the end.

Advancement to the top rank (whereupon the promoted one tells the secretaries to type merely "Professor" under one's name at the bottom of a business letter) is a small jump. In the spoken language of academia one is now a "full" professor. Along with this final elevation may come a small raise in salary and the expectation on the part of one's peers in rank that the full professor will take more responsibility in overseeing the conduct of the institution at large. From the position of full professor there is nowhere to go higher but into the dubious adventures of the administrative crab basket with its lowest designation of chairman and then to dean. Another way to rise from the position of full professor is to become a full professor at a more prestigious place. However, full professors move from one institution to another and better one only rarely.

Any teacher or researcher inside or outside the campus can asked to be addressed as "Doctor" if he or she has a doctor's degree (Ph.D., Ed.D., D.D., or some other). It is a fact in American professorial life that the more prestigious the institution, the less common is the address "Doctor." A professor of philosophy at UCLA or at Duke probably feels secure enough and is likely to prefer "Mister." However, educationalists everywhere need "Doctor" and glow appreciatively when they hear it. Most assistant, associate, and full professors may be addressed on the brick walk or on the letterhead as "Professor" and usually like it. The exceptions are the few hundred at Columbia or Berkeley or comparable great places who may feel demeaned by provincial elegancies.

Other titles tend to describe a position and are assumed by academics when they leave their departments (and thus their professorships) for administrative posts. A department chairman is still a professor. His boss, the dean, often is not. Nor is the next boss up who may be called a vice-president in charge of instruction at a small institution, or a provost (a rather new title in America) at a large one. A dean usually attempts to hold on to his professorial job in the department from which he rose. Tenure is a precious possession that one does not cast aside easily. The quasi-sacerdotal nature of academic employment and the distinctions in academic address have caused the gang bosses in the athletic departments (who usually answer administratively only to the president) to appropriate "Coach" preceding the surname. Sometimes the professor of physical education warms more to "Coach" than he would to "Doctor" and actually nods and blushes with pleasure when he hears it, for it certifies that he is a butch and a better man than the snobs who dominate the campus scene and who earn a little more than he does.

Which leads to professorial remuneration. Though important and of interest, the substance of the discussion can be brief. Professors' wages vary but little. It is important to stress here the enormous importance in professors' lives of prestige, which has been discussed above, and of working conditions and perquisites, which will be discussed in the next chapter.

A reasonable wage for the nine-month year for a full professor at a great university is $25,000 a year. A reasonable low wage for an assistant professor at a third-class state college is $12,500. Some important equalizers need to be mentioned at once. Progressive income taxes lessen the difference. On a particular campus and, more so, within a particular department, differences in salary are far narrower. These income figures are indeed lower than those of the diligent lawyers, the shameless insurance salesmen, the ignorant dentists, the vulgar retailers, the dumb high-school principals, and the colorless rentiers in whose neighborhoods the professors live. Since the variations in salary are so narrow and the rewards for maneuvering for higher wages are so paltry, it follows that those competitive lusts from which professors are not spared must find expression in nonfinancial areas of distinction and domain.

Some qualifications: A few hundred big shots at the great schools may earn somewhat more than $30,000 in salary. So do a few hundred professors of law, medicine, and business at lesser places. Instructors earn about $2,000 per year less than an assistant professor does for the same work. A nearly universal gentleman's agreement that will receive attention later keeps women's salaries about 15 per cent less than those of men with identical qualifications. Still, one can assume that someone meriting the address of "Professor" who has been on the job for a while earns roughly between $15,000 and $20,000 for the nine-month year.

Of course, only about one fourth of the professors collect just their basic salary (after deductions, naturally). The most usual and by far the largest aggregate supplement to professorial income is that for summer-school teaching. These jobs are available and indeed treasured at most places. However, summer-school teaching is sought only because of the money. The summer enrollees are usually the same students who failed the course when it was offered in the regular session or are public-school teachers whose certification requirements and the subsequent pay raises force them to take additional college courses. Almost all summer students are lazy and resentful. The weather is hot and steamy. Summer-school sessions may be from three to twelve weeks long, and salary formulas vary a great deal. Usually the teacher earns two thirds, or even far less, of what he earns per course in the regular session. Those professors whose improvidence forces them to teach in the summer are vengefully envious of those who somehow manage to regularize their outgo so that they do not have scheduled work beyond the statutory nine months. But how else is the usual academic going to make sure that the picture window in his living room will have blue draperies lined with white, that twelve-year-old Mark will have braces in order to articulate his speech and chew his food, that Elspeth can go to the music camp, that at the proper time one will have resources from which to pay the outrageous tuition for Mark and Elspeth at a university several cuts above the one where their father works during the hot summer?

In the struggle for plus points of prestige at the "great" institutions, one may slip in the eyes of his accomplished colleagues if he teaches summer school often. At the great places one is supposed to be researching even more intensely when the university is not in regular session and one is expected to find some outside source to subsidize this research. Royalties from a trade book published by Knopf or by Faber in London would be the very best, but a grant from a solid foundation ranks as a close second. In any case, at the upper levels of professorial life one risks taking on minus points if he takes a simple vacation. Even at a merely respectable school such as Montana State or Connecticut at Bridgeport the assistant professor facing the tenure decision errs if he lets it get about that he is, in fact, planning a summer bicycle tour of Sicily or a fling at satyriasis in the Greek islands. The proper strategy here would be to pretend scholarly seriousness and to concoct a fable about the urgent need to visit an obscure research institute or academy nearby (the American academies in Athens and Rome are handy for such purposes) and to be seen with scruffy manila files and an Olivetti Lettera 22 as one boards the charter flight. An even better coup for a young man on the way up would be to get a research grant to pay for the whole caper.

Which leads to the subject of research support. In contrast to academic salaries, the variations here are enormous. The physicists and chemists simply cannot do any research and often cannot teach without equipment, the costs of which boggle all their nonscientific colleagues. For decades now the financing for this equipment has come almost entirely from federal sources. Though the years of good harvests are past when one expected that government aid to science in the universities would forever increase exponentially, the scientists are still able to tap nice money wells. Indeed several insiders have claimed that much of the scientists' prestige in academia is due to their ability to spend lots of money that is not their own.

A track record helps. A physicist at the Santa Cruz campus of the University of California might legitimately apply for a $100,000 machine that will force mercury into a supercooled state so that it can be studied while solid. The biologists in the junior colleges in Alabama expect lots of sinks in their laboratories and good microscopes. But only scientists resident at Berkeley, Stanford, Illinois, Chicago, and a few other places fly to Washington to specify to those who will sign the checks for particle accelerators or cyclotrons. The Department of Defense gives tens of millions only to those groups of scientists with previous records of discretion and performance and where the recommendations (usually urgently stated for greater defense spending) are stamped with the cachet of an indisputably great university. Nothing succeeds like success.

A recurrent drama on the campuses now is the *Schadenfreude* of the humanists as they learn the average research grant in the sciences is down 35 per cent from the figures in 1971. Grants for chemists are now averaging only $20,000 per professor.

Experimental psychologists, whose work should approach scientific objectivity, can be costly—particularly if they require large numbers of healthy animals. The ape laboratories at Emory University and the University of Wisconsin at Madison are very expensive to keep in operation. Other academics are less costly to support. The sociologists like money to hire extra graduate students by the hour so that the flunkies can present questionnaires to housewives to learn how they feel about staying home all day or to determine with whom and how often teenagers climax sexually. Studies by political scientists are expensive, if they demand data not commonly found in reference books or census reports. "Area studies" (alas, never the same area for very long) can command lavish cash injections for offices, secretaries, consultantships, travel, and publication subsidies. The money flows and may stop as those in Washington or in the foundation board offices in New York who command the dollar cocks learn that we are deficient or oversupplied with information or people who can use it bearing on certain geographical-political hot spots.

Area studies usually call for the pooling of action by political scientists, historians, and language specialists. As a result of academic blooms now faded, we are now oversupplied with academic Russianists, Africanists, and South East Asianists. The Sinologists (Chinese specialists) who boomed when President Nixon switched to Mao are still coasting high but are, like their precursors, riding for a fall. The price fiat by the Arabs after the Yom Kippur war in October 1973 opened up several new honeypots. Energy studies, Arabic studies, and studies of the unemployed are now faddish. It has been claimed that poverty has been a goldmine for academics.

The usual humanists—the historians, the literature scholars, the students of dead art, the philosophers—are so easy to please. Many a secure professor at the State University of New York would well up with grateful tears for the dean who would give him five hundred dollars for air fare so he might spend twenty-two to forty-five days in the archives in Madrid, at the Bauhaus archives in Berlin, at the excavations at ancient Olympia, or with Turner's drawings at the Tate

Gallery in London. One way to improve morale in academic life would be to make these little goodies more generally available and not to ask for immediate results.

Some professors pick up extra cash by consulting. However, for many professors of business or agriculture in the state colleges and universities in California, Kansas, or Georgia, consulting is usually an expected (that is, nothing extra is paid) part of the job. Many engineers and chemists, fewer physicists, and still fewer economists still can pick up five hundred dollars a day for consulting. One hears of engineering professors who get very rich by payoffs for advising a governmental body to award a construction contract to firm A rather than to (nonbribing) firm B. Painters in the studio courses in the art departments get to keep the money for canvases they sell. Music professors can take private students. A clever professor of clinical psychology will arrange that his Thursdays will be free and his regular salary not docked so that he can talk with thirty or so patients for a weekly two-hundred-dollar day at the nearby state mental hospital. Almost any humanist or social scientist with a name is asked to read and judge book manuscripts for university, trade, or textbook presses for about one hundred dollars for two or three days of work.

The schedules and the supervision of them are loose enough to allow those who want to do so to do nonacademic moonlighting. Some two or three dozen professors (almost all of them at the great schools) have reaped great harvests as the authors of textbooks that are hustled by especially aggressive publishers. These big sellers might well claim that they "publish and flourish." These renowned successes have eased the way for rackets wherein editors are able to get other professors to sign textbook contracts. The professor spends five years of his considerable spare time while enjoying a total advance (doled out in fifths) of from $1,000 to $10,000. Usually the professors fail to ascertain that they will earn royalties of only 5 per cent of the retail price of the cheap paperback version. A bad show all the way around, for textbooks are not considered coin of the realm in the tallies of publication credits necessary for a promotion or a crack at a job at a better school.

A rather large proportion, perhaps even a half, of the professors in fields we might call traditionally exquisite such as literary history in English and other languages, philosophy, and classics do have family money. Some economists speculate in land or commodities or short selling in various over-the-counter markets. In one small college in

Iowa two forty-year-old professors of anthropology, one very skinny and one very fat, took evening jobs driving taxis—ostensibly for the money, but really for the prospect of casual lays. Both quit after a few weeks when it became clear that the women proffering the gifts were so repulsive and so low in the social scale that they were accustomed to offer all they had to all potential takers. In view of the fact that most professors at the low-pressure schools have offices that are sacrosanct, unlimited telephone use, the franking privilege, and large amounts of time to dispose of with no questions asked, it is curious that relatively few of them earn extra money except by summer-school teaching.

Illustration B:

MICHAEL DARCY OF
SOUTH INDISHOIS STATE UNIVERSITY

Michael Darcy's fluorescent-lit, eight-by-twelve office is in the starkly functional Humanities Building on the North Campus. Most of the interior surfaces are of gray plastic. The entire building reeked of industrial solvents for a year after its dedication. It was the tallest structure of President Albert Critie's second expansion program, which began in 1966. Superrational, with movable office partitions in eight-foot modules, the narrow building has, in the old-world fashion, its "first floor" one level above the ground floor, where the crowds enter the small automated elevators. That the ground floor is called the "rez-de-chaussée" is an elegance imposed by the Foreign Languages Department, which occupies floors eleven, twelve, and fourteen.

Students from the campus were once known as the "Aggies" and are still famed for their fervor at intercollegiate basketball games. In the 1950s the college's researches on soybean mutations and the artificial insemination of swine were more respected in Denmark and New Zealand than they were in the Indishois state capitol, some 135 miles away. Then in 1959 a band of local state legislators, in an unusual spell of optimistic co-operation, forced the trustees of the "University" (one stresses the third syllable rather hard in the usage at hand in order to indicate the enormous, 150-year-old land-grant institution in the capital itself) to consent to a doubling of enrollment at the old agricultural and normal college. The same local politicians and some town moguls who were land developers then worked through the board of trustees to force doddering President Sam Corcoree into academic pasture. Corcoree returned to the department of poultry husbandry, whence he had come in 1942. The new man, Al Critie, began at once to hire new deans for $17,500 (since then doubled) per year and promises. These deans in turn hired new department chairmen, using salaries of $14,500 per year (since doubled) and promises. The promises were for the last word in facilities and whole phalanxes of bright, new professors. In due course the money (and funded debt) flowed in, and reinforced concrete or red-brick-faced buildings towered or spread over the old research acreage, renamed "the North Campus." The new professors bought $25,000 houses (since doubled in price) which the developers thoughtfully provided on property nearby. New students duly appeared in ever-larger freshman classes. Enrollments did not double in ten years but rather quadrupled from 3,500 in 1959 as the budget of the old college (renamed "university"—but with a lighter stress on the third syllable) increased ten times over from 1959 to 1971. The "Al Critie" plan of 1960 slyly included a "major thrust" in the direction of cultural studies in order to counter the old epithet (which was not really disrespectful until 1959) of "cow college." Foreign tongues and books were necessary to indicate the installation of high culture in the rural southern part of the state, so a milieu of respect prevailed when Michael Darcy got his job as instructor in January of 1967, shortly after he had begun his dissertation at Chicago on "Irony in the Early Novels of Thomas Mann." His beginning salary was $10,250 for the nine-month year.

Hans Holm, Darcy's professor at the University of Chicago, in his letters of recommendation for the young man's employment dossier, raved over Mr. Darcy's "exquisite" mastery of his second language and his "extreme willingness to please." Holm felt that Darcy's six years as a graduate student was sufficient evidence that he was a procrastinator. No need to state this coarsely in a formal letter.

Actually, two of these years were spent in Berlin, where Michael had enrolled as a student at the Free University. Ostensibly he was "collecting materials and ideas" for some eventual dissertation in German literature, but his responsibilities at the university were negligible. In Berlin he had many acquaintances who were gentlemen much like himself. He had first encountered them in various places: the concert halls, the bars, the saunas, and sometimes late at night in one densely wooded park. The American was sinewy and tall, dark with blue eyes, and had large white teeth, which he eagerly flashed but which, alas, reeked of pyorrhea. He had long eyelashes. Despite his enthusiasm for things German, Michael dressed almost exclusively in American clothing in the so-called Ivy style.

In those years, the five hundred dollars a month sent him by his mother from Atlanta ("The Darcys always owned land near Atlanta") kept him very well in Berlin. He gave small parties where many of the guests had previously and briefly been his very intense friends. They drank white wines, smoked hashish, and talked about the cinema, the crises in German letters and theater, and people who were not present. Michael read and reread Heine and Fontane and especially Thomas Mann with the keenest pleasure.

On returning to the University of Chicago in September 1964, Michael's salon German wowed his professors. As a teaching assistant in the department (he did not need the $2,000 a year, but did need the "exposure"), he rather enjoyed meeting the ten-member classes of alert, appreciative, and amusing undergraduates, many of whom were Jewish but who were well brought up. Michael taught advanced German grammar and conversation. The gracefully carried panache of good-southern-family, his exceptional appearance, and his perfection in dress made his graduate career (as so much of his life) easy. However, Michael despised reading supposedly important, thick books on literary criticism or even short essays on the theory of literature and never could finish seminar papers on time. Michael's fascination with Thomas Mann intensified as his prestige eroded among the six professors of German at Chicago. Just before the Christmas break in 1967 the once-genial advisor, Hans Holm (whose field was Bertolt Brecht), commanded him to choose some dissertation topic so it could go on his curriculum vitae, which would circulate at the Modern Language Association meeting in New York.

Besides those under way, there were already extant six English, ten German, two French, and two Swedish dissertations plus sixty articles on irony in Thomas Mann's fiction, but Michael's vita looked correct to the new chairman of SIS's foreign language department. Dr. François Knaak's own specialty was Dante's Sicilian reputation. He had come to the MLA with orders from the dean (those were the great days!) to hire six "promising" young men.

Late in the afternoon on December 29, 1967, in Knaak's room in the new Hilton on Sixth Avenue Michael assured the harried, jovial doctor that the dissertation would be finished in two years, maybe less. A very good friend from the Berlin days who was now an editor at the University of Nebraska Press was "eager to take a look at it."

Yes, he was a happy teacher of beginning German already, but he did expect to be allowed to teach courses in German literature as well. Michael wore a three-piece gray herringbone-tweed suit (38 long) in the Brooks Brothers "346" line purchased two months before. His shirt was a Brooksweave blue Oxford-cloth button-down. His rep tie, ribbed wool socks, and shoes were from Brooks too. The black wingtips had *thin* soles. Just thirty minutes before the crucial interview Michael had installed his often-troublesome contact lenses and furiously brushed his big teeth to dispel the pesky, swampy smell characteristic of much older men. Knaak had been around long enough to know that Michael's slow, southern speech was authentically aristocratic.

The twenty-minute interview had proceeded gracefully, though it was rather devoid of specific questions on the part of either. At a couple of other interviews at the MLA Michael had been alarmed at the very direct, count-of-four stares and a few shockingly knowledgeable questions about Thomas Mann put by some young colleagues who were helping out their hiring chairmen.

When Michael came down to the SIS campus for the visit in late January, he brought two more Brooks outfits of "346" jackets and gray-black Majer slacks. His Bass Weejun loafers danced nimbly about the iced-over mud puddles all over the construction sites. The talk was of the new faculty club, climate, and rental prices for new one-bedroom apartments. Michael sedulously limited himself to one martini per supper and at the "getting-to-know-him" cocktail party. No one asked him anything about his views of teaching or his specific plans for making known to the world his presumably unique views of Thomas Mann and modern German literature—respectively his projected particular and general fields at SIS.

The dean gave Knaak a bargaining range of $9,000 to $10,500, which he said was "high for an A.B.D." (all but dissertation). In the course of some amiable phone calls during the week after Michael returned to Chicago, he settled for a nine-month beginning salary $250 under Knaak's upper limit. Michael was able to boast to his chums in Chicago that he had also been promised easy classes in order to have time to "finish that dissertation." He would endure the title "Instructor" until that dissertation was wrapped up.

In September 1968 he began to teach introductory German to teenaged graduates of the high schools in the southern part of the state. This was how twenty-eight-year-old Michael Darcy was introduced to the world of work. These children had not chosen the prettiest or the most immediately logical tongue in which to fulfill the language requirement for a B.A. He had the regular three-class teaching load, but the introductory language classes met with the professor only twice a week. The students were expected to spend much more time doing rote oral practice with the tape machines in the language labs. Michael appeared for six fifty-minute sessions in German 101 and explained grammatical points, drilled the students in pronunciation (his own *ö, ü,* and *ch* were all that could be desired), returned graded exercises, and maintained the stately pace of the very elementary textbook.

Or that was the way it was supposed to go. During the third week of the fifteen-week session Michael was astonished by the students' unselfconscious ignorance and sloppiness—which he chose to combat with supercilious humor. This technique had worked with the Jewish kids at the University of Chicago. By the end of the fourth week only two thirds of his total registration of ninety-two were maintaining the chapter-a-week pace of the text. The fifth week was devoted to some desperate sessions in which Michael succeeded in getting only half of his students to grasp what was meant by the dative case. Their baffled attempts to articulate the language Michael adored revolted him. By the drop date (that is, the final date on which students were allowed to withdraw from a course without taking a failing grade) late in the sixth week, half of the students had left, and some of those remaining were obviously too bewildered to realize that they could not escape the final grade of F. As Mr. Darcy congratulated himself on the witness of his scorn, the student gossip network began establishing the reputation of the new German teacher. A couple of genuinely interested students called on those of Michael's colleagues who liked to chat. For the three sessions of German 102 in the spring of 1969, his enrollment totaled fifty-three, but fifteen of these dropped during the first week. And Michael gave passing grades to only seventeen students after the final examination in May of 1969.

In the meantime a phone number proffered months before by a third party over a restaurant supper in Chicago led to a fast-moving acquaintance with a remarkably healthy but middle-aged lawyer in the town, and Michael grew accustomed to drinking bourbon with some gusto at small parties consisting of clever gentlemen from and around the booming college town. In preparation for the dissertation and for the promised course in "The German Novel Between the Wars," alone in his small apartment Michael reread, shivering with awe, *The Magic Mountain* and the whole Joseph series. That is he read until bourbon on ice befuddled him so that he had to go to bed for uneasy dreams. Every few weeks he raced his yellow Karmann-Ghia convertible up to Chicago, where he visited about and spent approximately equal amounts of time in the library at the great university and in the special steam baths. By the fall of 1969 Michael had outlined in detail the whole dissertation and rough-drafted a forty-page Preface. Alas, only six students appeared for the first meeting of the literature course on the fourth day of September. Three stayed to the end.

The academic years 1969–70 through 1972–73 were good and bad. Socially Michael was incessantly in motion. Besides the dreary departmental parties and a lot of formal functions inspired by the local Episcopal church which Michael had joined, he occasionally went to semisecret parties in handsomely furnished bachelor apartments in nearby towns and in the state capital, where the university (third syllable) was. Michael was a skilled mimic and raconteur. He took the character parts—usually those of the eccentrics in his department—when he told funny stories. In the spring of 1971 Michael was an especially appreciated guest at an orgy prepared for weeks in advance by a young biologist at a small experimental college sixty miles away.

A yearning for a firm friendship caused Michael to lease a large farmhouse with a young philosophy professor whose impotence had just ended his marriage of nineteen months. The men got on each other's nerves almost at once and they parted bitterly fourteen months later, but not before Michael had put a lot of work and $4,000 in Darcy money into painting and otherwise fixing up the place. He then settled into a $275-per-month three-room apartment within walking distance of his office.

In the summer of 1970 the university had provided $2,000 of research money so Michael could visit places sacred to Thomas Mann: Lübeck, where the boy was born and languished, Palestrina, where the young titan wrote *Buddenbrooks* and learned lascivious love, Frankfurt, Munich, Davos. He visited the ancient widow, Katja, in Zurich and charmed her as he stared at the skinny, dry neck, knowing that at that spot the great ironist had shouted while climaxing. The dissertation leaped forward. He finished a seventy-seven-page Introduction and wrote fifty-two pages of chapter two.

When Chairman Knaak called Instructor Michael Darcy in for a talk in the spring of 1972, he had before him a row of computer-printed figures that Michael could not see well. Knaak walked about his carpeted office with windows on two sides as Michael picked his cuticles while seated in an orange tweed swivel chair. The young man was ordered to attract, help, and pass more students. And he had to finish the dissertation—quickly. For a while Michael failed almost no one, thus arousing the open contempt of the few students who bothered to do his easy assignments and the secret sneers of the other three German teachers. On them would fall the burden of failing those whom Michael passed with B's.

In August 1972 Michael mailed the 927-page typescript to Professor Hans Holm, whom he had for several years evaded. By return mail Holm replied that he did not read dissertations over three hundred pages long. Mr. Darcy should have checked with him on that.

Then followed the desperate year 1972–73. Michael did cut the dissertation to 343 pages. He served (saying nothing) on the department's library committee and the university's Approval of New Courses Committee. A compulsive habit of grinding his teeth as he slept led to the long-delayed operation on his gums and the removal of six perfect-looking teeth which were replaced by a largely gold appliance. The dental work made him miss two weeks of classes, and he was erratic when he returned, being sardonic to good students who gossiped and gentle with bad students who he thought gossiped but who did not. Then, late in the summer of 1973, the dissertation was quickly accepted—largely because Holm believed Michael's claim that if it was not accepted, he was out of a job. So in October Michael was promoted to assistant professor, but without tenure.

After his two small morning classes this Tuesday in February when we observe him, Professor Darcy leaves his office to check his mailbox, which is on a wall in the bullpen that holds the four departmental secretaries. Before he can enter the room, he sees her seated on the blue plastic sofa in the corridor, gently rubbing her moist hands together. Maggie Vermehren was one of the first of the few students to get a crush on Mr. Darcy. And her fidelity held as she stayed on for years at SIS to get her master's degree in German. She was small and usually quiet. Her eyebrows moved a lot and her perfect, pale complexion blotched red when she spoke German or about

German. When she was in his office, Michael kept talking about Maggie's master's thesis, "Women in the Last Works of Thomas Mann," while deftly deflecting any conversations about Maggie or himself. Still, Maggie did not carefully separate her admiration for the great *bourgeois manqué* and her attachment to his local scholar. Once, while she stammered about the voluptuously bloody death of Rosalie von Trummler in *The Black Swan,* Michael watched horrified from his swivel chair as Maggie, who was standing, softly bounced her mons veneris against the opposite edge of his desk, just three feet away.

Now he speaks to Maggie in tones that he often used: "Oh, Maggie, I'm under the gun for some committee reports. Unh, and I've got to get up a fresh lecture for the goddamn Hesse class."

Maggie Vermehren, hot and passive, moves to the elevator to wait for the ticking bell and the hissing descent.

Professor Darcy leaps at the pile of fresh mail. Several book advertisements, including one on German history from Prentice-Hall and a text in introductory French from Houghton Mifflin, sixteen pages of mimeographed minutes from the faculty senate meeting two weeks ago, an announcement for a basketball breakfast, a schedule for the next two months of campus art movies, a dittoed departmental memo from Knaak demanding that those who vacate classrooms erase the boards of their diagrams and parsings, an air-mail letter from Buenos Aires to Professor *Barkey* in Engineering; an invitation—"Drinks and Munchables, 6:30–8?"—to a party given by an English professor and his wife three weeks hence. But there are no readers' reports from the University of Nebraska Press on his manuscript, "Incipient Irony in Thomas Mann's *Juvenalia*." Nor are there encouraging letters from department chairmen of foreign languages who might employ Michael in one of the many colleges and universities in the San Francisco Bay area. Only a letter from Mercy College in Oakland that is long and sincerely regretful—and mimeographed. Michael looks up to leave and freezes inwardly as he sights danger.

For three years the only language gaining in enrollments at SIS has been Spanish. Much of this isolated success is attributable to the energy of Mr. Tom Bajazzo, who, as usual, is smiling and greeting admirers. Bajazzo arrived at SIS in 1972 from Berkeley. He too has been having trouble finishing his dissertation, "Passion for Equity: The Proletarian Poets of Peru," and therefore Michael can call him

"Mister" a little pointedly. Bajazzo affects the Berkeley work-clothes style. He wears loose Lee Riders, Hickory shirts, and oiled-cowhide shoes with inner steel toes, even when he teaches. And Bajazzo teaches more than is necessary.

Bajazzo's office is next to Darcy's. The walls, as in all the new buildings, are thin. Some of Tom's visitors are students who despise Michael. Bajazzo's usual opener is, "Well, how's it going?" whereupon he kicks the door shut. The man is an incessant gossipist. He is, Michael has deduced, the intermediary by which stories of Michael's purported anti-Semitic and anti-Catholic slurs passed from the students to the teaching community. The perfect liberal, Bajazzo himself devotedly and laboriously tutors black athletes who take his introductory Spanish classes. He almost guarantees B's to those with dark complexions.

The Spanish teacher is almost always in that office. At night he uses university's freely provided telephone to gossip long-distance with the old Berkeley set. One night in his office Michael recognized at once a delicious odor. He smokes the stuff, too, though he naturally prefers hashish. He sat very still until he heard tiny giggles next door. Another evening shortly afterward Michael heard people enter Bajazzo's office and some irregular rustlings. Then, confirming his fears, a stifled and desperate female voice let go with, "Yes, that's it! Yes! Yes! Yes!" And then Bajazzo grunted softly, "Great! Great!" Michael fled with the hair rising on the back of his neck and slammed the door.

Michael's first class on the February Tuesday we see him had been German 102, the second half of the introductory year. There were just eleven students, making it the smallest of his three 102 classes. He had been patient. This past year he had succeeded in not pushing the students farther or faster than they could be cajoled into going. For his best students he had arranged advanced tutorial sessions in his office and occasionally in his apartment. Two years previously he had sought out and read some badly written, though helpful and detailed manuals on how to teach introductory language classes. A gentle cynicism, a realistic appraisal of the capabilities of his students, the seeking out of how-to literature, and, most importantly, fear for the future had made Michael Darcy a good teacher—seven years after he took the job.

Michael's second course, "The Novels of Herman Hesse in Translation," had been an attempt to take part in the popularity contest that he perceived (very late) he would have to enter in order to remain employed. He could not get permission to teach an undergraduate class on his literary hero, because the departmental and university committee knew he could not retain the required minimum of five students until the end of a session. On the other hand, of all the German writers, Hesse is the only one who has a campus following in America. Michael despised Hesse yet nevertheless read the critical literature on the sloppy, opportunistic mystic who wrote *Steppenwolf, Siddhartha,* and *Narcissus and Goldmund.* Sure enough, the dirtiest hippies applied. Since Michael needed the "count," he dramatized, flattered, and persuaded to see that they stayed. Occasionally when Michael praised the sweet sentiments of Hesse, a big boy who wore thick, steel-framed glasses supported him with, "Right on!"

But the adaption to circumstances had come late. The reformed Professor Darcy could not overcome his old reputation, and the students who appreciated his elegance in behavior and his diligence in the classroom were too few. There had been a budget crunch and, subsequently, a tenure crunch. In the department, he had no defenders. If he were gone, it would ease the way for those eleven instructors and assistant professors hired after him into the small number of likely tenure slots. He had only two little articles (one of which had been "in press" for eighteen months) and four book reviews to show as publications. Two weeks before, Knaak, in accordance with the AAUP rules wrote Michael a formal letter telling him that he would not be given tenure and that his teaching contract would expire a year from May.

Michael dutifully goes to the committee meeting scheduled for 3:30. It was Curriculum and New Courses and Michael remains awake as a fifty-year-old professor in biology argues with another from mathematics against a proposal from a three-man committee of the political science department to renumber "in a rational manner" the courses that could be taken by both undergraduate and graduate students. Mostly Michael doodles tiny, concentric circles. At 5:05 he votes "Aye" to approve or, really, "to send it up the line" so the faculty senate can approve it.

At 5:15 Michael puts on his Burberry and his low overshoes and walks home. At the apartment he eats a grilled chicken breast and cottage cheese with ice-cold California chablis. As he enjoys the three glasses of wine, he simultaneously regrets that they dull his determination to recommence the detailed outlining of the middle chapters of a projected biography of Thomas Mann. He had gone rather far on this project the previous summer when he rented a small cabin in the Smokies for three weeks, in the course of which he quit drinking. Nor can Michael concentrate on the articles in *Euphorion,* the *Deutsche Vierteljahresschrift,* or even in *Der Spiegel,* which he has airmailed from Hamburg at considerable expense. Nor are the records of Artur Schnabel playing Mozart's piano music anything but stingingly irritating.

Instead, Assistant Professor Michael Darcy, as has so often been the case lately, sits in his six-hundred-dollar black Eames lounge chair and switches to scotch on ice. He stares before him with a fascination that is endless at the patterns of a magnificent, very old Moroccan rug, a bargain that he bought at an auction in Chicago for $875 two years before. And he broods ever less precisely about what he might do after he finishes teaching the next academic year, which will be his last at South Indishois State University.

IV

Perquisites and Hazards

When it comes to choosing between a usual profession and a job in academia, there is no contest. However, as was made clear, the attractions of professorial work lie less in the wages paid than in the atmosphere and the perquisites.

In the following it will be necessary to refer often to the prestige rankings for institutions and for professorial specialties discussed in the previous chapter. Working conditions at Florissant Valley Community College (established 1963) in St. Louis are far less delightful than they are at Dartmouth. Still, the increasingly severe competition for jobs in the academic provinces is proof that for our oversupply of intellectuals these posts are preferable to traineeships at Sears, at Minnesota Mining and Manufacturing, or at some branch bank. At whatever place one is a professor, one's assigned task is to discover, to preserve, and to communicate truth. How marvelous that providence has provided more than a third of a million people with the paid opportunity to attempt to do just that!

The key figure that the professor uses to gauge the quality of his own job vis-à-vis those of his old friends from graduate school is his "teaching load." What this means is how many hours (sometimes called "*contact* hours") the professor must appear before his classes for each week that school is regularly in session. These figures rather than salaries, which are almost a taboo subject in nonacademic circles to which the professors belong, are an extremely common topic of informal communication in academia. Dilation will bring with it revelations.

Not so long ago, say when professors now fifty years old began their graduate work at the age of twenty-two to twenty-five, it was expected that in a medium-ranked institution one would teach five classes a week, each of them a three-credit class meeting three hours a week. Thus we explain the "credit hour" unit of academic accounting. At the same time, each student's full "load" of classes was about five, each of which met two to four, but usually three times a week. A rough assumption which is almost never blatantly stated is that for each hour in class the professor as well as students should devote two hours to preparation and to study respectively. The professor's teaching workweek was fifteen hours on the job, thirty hours of preparation. Therefore, he had a forty-five-hour workweek.

It is necessary to make the qualification at once that the teaching hour does not last sixty minutes but fifty minutes. In most three-credit classes that meet on Monday, Wednesday, and Friday, the class begins on the hour, with ten minutes for getting to and from class. A variation is to have a three-credit class meet just twice a week (most often on Tuesdays and Thursdays) for seventy-five minutes each time. This latter schedule can permit a professor to exclaim on the last day of his workweek, "Thank God it's Thursday!"

A three-credit class need not physically assemble before the responsible professor for 150 minutes a week. For example, a three-credit biology, chemistry, physics, or accounting class may meet for two hours of lectures and demonstrations by the professor and for three to five hours in laboratories for do-it-yourself experiments supervised by graduate-student laboratory assistants. Similarly a four-credit introductory language class requiring pronunciation and rote practice before playback tape machines may meet only twice for fifty minutes before a properly credentialed assistant professor. The student will be expected to spend three or more hours on his own wearing earphones and muttering in strange tongues in the "language laboratory." Another variation is the three-credit "seminar" (usually a small discussion class held for graduate students alone) which customarily meets just once a week or less often. It is expected that the restricted number of seminar "members" (usually four to twelve) will meet only to offer for criticism (purportedly) laboriously assembled and novel findings. The point of the above discussion is this: The declared number of hours in the professorial working week—as delightfully loose as these are officially—always turns out to be more than the actual number. Besides these shortcuts there are other ways, moral and dubious, for the professors to chisel.

It has been the case that, since research was acknowledged as a leading task for the best American universities, these institutions provided for research by requiring fewer formal teaching hours of their distinguished faculty. The time left over would be devoted, as it was in nineteenth-century German academic life, to pushing back the frontiers of knowledge. Institutions thereby merited acknowledgment of their greatness by producing evidence of discovery and thus a momentum favoring and fostering research was launched in American higher education.

Institutions originally established to serve local constituencies and wishing to be considered a little more than merely respectable had to provide the ambiance and the facilities for research. For the candidates looking for the best professorial position, convincing evidence of their employer's commitment to research was a reduced statutory teaching load. And sure enough, famous researchers have almost always settled where research was encouraged by the formal release from teaching duties. Their fame attracted additional faculty members and, usually, an academically inclined student body, which (to move way ahead of the narrative line of this book) needs professors but little, but which largely educates itself. Harvard led in fostering greatness by reducing teaching hours, though Johns Hopkins and the University of Chicago were research pioneers too. The most successful purchaser of great academic prestige by the technique of reducing teaching hours was the University of California at Berkeley in the twenty-five years before 1960.

After the excitement engendered by Sputnik, other ambitious boards of regents or trustees nodded in agreement to explanations of persuasive presidents, deans, and members of the American Association of University Professors that a great professor is great because of the countless hours of research that go directly or indirectly into the preparation of his brief and (increasingly) infrequent performances before postadolescents or emulating graduate students. Since the salary possibilities for almost any professor rarely vary more than 10 per cent up or down from what he earns at present, the most convincing (there are no near rivals) evidence of a commitment to excellence that a hiring chairman can offer to a job candidate is a smaller-than-average teaching load. Prestige matters to professors, and since 1950 or so, the single indication most emphatically demonstrating high prestige is a small number of weekly teaching hours.

This figure is, incidentally, a taboo topic outside the corridors and offices. A story common in academia is in order here: Recently, when questioned by a state legislator who was alarmed at the increase in the state university's budget as to how many hours he taught, a professor replied, "Nine." The legislator was reassured, for he assumed that this was a daily total, not a weekly one.

To return to recent history. In the 1960s, as professors were supposed to be in short supply, those on the job taught ever less. By 1964 hirelings at expanding four-year colleges found they could ask for twelve-hour teaching schedules and get them. To set themselves apart from those beneath them, professors at the big private and state universities demanded time (as well as money) to fight at those stubborn frontiers of knowledge. Teaching loads fell to nine hours a week. At Harvard, Chicago, and Berkeley they descended to six. Then a new round of reductions began. Teaching loads will go no lower than they are at present.

Those personages with a professor's rank at the top twenty or thirty universities can expect to have six assigned hours of teaching a week. At these places a typical schedule for a semester (fourteen or fifteen weeks) or a quarter (ten weeks) is one three-credit lecture course and one three-credit seminar. At the next ranking hundred or so institutions, the usual load is nine hours a week. At four-year schools which merely pretend to support research, the teaching load is usually twelve hours. At the two-year junior colleges, and in much of academic "Siberia" the professors still expect to teach fifteen hours a week.

However, all along the way there are methods to chisel. And, as happiness comes in bunches, chiseling on one's stated duties is easiest where the teaching demands are least. Moreover, one's success in chiseling away at the teaching load also increases one's prestige.

At the better 150 or so colleges and universities, the professor who is not in disfavor can occasionally request his chairman to reduce his burden of two or three courses a semester by one course. He is "under the gun" for some correlations, for his chapter in a collective work, for a bibliographical essay, for a seventy-page research report he agreed to do for the Provost's Committee on the Reform of the Undergraduate Curriculum. No self-respecting chairman would have accepted his job if he was not assured of these goodies to apportion to his supporters. In fact, such gifts may be the sole effective means of a chairman's control over some of his troops.

At many institutions, the full professors teach one less course than the associates and assistants. The smaller load raises the status of the full professor and, if he does little or no research (which is overwhelmingly the case at middle-ranked institutions), the boon is justified by the professor's committee work—which usually produces little of substance either.

If a professor is sly, he can lower his teaching load in other ways, but mostly this requires a staff of eager-to-please graduate students. Even without formal assistance one can get by for less. The first meeting that begins a semester of classes is usually brief: The professor writes his name on the board, says that it is pronounced with a long "a" and with the accent on the third syllable, distributes a prospectus, and repeats much of the information in it, to wit, the name of the textbook, that tardiness predisposes him to migraine, that sleepers must not snore, and that he will not allow eating, drinking, or newspaper reading while he talks. Ten minutes.

Except in courses in social history, abnormal psychology, the sociology of marriage, the continental novel, or American foreign policy —all of which are difficult to make dull—most students resent having to sit still for fifty minutes. If the fall or spring weather is especially priapic, if (as is now rarely the case) rumors of political riots make him nervous, if he has a sore throat that makes his voice waver, the professor can dismiss his class ten to twenty minutes early. The mesomorphic males whoop with joy.

Twice or more during the semester the secure professor may decide not to appear but instead to stay put in his home's fourth bedroom, which he converted to a study. He stays there to nurse his hangover, to finish his income tax, or to catch up on recent journals in his scholarly specialties. He merely phones the departmental secretary to write on the green composition board in room 205 in Glover Hall that "Professor (long 'a'—stress on the third syllable) cannot meet his classes at 10:00 and at 12:00 today." Students entering the lecture hall sigh with relief as they see those words, but agree that it would have been ever so much nicer if the "cut" had been announced in advance. Like that time he had to attend those meetings in Knoxville. The professor who "cuts" a class, however, must not be seen that day playing golf or emerging accompanied from a motel a few miles outside the town limits. Word will get back to his enemies and thence to the chairman, who can refuse goodies as well as grant them.

Besides his hours devoted to teaching, the professor has more, but still very flexible requirements for service. He must have office hours.

He establishes these hours by announcing them in the first meeting of the class and by an appropriately inscribed three-by-five card taped to his office door. He promises to be on hand for consultation with students for two or three hours a week—usually in the afternoons after his lectures. Except at the big research institutions, where the professors are indeed pestered by graduate students needing reassurances, the professional activities during office hours are scarcely ennobling:

"I thought I had you psyched out for that snap quiz, and here you gave me a D-minus."

"I can't read your assistant's handwriting in my bluebook."

"The coach says that you want us to read so much that it is cutting into our workouts."

"Dr. Schneider, I know that my term paper looks just like the article you found in *Horizon,* but honest, I swear to God, I *did* write it myself!"

"On the final exam, are you going to ask us important questions, or are you going to make us remember a lot of picky names and dates?"

"I was also disappointed that I only got a C in your course the year before last—especially since I loved your fascinating lectures. But do you think you could give me a good recommendation for the architecture school at Rice University in Houston anyway? Thank you so much!"

Committee service is not a statutory requirement. There are no stated minimums for committee performance. However, the ancient and faithfully maintained myth of "self-governance"—which holds that the professors themselves should run the university—requires devotion. The professor who is not making evident the fact that he is researching (that is, he is not publishing) prudently gives himself public exposure near at hand. There are all sorts of committees: those within a department (Library, Undergraduate, New Courses, Forward Planning, etc.), those presumably leading or watching universitywide functions (Athletic, Faculty Welfare, Provost's Advisory, Discipline, Forward Planning, etc.), and those reassuring the outside community (called "town and gown" committees). At its easiest— which is most often the case—committee work consists of looking attentive and paying only enough attention to guess correctly which way a vote will go. (A bibliographical insertion is in order here: Some of the most cynical admonitory writing by professors for professors is on the sensible way to behave in university committees. However, since committees provide ritual functions that accomplish little of substance, this book will dwell but little on this topic. Disillusioned professors write so much about silliness in committees because only at these times do they see in action those of their colleagues who are not close friends.) Valuable committee service can be directed to making sure that the professor's department's interests are preserved in conflicts with upstart disciplines (examples are area studies, speech departments, programs for creative writing, etc.), to defending friends in discipline disputes with students, to pushing approval for departmental colleagues' new courses, to sponsoring their grade changes, to lobbying for a bigger parking garage and lower parking fees near the building where the departmental offices are.

The busiest professors (an economist at the Brockport Campus of SUNY calls such personages "whirling dervishes") on the campus ascribe most enthusiastically to "self-governance." They appear to be genuinely determined to reform the university and may fritter their lives away at this great task. Alas, the big decisions (if indeed they are big) in universities are made elsewhere, and even these decisions are impossible to put into action if they demand sensible shifts from past procedure. For universities are almost incapable of being steered; they drift with the times and more particularly with the finances. Committee meetings are so common and so well attended because many responsible professors must meritoriously fill their working days.

There are fewer working days than commonly believed. True, their basic salary after withholding is paid out in nine equal lumps, signifying (as is officially stated) that the academics work nine months a year. But a closer look at the professors' working year exposes the stretch-out. The academic year commonly begins just after Labor Day and ends nine months later. Almost all American campuses are on the semester or quarter system, which means respectively that courses with their appropriate credits are in two fourteen- or fifteen-week sessions or in three ten-week sessions. It is true that professors must hang around during the two days before each session while students "register" (that is, sign up and pay for) the classes they will take. Professors are responsible for the supervision and grading of the final examinations that are spread over the ten days to two weeks after each session. However, the academic workyear also encompasses a Christmas vacation, an Easter vacation (which sometimes is called a "spring break"), a four-day holiday for Thanksgiving, and perhaps two to four other long weekends. Ignoring the fact that few professors meet their classes every time they are scheduled (see the remarks on chiseling above and the discussions on how to use graduate students below) this means that a professor on the semester system apparently meets with each three-credit class thirty-five hours (14 weeks times 3 classes of 50 minutes each equals 2100 minutes, which is then divided by 60). The standard teaching load at a respectable place is three courses per semester or six per year. Simple multiplication of 6 times 35 gives us the figure of 210 hours of actual teaching work for the professional year. This book will employ few statistics, but the above calculations and their results are essential to get at the secrets the professors have kept to themselves.

Some more open calculations are necessary. Assuming a low salary of $14,000 per year, we can deduce that a professor enjoying (the effective) seven-month year and the nine-hour week earns $2,000 per month and $66 per hour taught. The teaching hours of a full professor at great institutions are fewer and he is more highly paid. He can earn $200 per teaching hour and sometimes much more. Even in academic Siberia, where people teach (usually desultorily) as much as fifteen hours a week, professorial wages rarely fall below $35 per hour spent in teaching. We have now arrived at the crucial figures that show how attractive the occupation is and why professors are such peculiar people. *For what they do, professors are very well paid and they have great amounts of time to dispose of exactly as they wish.* Most of the distinctive charades of professorial life are attributable to the usually obsessive, sometimes playfully indulged in, need for professors to hide from each other and, vastly more important, from the outside world the facts in the sentence italicized above.

Withholding until a later chapter some descriptions of how professors actually work in the classroom or laboratory, it is appropriate to discuss class sizes, which vary from about two to about 2,000. In the ceaseless struggle for prestige, it is considered desirable for professors to teach either (but, even better, both) very small classes or very large ones. The professor at Ohio State who draws 1,000 to his electronically amplified lectures on the continental novel ("Suzy, he makes Balzac live!") may have to give machine-graded tests to get his final grades in on time, but he demonstrates to his colleagues that he is a performer and a maintainer of enrollments worth deferring to. The same man, if he wishes to enhance his reputation further and to arm himself against those snipers who call him a "popularizer" or possibly a "whore," can turn away from his yearly graduate seminars on the continental novel applicants who do not easily read French, German, Russian, or Italian and thus restrict his seminar enrollment to four or even less. The "star" will be yet more careful about whom he takes as a dissertation student and intrigue in the national network of his discipline to find jobs for his Ph.D. students at "decent" schools.

The above suggests a scenario of academic heroism and almost no one can play it. Classes are usually both smaller and larger. To vibrate the eardrums of fifty to a hundred in a classroom requires good diaphragm control. Still, with a class of this size one cannot learn the names of more than a few students in a ten-to-fourteen-week session. A class of fifteen to forty is worse, for after the third week one knows them all and sees as he dramatizes, explains, or demonstrates that, whatever the intensity of his preparations or however exquisite his knowledge, few care very much for what is his spiritual and professional blood. As to calculations: The students at Ohio State who are enchanted as the professor resuscitates Honoré de Balzac are furnishing him about twenty cents apiece for each performance; his four seminar students, about fifty dollars for each hour. However, one can assume that at a middling state university the average student in an average class is the agent by which the average professor collects about two dollars. The route by which the student pays the professor two dollars for each hour he sits in class is circuitous, it is true, but the student or those bankrolling him or her might keep the figure in mind as a basis for demanding their money's worth.

High-school guidance counselors and the college catalogs tell students that they can call on the professors for independent study (that is, one-to-one intellectual nourishment) outside of class hours. Indeed, the case could be made that professors at universities financed almost wholly by public funds might be legitimately demanded for their expertise by anyone inside or outside of the university. Few, except the paranoid, obsequious graduate students are so importunate.

At the universities proud of their large graduate programs, the undergraduates have far fewer professorial contacts than might be suggested above. It is expected that almost all graduate students will do various kinds of preprofessional work to finance their withdrawal from the job market as they prepare for a later attack on that market. Big universities have thousands of graduate assistants, laboratory assistants, or teaching assistants. Here, too, there are invariably fewer jobs than seekers for them. Their remuneration customarily is the cancellation of all or part of the regular tuition and $2,000 to $3,000 more in payment for the academic year. The assistants are assigned one or more to a professor, often with few specifics as to how they will earn their keep. They are there in order to please (indeed, their subsequent prosperity depends on it), and the opportunistic professor is well aware of the benefits to be gained from their use. At the immense state universities T.A.'s usually do most of the teaching in the "lower division" (that is, the first and second year of the college curriculum). In the three-credit "History of Western Civilization" course at Wisconsin or the State University of New York at Buffalo the professor himself may lecture twice a week for fifty minutes to seven hundred persons. For two more fifty-minute hours, whole phalanxes of T.A.'s meet groups of ten to fifteen students to argue over some controversial historical document or a piece of history writing they all presumably have read with care beforehand. The T.A.'s grade all the essay examinations and term papers, keep their own office hours in a large room with many little desks and straight chairs they all share, and keep records of each student's performance. At the universities with total enrollments of more than 20,000, the introductory English "theme-a-week" and grammar courses are taught almost exclusively by advanced graduate students. So are the introductory sociology, political science, psychology, mathematics, and foreign-language courses. At a big university all but the most advanced laboratory science classes are run by paid graduate assistants.

Instruction from graduate students costs less (for the university, that is) than professorial instruction, but one should not assume that it is inferior. The T.A.'s at Stanford or Columbia are likely to be far better informed, eager, conscientious, and sympathetic than their supervising professors and can be expected to be more energetic and more respectful toward the students than some sour professors teaching the same courses at the second-rank state colleges in Arizona or Maryland. A further distinction to establish is that the T.A.'s at Chicago or Princeton or UCLA are likely to be in a different league both intellectually and pedagogically from the graduate students at Bowling Green State or the University of Arkansas. It is only to restate the obvious to claim that the quality of an education depends but little on the quality of the degrees of those who dole it out.

Higher education is most assuredly gleaned where tradition, the majority of students on hand, and the ineffable atmosphere all favor it. Several mutually supporting momentums of already proven excellence tend to concentrate prepared and motivated undergraduates, energetic graduate students, good libraries, spiritually ennobling extracurricular activities, and a healthy, trusting ambiance at only a few American colleges and universities. While better-rewarded and famous professors happen to teach, research, and scheme at such places, it is wrong to attribute more than a part of the happy and lively intellectual atmosphere to those professors alone. At an established place where almost all embrace the grand tradition, students and professors all educate themselves and one another.

To return to graduate assistants and their use: They can also be used to record experimental data of scientific validity. They write down long series of physics calibrations, run rats repeatedly through mazes, write out book orders for the library, and verify footnotes and translations. When a student does most of the drudgery for a scholarly article, he should be (according to professorial good manners) but often is not listed as a second author of the resulting publication.

Though it is against the rules, graduate assistants can be summoned to fetch the boss after a stupefying drunk at a suburban roadhouse, to babysit, and to tend bar at big parties. One hears of graduate students washing walls, mowing lawns, and comforting professors through their own or their spouses' menopauses. As is implicit in the master-slave relationship suggested above, circumstances conspire to draw assistants and professors together intimately. That these relationships occasionally climax erotically should astonish no one.

Perquisites that require elaboration, if only to establish their small importance in the aggregate, are research grants. A popular hero in American fiction—inspired perhaps by a central problem thoroughly investigated by Henry James—is the Yankee intellectual in Europe. For many years now, the hero of many such novels has been a Fulbright "fellow" (that is the holder of a stipend which supports the scholar while he is away from his job). Contemporaneous with high academic euphoria in the 1960s was an ad man's slogan "While you're up, get me a Grant's," which hustled an inferior brand of scotch. Some professors snatched this and, in the faculty lounges after bitching at length about their present working conditions, would call to a colleague rising from his armchair, "While you're up, get me a grant."

One must distinguish here between research support, which consists of such things as equipment, salaries for others, publication subsidies (that is, a gift to a press in order to convince the press to turn out a book in an edition which is below the normal break-even number for that press), and vastly-to-be preferred fellowship grants, which furnish the professor with something like the equivalent of his salary and which free him from teaching—in essence, something for nothing. There are a bewildering number of foundations, institutes for advanced study (sometimes called "think tanks"), and boards which invite professors to apply for freebies (see the *Annual Register of Grant Support,* Chicago: Marquis, yearly editions). And apply they do for the boodle that would include round-trip economy air fare to Kyoto or Canberra, the equivalent of nine months of salary ("affidavit required" say some application blanks), and expenses for books and local travel while on the scene. For the Fulbright awards and for the National (that is, financed by the federal government) Endowments for Science, the Humanities, and the Arts, the deadlines are in June for the academic year that begins fifteen months later. Guggenheim, the American Council of Learned Societies, and the various academies want their applications in October. Yearly, many thousands of academics fill in the forms and append supplemental sheets typed in double spaces with descriptions of their intended project. Angry at being forced to humble themselves, they beg for letters of support from professors with greater names than their own. That the requester may despise the requestee makes the exercise yet more painful. Some professors are smug. They believe they have discovered a shy, right-wing foundation with bags of CIA money that no one else knows about or applies for. A good friend at Northwestern who has already won a decent award assures a candidate that his project is "sexy, but not too sexy."

Anxious waiting follows the stamp licking. In February the professor meets with his chairman to make certain that his classes already scheduled for next fall can be taken by others or safely cancelled. One seeks out a tenant for the furnished house who will cover the mortgage payment of $299.63 for the precise period August 15, 197–, to April 30, 197–+1, and who will also polish the dark-wood furniture and care for the fruit trees and the collie. One phones to hear of Delphic hints, which are interpreted favorably, from friends of friends on the reviewing boards. Then on March 15 bad news from everybody—the Ford Foundation, the Stanford think tank, and the little-known foundation in Pittsburgh alike:

"We regret that. . . ."

"I am sorry to tell you that. . . . There were 2,773 applications for only 305 awards."

". . . The committee has regretfully been obliged to disappoint many deserving scholars."

"The competition remains keen and the funds limited."

Of course, some few hundred professors do indeed get these academic brass rings. But the winners are distant in more than mere miles from the working stiffs at the California State College at Chico, New Mexico Highlands University, or the Greensboro campus of the University of North Carolina. The winners have won before. They presented their projects in assured, terse, honed language. They arranged far in advance for delirious encomiums (which in many cases the contestant himself drafted and then sent on to the recommenders) from professors as eminent as themselves whom they will in turn help in later years and who just now preside over research institutes of African languages in Hamburg, Etruscan archeological digs near Naples, or lavish offices set aside for pensiveness near Santa Barbara.

Long ago some foundations were originally set up to liberate as-yet-unproved professorial researchers from their considerable teaching duties. But no foundation has been able to maintain its professed after Sputnik, any Russianist who had published an article could pick preference for the young and/or hidden. The members of reviewing boards are chosen from the splendid places, and they quickly winnow out those who have no track record or who offer no prospect of someday returning favors.

The fashions that sweep academia can bring about windfalls. Just up grants of free time to intensify his Russian expertise—even if he wished to investigate the press in Odessa in 1910 or the prerevolutionary Orthodox Church or the Soviet cinema in the 1920s. Similar waves of benefaction have washed and receded from South America, Africa, Southeast Asia, and China. Now it is the Arabic Middle East. Environmentalists whose eyes well up with outrage and who are agreeable public speakers have been hot for some years now. Black males, especially those who articulate standard, middle-western English, in grantmanship, as in other academic subdivisions, have long been the cocks of the walk.

Small grants ranging from one hundred to five hundred dollars are plentiful game in ambitious universities. Chairmen who wish to give their departments yet more "exposure" usually can award a pleading researcher a "special assignment" which gives him a summer-school salary without teaching as he labors to put his novelties into publishable form. Many colleges and universities have special faculty committees which are given several thousands of dollars to allot in gobbets to those who fill in the furnished application forms. The applicants beg for payment in advance for manuscript typing, microfilms of scarce newspapers, two weeks at thirty-five dollars per day to look closely at the lichens atop of Mount Bierstadt, expenses for the 2,000 miles of driving necessary to interview Jean-Paul Sartre's American disciples, or tuition, room, and board for a summer refresher course in the bass fiddle at Interlachen. Here again, funds are always short. A track record is helpful. So is the prospect of being able to return favors.

The sabbatical year is a common perquisite, though far from universal (the Universities of North Carolina and Texas, Ohio State University, and many other places do not have a sabbatical plan—though they may assign "research leave"). Most colleges or universities above the third rank do offer sabbaticals. After each six years of full-time service, the professor claims he is stale and applies for a half year at full pay or a full year at half pay during which he is expected to go elsewhere. Presumably he will finish the research on the "monograph" (that is, a detailed book on a narrow topic—to be distinguished from the less-detailed, broader "survey" of research) from which, as he ceaselessly complains, his onerous teaching schedule keeps him. So he leaves to hang around Berkeley, Oxford, Heidelberg, or Florence for a few months in a furnished house rented for $450 per month to "find out what the people there are doing."

One's chances of being sent off are increased if he wins on his own a fellowship from a prestigious foundation—for example, a Guggenheim—that pays skimpily. The university makes up the difference with a sabbatical. In the academic world, the sabbatical is not a right. These chunky gifts are ultimately bestowed by deans and vice-presidents in charge of instruction. They are supposed to acknowledge energy given to teaching ("Poor thing needs a rest") and research distinction, but sabbaticals also reward loyalists who accurately and consistently inform on their chairmen.

There are other perquisites that make professors' jobs worth struggling for and hanging on to. The professor has an office. During the early years of the boom, academics in some popular places were required to share offices originally intended for one person. This made enemies of smokers and nonsmokers, teeth suckers and those who could not bear the sound, young and old, right liberal and left liberal. The chairman of an English department in Oregon acquired deathless affection in 1959 when he demanded that the architect for his new building specify faculty offices exactly seven feet by seven feet square, that is, barely acceptable for one person and distinctly too small for two. When additional new professors were projected, he thus forced the administration to build yet another building to house them. Since about 1966, offices in new buildings have been getting larger. The typical professor pleads to be able to hold little seminars in his office so as to reach for his own books in order grandly to offer a quotation, bibliographical citation, or statistical table that would prove him correct after all. Woe to the academic vice-president who allows the law professors to specify to their architect offices much larger than those at present enjoyed by those in business or education. Senior professors (that is, those with tenure) will fight like actresses to have offices with windows (many new buildings have "inside" offices, that is, without windows) and near the toilets. The new offices are customarily wall-to-wall carpeted. On the walls are blackboards for the mathematicians, maps ("Burgundy at the Time of Charles V," "England at the Time of the Conquest") and fourteenth-century brass rubbings from Bristol for the historians; travel posters ("Fly Avianca!" "Beautiful Tegucigalpa!") for the foreign-language teachers. There are lots of pale green or pale gray steel bookcases, a large plastic-topped desk, a vinyl-upholstered, swivel-tilt armchair that squeaks, a couple of institutional straight chairs (for book salesmen or for students—professors rarely gossip in their offices), a four-drawer file cabinet, an ugly steel table holding an old electric typewriter and a black telephone.

Local calls are free. Dial 9 for out. The top hundred universities also provide tie-lines or WATS systems for long-distance calls. The universities pay for the postage on what the professors mail out too. They also provide letterhead paper, envelopes, paper clips, staples, and secretarial help, though the last-mentioned service is always inadequate in supply and especially lacking in quality. Astonishingly few professors take advantage of the world that is within grasp from their sacrosanct offices. Very few play the horses or the stock market, run little mail-order businesses, or do comparable things "on the side" as it were. A tale has it that a professor of Romance languages grew rich (that is, his house had ten rooms and he bought a new Lincoln every even-numbered year) over a ten-year period by importing and wholesaling Portuguese wines. The warehouse he visited only rarely was at the end of a railroad siding near the docks. His office, phone, and mail services (a morning and an afternoon delivery) were provided by a branch of a university in New England.

To encourage "keeping abreast of one's field," departments have an erratic travel budget. Twice a year professors not in academic Siberia should expect to get either *per diem* of about thirty dollars a day or economy jet fare, whichever is less, to attend scholarly meetings. If the professor's name is "on the program" (that is, if he is the chairman of a session, presenting a paper [a short research report read aloud], or commenting on someone's paper about recent findings), his chairman should give him both *per diem* and the travel money. Travel funds, however, are the first to be sacrificed in economy campaigns.

Students, wives, and trustees always suspect that the professors screw like cats while they are away. Not so. Once after a convention in Memphis, a professor who was the last to leave met a tired cleaning woman in his room. She asked, "What kind of a convention was it that just finished?"

"Why it was the Southern Historical Association, ma'am," the professor replied.

She shook her head and murmured, "I never in my life have seen a group of men who drank more and fucked less."

Regarding travel expenses for administrators, it is expected that chairmen, deans, and the bureaucrats above them will travel wherever, whenever, and however they wish at university expense, money crunches or no.

Faculty clubs are, increasingly, relics of a more genteel past. At the newly big places they are usually an automobile drive away and so are shunned, since the professors fear the loss of their parking places upon returning from lunch. The faculty club at Harvard is as elegant as one might expect. Some luncheon specialties are chicken cordon bleu, stuffed baked shrimp, and strawberry parfait.

A professor at Brandeis recalled his first visit to his faculty club:

> . . . on the menu . . . was corned beef and potato *lotkes* with sour cream. It wasn't kosher, but you knew you were eating Jewish. It was very good, and I had finished the meal and was talking to one of the faculty and looked at the dessert menu of which there were about ten or eleven, and the waitress asked me if I wanted one and I said, "No." And she looked down and said, "Come on, this one . . ." And I said, "No, I'm really on a diet." And she said, "Ach, a little dessert—what will it matter."[1]

Most of the more than a quarter million American academics have no access to certain other elegancies that professors had when a professor was a *rara avis*. Very few professors get waiter service, kosher or nonkosher at wainscoted faculty dining rooms. At present only the better-heeled private colleges and universities have agreements with their friendly competitors for the mutual remission of tuition for children of faculty members. The large houses that colleges once gave rent-free to their miserably paid professors have been turned over to the Lutheran students or have long since been bulldozed for parking garages. However, the professors have the same privileges that students have regarding access to special lectures, concerts, art movies, the snack bars, swimming pools, and gymnasiums.

Professors have first crack or second crack (after the alumni) at tickets for football or basketball games. These are paltry bribes for the professors' conscienceless endurance of the intercollegiate athletic programs. The absolute unassailability of the universities' athletic programs has a long history which remains unwritten. The professors, by betraying their obligation to criticize—actually maintain intercollegiate sport as a quasi-sacred realm that attracts and holds the opponents of the professors' tasks to seek, preserve, and communicate truth. The athletic directors, most especially the football coaches, squander millions and damage and occasionally destroy (there have in the past century been dozens of cases of murder on the football fields) young men called students.

One of the essential (and never admitted) duties of an American university president is to oversee the membership of the faculty athletic committee to make sure that it remains quiescent and continues to legitimize what is an illegitimate and indeed antiacademic operation. Few campus issues cause so much unexpressed soul-examining among the competent or idealistic faculty. Unlike the recent leftist political agitation, which was far less divisive or threatening to intellectual inquiry in the universities, this imperishable issue never hits the local newspapers. For the sports editors will not allow it. The trustees will not tolerate a professorial examination of the athletic budget or any sort of sniping at the program. This issue causes many professors to view the trustees as swine. Curiously, the professors are rarely bitter at the coaches as persons. They too are partly dazzled by the charisma of omnipotent machismo, and many grudgingly admire the nifty, long-standing hustle. Professors who vocally oppose the athletic program are treated as hand-biting ingrates by the trustees, who await opportunities for revenge. The coaches, who are only, after all, trying to do their job, which is to win (and this has nothing to do with education or research or service), view almost all professors as flaccid stumblebums, jock-strap sniffers, twittering faggots.

We can leave this bitter topic for some sweeter ones—the tax advantages available almost exclusively to academics. The substantiation for the claims (all of them by now decided in the courts) listed below is that they are deductible as research costs. Professors can depreciate as though it were a business expense the retail cost of their libraries over a ten-year period. If his travel expenses come out of his own pocket, the professor claims these as research expenses. Of course, a lot of fudging goes on here. In order to assure his colleagues that he is a scholar and not a *bon vivant* and to raise a smoke screen for the Internal Revenue, a historian from Boston College who wants to show the wife and kids Italy in the month of June declares to all that archives or digs are his object. The psychologist from Kentucky State University who wants to experience for himself two weeks of poppers and discothèques in Amsterdam, learns to pronounce the name of a research institute for old age nearby. The teacher of composition for stringed instruments at the University of Colorado who wishes to gossip all summer with dear friends from graduate school who now live, respectively, in Evanston, Bloomington, and Wilmington declares that the avant-garde concerts in New York City are his object. He packs the VW camper with the five kids and their sleeping bags. And all these travelers keep receipts—some of them forged.

There are special attractions for the big fellowships that require residence abroad. One deducts moving expenses coming and going from the home town. For the duration of the grant, the tax regulations allow for the deduction of three hundred dollars per month as research expenses that need not be specified.

Until the tax reform of 1976, a professor who installed a long table with a pencil holder on it in one room of his seven-room house could claim one-seventh of all his housing expenses—mortgage costs, taxes, insurance, utilities—as research expenses.

There is one advantage, or complex of advantages, which the professors enjoy and which, though quietly speculated about by outsiders, is almost never revealed for what it is.[2] The American professor spends his working life among the healthiest, the liveliest, the most voluptuously decked-out humans that have ever ornamented the earth. These are American college students. Almost all professors are voyeurs and fear admitting to outsiders (for even more of them would want their jobs) the raptures, the swooning pleasures that are to be had from this looking and the fantasies that the looking inspires.

The quality of erotic looking varies, from the ecstatic to the merely amusing. Eyeballing is best in southern California. The youths are always in the fresh air. Big blonds wearing loose cut-off Levi's from which strut hard brown legs that one yearns to slap. Sun-bleached, kinky hair on the men's legs. Burned skin flakes from their pink noses. Their teeth are wet and white. Sometimes the dark girls are greasy and have little rivulets of sweat behind their ears. One smells from afar their crotches, their armpits, and their feet—always good. Direct staring and sniffing is always most perilous in California because devoted esthetic peering could well be misinterpreted by the objects that perceive it and answered with a deliberate tease or a "Why not?" invitation.

The reader might imagine a clear, warm afternoon in April at the campus of Duke University. The dozens of girls vary little from the perfect, clean type. Polka-dot dresses, clean, thin jeans, light voices. They walk in little steps, they lick their lips, smile grandly, and wave their eyelashes at everybody—even at the quiet stranger, probably a professor, whom they have never seen before. They cannot see what shrill, bitter-sweet happiness, what desperate yearning and desperate disappointment they cause to churn within him. Nearby, at dusk on the Chapel Hill campus of the University of North Carolina, the same professor strolls, apparently self-involved, through groups of males and females dressed in soft work clothes. Heavy, hard-nippled breasts sway in thin, patterned blouses. One girl has a fold of old denim far up between her crotch lips. They are noisy. The girls stand close to graze big boys who have heavy, coiled baskets of strength below their hips. How can the voyeur know in the near darkness if their cocks unfurl? He will imagine it.

At Chapel Hill and at other places there are so many hundreds of voluptuously healthy, happy people about that even the few supreme beings become oblivious to their distinction. They forget that they have sensual beauty to so keen a degree and therefore are relaxed and unselfconscious, which causes the esthetic voyeur to adore them yet more hotly.

At his own campus, the professor has his favorites. The thin black girl with short hair and a hooked nose whose posture is one of unassailable pride. Twins with large behinds and long yellow hair. An engineering student who has big shoulders, and who walks a little pigeon-toed as he carries a small filthy rucksack. He can recall sadness at the long drama of observing an especially handsome, angelic boy, selected for watching when he was a freshman, grow slightly fat and coarse as he betrays the loveliness given him and overeats, overdrinks, and oversleeps for four years. The loveliest girls usually hold up.

On the northern campuses the academic year occupies the heavy clothing seasons. All the same, well-covered students who are handsome still inspire the wicked imagination of a refined voyeur. He relishes distinctive walking styles and watches pairs, imagining the powerful, cunningly skilled postpubescents grunting, socking, overflowing with ooze. In the winter the student union is a hearty place to drink a cup of coffee and to appear distracted with weighty matters at the very time one has reveries of participation in stinking, lightly bloody orgies in semidarkness with teenagers. An especially good time for erotic looking is when the professor "proctors" (that is, patrols or oversees, looking for cheaters) an examination. The atmosphere is far more sensual than it is during a lecture when the dominant professor is too preoccupied with the presentation of self and subject matter to appreciate the little, chubby girl in the front row whose eyes are glazed as she softly taps her bare knees together. During the test students stare with puzzled absorption at the questions and mark the little spaces on the machine-graded forms. The professor frowns as he strolls, ready to trap the dishonest. He is really looking down blouses, comparing strong, young necks, probing with his eyes lickable cheeks, arms, and legs. Do the students notice that the professor has tears in his eyes and is softly rubbing his lips?

If the professor is not too fat or too old, with reassuring frequency (say, twice a semester) something like the following playlet will ensue:

A girl with a bad complexion comes to his office and, after closing the door behind her, confesses her enjoyment of the lecture on the tragic life of Gustav Mahler and, in a curious transition, comments on his (the professor's) mustache. As the one-sided conversation advances, she remarks that, if she seems depressed lately, it is because she is lonesome after breaking up with her last boyfriend whom she trusted so deeply for seven whole months.

Sometimes exciting prospects are more directly offered:

"Since my parents went off to the Bahamas for a month, all I have been doing lately is sitting home alone in that big house and listening to the kind of music you like and writing poetry."

"Dr. Settembrini, what can I do to get a B in symbolic logic?" The poor dumb thing's eyes well up with abject sincerity. Should the professor reach across the room to embrace her and assure the child that everything will work out for the best?

One hears from time to time of the anguish of a homely and serious virgin, a student in her twenties. After hinting at coming crises in her life, she rocks back and forth on her heels and threatens a descent into lesbianism if the young professor she has come to admire and trust will not help out with overdue, extraprofessorial lessons.

The males are more lighthearted. They mumble equivocal inconsequentialities that are intended to lead to sexual discussions of one sort or another. The leads become ever more obvious until the professor gets fidgety and looks pointedly at his watch. The boys blush, shuffle their big feet, and, when it is clear that there will be no nibbling at the bait, abruptly leave the office with a smile so large it borders on a guffaw. Whew!

It will sadden some and cheer others to learn that the girls who proffer the most personal gifts are rarely the campus beauties while the boys who do often are. Also, it is proper to add the reassurance that, with some generic exceptions noted in the course of the book, there are near taboos, which are never explicitly expressed yet are nevertheless very much in force. Perhaps the professor atavistically views himself as a priest; perhaps there is something in the tribal atmosphere in the university; perhaps there are between professor and student certain residuals of a family relationship. In any case, there are implicit prohibitions against sexual congress with undergraduates. With graduate students and especially with departmental secretaries, the taboos are looser.

Before exposing some of the hazards of this agreeable occupation, there must be a few restatements. Unless they are the few hundred big shots at the great places, and have dozens of graduate students each and publication deadlines to boot, or they take their committee duties far too seriously, almost all professors have a lot of time to use however they wish. Most of the hazards of the profession are traceable to its lack of specific, exterior goads. Professors work in a milieu where the means of appraising and awarding accomplishment are so imprecise or even perverse as to make it nearly impossible for them to be sure of where they stand or how secure they are either in the academic community or in the outside world. Within their institutions, significant communication is overwhelmingly verbal and professors will have their most vivid contacts with the outside world by means of the spoken and written word. Otherwise stated, to use Marshall McLuhan's terminology, professors are old-fashioned print men. Professors are still subject to the at-once cancerous and optimistic consumerism that keeps their neighbors busy. Professors (whatever obfuscations or flagrant exceptions they or their critics may unearth) are smart and are conservative.

The biggest hazard in the life of a professor is the same liquid that has always devastated fretful white men with time on their hands. Tales of the stepped procession into rotten alcoholism are too familiar to us all to merit more than a schematic, occupationally specific retelling here. Usually the regular drinking begins in graduate school. Two tumblers of red wine from a gallon jug in order to sleep after having spent days looking for the "theses" (for so are phrased the questions on comprehensive examinations) in the three volumes of Rostovstev's *Social and Economic History of the Hellenistic World* or Lyashchenko's 880-page *History of the National Economy of Russia*. Later, an assistant's salary of $12,500 permits one to pay for surer and harder jolts of middling-quality bourbon and scotch. The usual academic cocktail is the olived, super-iced, and devastating martini.

The inescapable frustrations of academic life are incessant and difficult to specify, since they seem like mere annoyances and pinpricks when related to outsiders. The pleasures of bourbon over ice in a cut-crystal glass are immediate and irresistible. The bachelors in their thirties and forties fondle them while brooding over small hurts. When they appear in the corridors the next morning, the bachelors know that others know that the Certs have not covered the tainted breath. Their affable colleagues mask their perception of a drunk. The drunks wallow in shame and, if they are still young and fairly tough, may not drink a drop for the next four nights running.

The awarding of tenure is devastating for the delitescent alcoholic, for he is insulated from many previous restraints. He chisels irregularly on duties considered irreducible and the self-indulgence which his quiet addiction has already confirmed speeds his decay. To the administration and to vigorous younger colleagues he is viewed as irremovable and becomes (dreadful academic condemnation!) "deadwood." Sometimes the drunk becomes popular with students because he grades generously and his eruditely anecdotal lectures provide intervals of buffoonery ("better than Johnny Carson, on his good days") or are mysteriously canceled.

Like their neighbors, who usually have more to spend, some professors, particularly those who assume their marriages will last forever, try to live graciously. They are inspired by the tone of the ads in *The New Yorker, Atlantic,* or the New York *Times Magazine.* They tell themselves and their guests that it is a "hobby" to buy case lots of good German whites, bargains in French reds or little-known (that is, costly) California wines of all sorts. They also collect dozens of sticky, unusual-shaped bottles of liqueurs concocted in Swiss monasteries or Sicilian caves. These professors have rows of cookbooks and may collect these too. Between the cookbooks are yellowed recipes clipped from the New York *Times.* Suppers at some of their houses can be memorable and pleasurable experiences. A visiting French music historian who was much invited out during his year at Cornell University was astonished that "when the Americans wish to eat very well, they eat at home." However, at these parties, as at all others, professors drink too much and gossip compulsively about those not present.

One can find limitations of the expensive, good life in the academic provinces, but as one moves away from the old academic disciplines and westward and southward from the clustered, first-class schools, the parties are both more frequent and clumsier. Little Bennington College in Vermont is a fairly classy place, and when their young president, Gail Parker, served hastily prepared and bad food, it was held against her. However, the wife of an accounting professor in Ames, Iowa, can, as the other dinner guests look on, *present* a distinguished guest with a $2.89 bottle of Liebfraumilch (the name and the wine make some Germans retch) at room temperature for drinking on the spot. A professor of educational psychology at Armstrong State College in Savannah regularly serves chilled Mogen David with Chef Boy-Ar-Dee spaghetti at his dinner parties.

At a large "duty" party (one invites the whole department and a couple of deans) there is usually an alcoholic punch that is too sweet and a nonalcoholic punch that is too sweet. For duty parties the hostess crowds the extended dining-room table with bowls of substantial potato chips, celery sticks, carrot sticks, bits of cauliflower, and, in earthenware pots, mixtures of sour cream and dried soups to dip them in. Everybody eats this crap. Conversation at an academic party where the invitation net has been widely cast is boisterous about sports and the weather, and more restrained about child raising, the public schools, and plans for next summer. Except for one or two groups of three distracted, chuckling, rapidly sousing professors in far corners of the study or the garden, talk of campus matters is allusive or is responsibly deflected. One talks of serious matters only with trusted friends.

The television coverage of some campus disturbances in the late 1960s indicated that a lot of professors are loose radicals. George Wallace's scorn for professors who can't park their bicycles straight tends to build an image of professorial impracticality. There are a few quotable *real* revolutionaries still minable for journalistic copy. All these tend to confirm a long-standing impression of John Q. Public that professors are subversives at heart. Many professors are odd, but J.Q.P. is dead wrong.

In the classroom, in a commencement speech, in writing down criteria for judging promotability, in theoretical articles, in faculty club grousing over current events, it is immensely difficult for a professor to maintain face among his peers while professing other than middle-liberal views. More specifically, professors sound like they are prointegration, pro-ERA, pro–welfare state, prodétente, egalitarian democrats. A professor who declares that he holds other views may be made to suffer keenly. Witness the harassment of Professor William B. Shockley of Stanford, who has published articles postulating IQ differences between black and white children. Or Willmoore Kendall, an argumentative elitist, who got Yale to buy his tenure from him for $60,000 in 1960. Racist slurs as jokes are taboo even among close friends. If one is not Jewish and tells even one Jewish joke when drunk, he may suddenly find himself no longer invited to parties. Very late in the Viet Nam and Watergate crises, the professors competed with one another to invent fresh and cutting rhetoric applicable to their elected national leaders.

But professors do very little that is actively political. In the aggregate, they have rarely voted more than ordinary citizens and rarely even sign petitions. This persistent laziness should be proof of academia's deep conservatism and timidity. Historical substantiations abound. The German academics (upon whom our notions of proper social status were partly modeled, be it remembered) scarcely twitched in resistance to resistable, diabolical politics in the period 1920–45. The quiet, going-along-with-it of professors in southern universities during the (still ongoing) integration struggle also come to mind. One disturbing aspect of the California oath controversy of 1949–52 is that so few of the enormous faculty actually acted on principles. A few distinguished men quietly allied with the non-signers, but

> . . . there are many others of the institution's famous personages who remained nearly or wholly aloof throughout the controversy, for example, Professors Earnest O. Lawrence, Edwin M. McMillan, Glenn T. Seaborg, Emilio G. Segre, William F. Gaiuque, John H. Northrop, Luis W. Alvarez and others; and one can only speculate if the Regents would have dismissed, for not signing, men such as these on whose reputations the University's scientific fame in substantial part lay.[3]

Parents who worry that clean-cut Michael or Susan will, upon arriving on the state college campus, become zapped weirdos, mouthing the slogans of dumb idealism and scary anarchy, have good cause for concern. But Mike and Sue were already softened by junk television and the rhetoric of dope while in high school and will intensify their appreciation of the new ways together with kids from equally nice neighborhoods who now live in the dorms. Together they will talk earnestly of deep matters while being inspired by the sloppy lyrics of magnificently seductive rock music. At bad universities as at good, most of what the kids actually learn, they learn from each other. The professors at the less-than-first-rank institutions despise the garish evidence of cultural degradation about them but do nothing to resist it. They complain and gossip.

Professors are only rarely television addicts, amateur craftsmen, athletes, or passionate collectors. All studies of how professors use their ample leisure demonstrate that they read a great deal. Their social life is odd and curiously limited, for they confine their friends to academics like themselves. Even in a college with a student body of 5,000 and a faculty of 300, they clump socially as well as organizationally into predictable groups. Interdepartmental friendships follow the expected lines: For example, the art historian in the art department lunches often with the cultural historian in the history department. The wives of an educational psychologist and of a supervisor of beginning teachers will buy bulk vegetables together at the local farmers' market. Social scientists from several disciplines will play golf or bridge with statisticians or computer scientists. In the neighborhoods the professors are only pleasant with their next-door neighbors, for they are likely to be bigots and harsh disciplinarians with children. The neighbors may have complained to his face that the professor is not caring properly for his lawn, car, and house. Their specializations have caused professors to travel far to take their jobs, so they have only occasional meetings with their parents or other near relatives. For many professors, their closest personal contacts with the outside, adult world are their not infrequent meetings with insurance salesmen.

Another social peculiarity of professors is the durability of their friendships that were originally professional. Those who stuck it through together at the same big graduate schools are plugged into chum-colleague networks stretching from San Diego to Nova Scotia. On the Friday night before the Easter vacation a six-member family, delirious with happy anticipation, will load the rusty Plymouth station wagon for the overnight, nineteen-hour drive from Albany, New York, to Athens, Georgia, to visit people met and adored in Berkeley fourteen years before. For a week the families (joined perhaps by yet another Berkeley family or two) will overeat, overdrink, and toss the Frisbee just as they did so long ago in Tilden Park. And they will tell and retell stories on their former and present colleagues. They will talk and talk, reveling in the prolonged opportunity to do so. They will talk until their jaws grow tired.

As on a tramp steamer (the parallel is not idly chosen), the skilled storyteller in academia has privileged status and can be influential to a high degree in intrauniversity power politics. In no other kind of organization is there such a gulf between the formal communication network, which is laughably ineffectual, and the informal communication network, which is unspecifiable and secret but which works all the same. The substance of the informal network is gossip. The gossip organization has ranked executives without titles. The academic gossips move slowly and make reputations and destroy them.

Academics must gossip. There exists no other way for them to learn just what is going on. How else can a professor learn if his colleagues are competent, doing their share of the work, benevolent, or malevolent? The offices are sacred. The professors cannot visit each other's classes and are incapable of judging each other's published research. Therefore, vast amounts of control and influence accrue to the storyteller, the assembler, fashioner, and distributor of news. The master storyteller or gossip does not himself gather raw data. The gossip collects his stuff from malcontent students, particularly graduate students, and also from colleagues who thus repay him in kind for the nicely told stories.

"Have you heard what kind of new Mickey Mouse courses Sumpkin is working up now?" he slips in at a dinner party with a sideways glance.

"Did you know that the fellow from Montana who wrote the ecstatic review of Granby's little book in the *Journal of Social History* is trying to get Granby to write him an equally ecstatic letter for a Guggenheim?"

The gossip can pose as a defender of those who are slipping and, while playing the good guy, speed their decline.

"Funk has been unjustly maligned," intoned sincerely in a condescending voice to three others, none of them Funk himself.

"He seems determined to stay off the sauce for more than a few weeks this time."

"Bourden at Harvard says that Stern's little book [everyone knows that the publication was subsidized, that it took nine years to finish, and that Stern is already forty-four years old] shows great promise."

It is perhaps regrettable, but it is true that academic gossip is true gossip. A caveat: Academic gossip here means gossip gathered and examined by professors only. Student gossip is unreliable. The reputation of a great academic gossip is as much due to the consistent accuracy of what he (rarely she, incidentally) purveys as to its skilled presentation. Many of the notorious, emotion-searing divisions of al-

legiances in academic departments originate when an upstart raconteur campaigns for control and influence. The malcontent tells carefully honed, accurate tales about the incumbent gossip and his
feeders. Obsessive hatreds take root that are as keen as those among
merchant seamen. Everyone dreads young and ongoing enmities
which look like they will never end. Things were better before all this
started. Better stick with the old gossip and crush the upstart by
snubbing him.

It should be emphasized in fairness here that diligence, competence, and, most especially, departmental loyalty are usual categories
of judgment set forth by the gossipists. However, since almost all
professors are lazy and incompetent in one way or more, almost all
are easy marks. Some matters are considered out of bounds. Professors A and B will exchange facts about Professor C's atypical sexual
orientation, his salary, his allegiance to Catholicism or Judaism, his
manner of dressing, or his inherited money only late at night and
when A and B have drunk far too much. The talk is awkward and in
whispers, for A and B know they are doing wrong. But word—even
of these things—does get around.

Their isolation from kitsch culture, their literacy, their intradis-
ciplinary bases for social life, and their allegiance to distant friends
should not obscure the fact that the overwhelming majority of professors are forces for stability, not change. More evidence is in order.

The professors' cars are noteworthy because they are at first glance
so uninteresting. It takes considerable courage for a professor to buy
any new car—much more so an obviously expensive one. Anyone
who has been in academic life for ten or twelve years has observed
the cheeky ones move from buying a light brown four-door Ford
with an automatic transmission every five years to the regular
purchase every three years of a small Dodge or Oldsmobile similarly
colored and equipped. The man with three children (this is the acceptable maximum; the wife who exceeds this number risks at parties
drunken insults from members of Planned Parenthood) may buy
through the want ads a tarnished four-year-old station wagon which
a trusted mechanic pronounces sound from an engineering point of
view.

The car one is expected to bring back from Europe is an off-white
Volvo or a Volkswagen camper. The strenuously advertised safety
and durability of the Swedish car snag many academics. The camper
is a four-wheeled burlesque of practicality. New, each of these cars is

very expensive. But the returner from abroad explains to his colleagues that he saved three hundred dollars over the best price offered by the local dealers for autos as completely equipped with accessories. So much for the radical, starving professors.

Energetic walkers and bicycle commuters are less required to maintain a stock of defensive repartee than they were a few years ago. As up-to-date liberals, the academics must profess environmentalism. And, though rarely participating sportsmen, all ascribe to the motto (behind which some of the coaches hide too) *mens sana in corpore sano,* which means that a sound body should serve a sound mind. Even if the professors recall nostalgically having played softball and basketball, few risk displaying their present incapacity in the campus intramural (from Latin, "within the walls," meaning in sports' language the assembling of teams from groups—most often fraternities—from within the campus) leagues. Exceptions here are the university professors resident along the Northwest coast and most physical educationalists. Every professor has a colleague who talks a good handball game, but who has never been seen playing. Since golf and tennis are played by the technicians and managers who live in nicely kept houses costing 25 per cent more than those of the professors, those sports are considered commendable for the same reasons that bowling and roller skating are not.

Professors eat in the company of one another and eat too much. Gossip is often exchanged at leisure over a big lunch, a lengthy and excellent supper at home, a large potluck buffet, or, minimally, a sugared coffee. Academic wives are intelligent, though cooking may be one of the few areas in which their husbands permit them to achieve creative distinction. Commensalism is the most usual academic entertainment. They stay long at table—even after second portions of the trifle or flan or key lime pie have been spooned in— for few professors play bridge. While at Yale or Columbia or Bloomington or Ann Arbor as graduate students having babies, they played charades or co-operatively filled in 85 per cent of the Sunday New York *Times* crossword puzzle with dear friends now scattered, but no more. The diet crazes that rush through the prosperous bourgeoisie captivate academics too. This despite the warnings published in the student newspaper by a stern biologist or an authoritative nutritionist that the diets are dangerous or useless. He who loses three pounds a week for five weeks running is vigorously congratulated in the faculty lounge. No one remarks (at least to his face) when he gives up to eat enormously and so gains three pounds a week for five weeks running.

Less so than others now earning from $17,000 to $27,000 per year (these figures are higher than the nine-month salaries given earlier; summer school teaching is included), the professors were lulled to optimism for ten years before 1972 or so. However, many imprudently barreled themselves into mortgages, insurance policies (conservatism again), and annuity plans for Mark and Elspeth to go to Yale or Princeton or to Vassar or Radcliffe. In the sixties, academics' paychecks were rising much faster than those of their neighbors and brothers and faster than the cost of living. Many paid off old mortgages and traded up. They projected past improvements into the future. Some of these academics are now just barely hanging on. Those with several children use powdered milk and have given up the tutoring in French. The flute lessons go next; then the ballet lessons; then August in the cabin at Lake Oconee. Even for those tenured and still earning fairly well, the inflated future is cheerless.

Does the professor trick? With his wife (*"ma régulière,"* as the French professor says) he does. Despite continuous presence of splendid, subservient youths in fantasy-inspiring situations, they do not rub and grunt in the flesh with the undergraduates. The atavistic view of themselves as guardians of ritual or surrogate parents which was mentioned earlier holds them back. There are other partial explanations. The professor lives in a world where one's stock goes up or down, where one is weak or strong, according to how much can be held against him by the gossipists. An aged man may warn a susceptible assistant professor with, "You never piss where you swim."

Young and loose sociologists (who may not be prizes themselves) may suggest that the humanists and scientists are not getting anything young and cute because the seekers are so humorless and ugly. Actually, only a few professors are choice pieces, but old-fashioned erotic standards are likely to be of small importance to many of the postpubescents of the present. Pilled, or overexperienced at age twenty, they will open their legs or mouths, uncork their fists, or raise their behinds out of boredom or on a dare. A terrifying fantasy that short-circuits many searingly delicious professorial reveries has the hero walking toward the library when he sees a recent trick nod to her sorority sister (both have dirty necks and gold hoop earrings) and mutter, "See the one with the combed-over bald spot and the pipe? I nailed him on the floor of his office late last Tuesday afternoon. He shot too quick and his cock is teeny."

Outsiders are fair game. In the absolutely strictest confidence a specialist in Latin rhetoric has delightedly showed his closest friends an oddly printed piece of 8½-by-14-inch paper. A dear friend in Champaign-Urbana—in fact, his dissertation director's wife—had sat naked on the plate of a Xerox machine, dropped in the nickel, and sent off the resulting picture of that part of herself which he had often exclaimed tasted sweetest. It is well known that a distinguished scholar of the medieval lyric regularly brings back from Paris strikingly young and pretty "delinquent boys" and sets about to rehabilitate them. He takes each one with him to movies and to cocktail parties until, after four months or so, the youths just disappear. However, from New Orleans or San Francisco they send affectionate postcards, which the scholar shows to all.

The notion of professors mate-swapping dismisses itself. One reason for the salacious joy many professors took in the gossip out of Bennington is that Gail Parker's shacking with Rush Welter (also married) was so enviable and unusual. Almost all professors are too tight in their ways and, though they have reveries of unusual erotic adventures and the time and freedom for them, they use the time for old-fashioned pursuits like reading, drinking, listening to music acknowledged to be good, gardening, thinking, or talking.

As in so many of these categorizations, one has to make exceptions of the sociologists-psychologists-anthropologists (shortened to S.P.A.'s earlier), who almost always consider themselves cultural relativists. These grown-up academic children refuse to acknowledge any standards of behavior as correct. They hesitate not to screw just about anybody and might demand that those in their power come across. It is not unusual to hear that the female graduate students in one of these departments will have a meeting in which they vow to one another that no longer will any of them put out for their professors. But then, the S.P.A.'s are boors in committee meetings since they smoke cigars, scratch their crotches, and will not learn parliamentary procedure. They do not ever have to learn to write correctly and, unlike the educationalists, who merely write lots of nothing, they obfuscate and brutalize the language. They boast to all that three of them have together written a theoretical article, later prominently published, while all were convulsed with hilarity from blowing grass. They are the only academics who use dope.

That their more conventional colleagues will not enjoy marijuana is everybody's little loss. The harmless euphoriant could brighten many sour professorial lives and make more cheery the campus landscape. Many young professors do try. The universally specific benefits of the herb are overproselytized by an S., or P., or A., who lives in the shabby colonial across the street from the scientist or humanist. The more conventional initiates, trying what most kids now do at age fourteen, are—despite all the assurances, they have read or heard—too terrified to open themselves to new, small pleasures.

There may be no way to convince such conservatives to experiment with the hallucinogens which are more difficult to obtain, or once obtained, to trust. Pity. An occasional, managed jolt of LSD could jangle stale minds or reanimate the keen pleasures in internal things that inspired professors to begin the long preparation for their occupations. It is unfortunate for the torpid professors that the reputations of the hallucinogens have been made by empty heads who take them seriously.

Acid would be especially beneficial for oversecure academics in their forties or fifties. It would not change the essential patterns of their lives. The cynical physical scientists are cheating themselves by avoiding a healthy way to be reinspired by the clouds and leaves of sweet nature. The humanists might suck a tab of something dependable and an hour later reread Rupert Brooke's longer poems or relisten to the Scarlatti harpsichord sonatas that made them shiver with ecstasy and devotion when they were young.

Illustration C:

ADELE GOHEEN DAHEIM OF
EAST PALMYRA STATE

Like many California commuters, Adele can enjoy two distinct mental lives while on the freeway. On this November morning the traffic is, as usual, dense and fast. With pride and familiar skill, Adele shoots the little Datsun over three-lane spans and shifts from third to fourth gear and back again without rippling her reveries. This morning the fantasies are her favorite kind. Adele is with a huge, androgynous companion, who is strong and tender. They walk hand in hand slowly over paths of pine straw in deep green forests. They stop frequently at cool springs. The friend of the reveries nods in sympathy to Adele's stories and responds cheerfully and well to Adele's voluptuous needs. The vacation dream makes the thirty-three-mile drive from Santa Monica to the campus pass most quickly.

More often Dr. Adele G. Daheim's passage from home to work is preoccupied with the same subject matter that has always made professors pensive as they walk, cycle, or drive to where they must fulfill their professional obligations. After she locks the car's door, she excludes the domestic world of her house and children from her mind and starts to plan the content of her two morning and one evening lectures. She recalls with annoyance the already delayed paperwork in her desk and the scheduled, inevitable meetings. Along the walk from parking lot L she reviews the day's obligations in her "liberated woman's appointment calendar." Naturally she plans in anticipation the strategies she would have to take in the usually abrasive encounters with many of her thirty male colleagues in the psychology department at the California State University at East Palmyra. Her ten-year career at the college had included many humiliations for a proud woman.

A basic cause of Adele's trouble in a man's world had been her striking appearance. She was petite and very dark—even more swarthy than her former husband, Al Daheim, who was Jewish. Though she was thirty-nine, the anguish of the past years had not done much damage, and the sole distractions of the fine face were just under her bright brown eyes. Those dark sacks were likely to stay reddish after weeping. She had a slim, muscular body and rather large breasts, which attracted too much attention. Adele would have liked to have been viewed in her professional life as something other than an exceptionally pretty and shapely female. She was a responsible mother, a professor to whom were due (indeed overdue) all the rewards that accompanied that position, and a dedicated battler for human dignity—her own and that of others. But such thoughts were dangerous for her just now. Angry thoughts always raised Adele into a defensively proud posture and also put her on the verge of tears that could mar the workmanlike presentation of lectures she had given twenty times before.

In the lecture hall she stands before a lectern at 10:00 A.M. for Psychology 101, the introductory course. It is late in the ten-week first quarter. Of the eighty-four students who registered nine weeks before, thus filling all the seats, only forty-seven are on hand in the eight-year-old, dirty classroom. The state college system accepts all California high-school graduates. Though professors at East Palmyra become accustomed to lackluster student performance after a few years on the job, most still demand evidence on their tests of some disciplined reading and of the students' respect for their lectures. So listless are most of the beginning students and so manifold the attractions of Los Angeles around them that only 65 per cent of the freshmen return for a second year; only 35 per cent graduate in five years or less. Adele herself does not compromise to Southern California *dolce far niente*. Her psychology lectures avoid diverting anecdotes of psychotherapy, ESP, insanity, and kinky sex. Expectations of such diversions had, of course, led many students to register for psychology in the first place.

For three weeks now Adele has dwelled on learning theory, for her 1969 dissertation at the University of California at Los Angeles was in this area of experimental psychology. Her textbook is the simple, general one imposed for consistency by a departmental committee on all sections of the course. However, the book of readings, which Adele was allowed to choose, is a collection of crucial (to learning theorists, in any case) articles about hungry rats running through mazes and hungry pigeons pecking at buttons. Adele's lectures tend to dwell on the controversies of the 1950s and 1960s that preoccupied working, experimental psychologists. Adele uses no movies or pictorial slides in her lectures, but occasionally employs an overhead projector to show the students graphs of experimental variables, such as changes in the rates of pecking that followed alterations in reinforcement schedules.

Adele's voice is strong, but noncommittal. Almost all the students are restless in the healthy way of youth and are bored. Those on hand have learned that there is little connection between the few things that Dr. Daheim says shrilly and loudly and what is likely to be on her examinations—old copies of which can be purchased for five dollars in xeroxed form on the organized campus blackmarket. During lectures a few students read the campus newspaper or (less often) the Los Angeles *Times*. Some doze uneasily; some chat or giggle very softly. For the lecturer, the fifty minutes pass quickly. At exactly 10:50, she announces the time and place of the three-hour multiple-choice final examination and dashes to a coffee machine near her office. She smooths the fabric of her polyester black slacks and her ruffled, V-neck blouse and stretches in an oak straight chair while trying to relax. The next class is in the same room on the same subject, and she must be ready to go at 11:00. Adele has presented her version of Psychology 101 so many times at East Palmyra that she no longer makes distinctions between lectures separated by three years, a few days, or ten minutes except that after she gives two back-to-back lectures, as today, she feels relieved but rather played out.

Years ago she had foreseen better things. Adele Goheen was the second child of a Philadelphia physician and a librarian with whom she still exchanges affectionate twenty-minute phone calls at the night rate. At Swarthmore she was popular with the boys and resented by the girls. She was a marginal student in philosophy and upon graduating in 1957 she told her friends and classmates that she would travel in Europe or work as a cocktail waitress. However, lacking courage to move far from familiar surroundings, she applied late for admission to do graduate work in psychology at Penn State.

The subject was more interesting than any other and suggested that its mastery might make her useful to troubled people.

She met Al Daheim, a twenty-seven-year-old army veteran and a would-be biologist, at a folk dance two weeks after her arrival. The courtship was swift and was anguishing because of her mother's bitter, though quietly voiced, objections to Al's Jewishness and to his unmoneyed family. They married and smartened up their cheap one-room apartment. The roof leaked. They had spaghetti parties and made and bottled their own beer, ten gallons at a time.

In June 1959 they both got their M.A.'s and left at once in a tattered and heavily loaded DeSoto for Los Angeles. One or the other of them had been accepted for Ph.D. work at several good universities, but UCLA had accepted them both and had offered Al a $1,750 assistantship besides. Pride prevented the couple from begging for Goheen money, and it soon was apparent that only one could be suitably financed. So Adele found undemanding jobs as an assistant researcher around the campus. In the biology department Al's prestige was high.

A set of unconventionally witty graduates of Reed and of the Claremont Colleges asked them to many parties and picnics. They had fun and spent little money. In a couple of years they actually saved $5,000 and Al was earning $3,000 a year as a teaching assistant, so they had their child, Margot, according to plan in 1962. Despite the objections of the psychology department's more distinguished professors, who felt that a mother belonged always at home, Adele was admitted to begin her own Ph.D. work in the fall of 1964. The arrival of Alex in April 1965 (births were easy for Adele—"A marble down a shute," Al boasted) caused her to miss just three days of classes, but her firmness about bringing Alex with her to the departmental library and to some meetings stung the same men who had opposed her admission to Ph.D. work. However, many crowded around for peeks when she nursed her son. Some younger men were heard to murmur, "Touching!" or, "Marvelous!" Alex cooed and Adele chattered affectionately at him.

The Daheims were steadily busy. Al scored richly when he got a full-time research job at the Scripps Institution of Oceanography at La Jolla that paid $8,000 a year and also allowed him to collect data for his dissertation on sea urchins. He had to commute a hundred miles each way and sometimes stayed overnight. Adele could not avoid her well-placed critics. One who felt mothers had to stay home failed her in his seminar course, which was a requirement for all Ph.D. students. She knew her work was better than the average for the course. When she gathered the courage to call on the famous professor during his office hours (3:30 to 5:00 on Tuesdays) for explanations, he said firmly and not without kindness in his voice, "I hope this teaches you a lesson, Mrs. Daheim." However, another great professor, who was the persecutor's enemy, also offered the course and gave her an A the second time she took it. The second great man protected Adele. He despised the men who failed her. He determined that she should indeed get the Ph.D. and enlisted some younger professors to their cause.

During these political maneuvers one of the newly hired assistant professors who sided with Adele's protector asked her often, "Don't you get lonely with Al away so much?" Once, after she broke into tears while narrating some recent causes for her hurt feelings, he rushed around his desk to embrace her. When she bent to him, he grabbed roughly at the tips of her breasts and sucked at her neck. She was frightened and ran from the office. He phoned her several times at home to apologize and expressed a desire to remain good friends.

She hired a series of maids to look after the children when she and Al had to be away. Two in a row were drunks. Another was a militant Christian who frightened little Margot with descriptions of the imminent apocalypse. One who seemed satisfactory for several months was caught forcing both children to take strong tranquilizers. Then came the year that Adele and Al were "honest with each other." The long talks began when, in a lapse of common sense, Al confessed to a few tosses with a secretary at Scripps. The girl had moved on when the talks petered out a year later. However, Al and Adele had questioned and had answered one another too deeply and too honestly. Each learned that the other was quite nasty and eventually boring. They learned that they could not bear one another's company any longer. So Al took a job as assistant professor in Connecticut. He agreed to finance Adele through to the Ph.D., for she had just passed the comprehensive examinations. After Al left, she had some affairs with Santa Monica studs who tickled or teased Margot and Alex cruelly and who lost interest in her after they mouthed her chest for a few nights.

She made a down payment on the Santa Monica beach house. The mortgage payments were $214 per month. Just after Al left in August 1967, an unexpected boost in enrollments at East Palmyra State College caused the chairman of psychology to call about frantically for competent people to teach those required freshman courses with large enrollments which the permanent members of his department avoided in preference to the more prestigious upper-division courses. Adele taught two sections of Psychology 101 in the late afternoon and got $600 per course per quarter, or $3,600 per year.

By assembling a committee of young and sympathetic faculty members, in 1973 she finished her degree. The dissertation was based on an experiment using three hundred UCLA students, each of whom chased an electrically charged disk on a twirling turntable with an electrically charged little stick. The title of the dissertation was "Positive Reinforcement, Vicarious Reinforcement, and Partial Reinforcement as Related to Persistence in a Perceptual-Muscular Co-ordination Task Employing the Pursuit Rotor for a Human Research Paradigm."

During one summer, Adele and a middle-aged professor of nursing she had met in a woman's encounter group late in 1969 wrote a short textbook, *Psychology for Nurses,* which was published by a small press in Illinois. She kept up with the current literature of female emancipation and assertion.

Most of Adele's friends stayed with the leftward moving crest of the feminist wave, and Adele moved with them. She attended countless meetings, circulated petitions, sent contributions, and subscribed to the latest women's periodicals. Two radical newsletters called *Off Our Backs* and *The Big Mama Rag* came unwrapped to her mailbox at the psychology department, where they were surreptitiously scanned by some male professors, who were scared out of their wits.

One night just after she finished her dissertation, two childless divorcees bullied her into nodding in agreement that to continue to accept Al's monthly $300 for alimony was "immoral" and "degrading." She wrote the necessary letter and regretted it instantly, for except for the $250 for child support (which Al continued to send) she was now dependent upon her wages as a "temporary" instructor at EPS.

All this as background.

On the November afternoon that we rejoin her, Adele sips machine-made coffee at her Formica-topped desk in the windowless office which has an adjoining toilet. She shares the room and facilities with three other women. Unlike the other hundred or so rooms in El Dorado Hall, the office is now clean and even reeks of disinfectant. It has been spotless ever since she claimed in her legal brief that the dean had ordered a cessation in its maintenance in one strategy to drive her from her job. She sits quite alone, for her officemates have different schedules and the students at the commuter college rarely call on Adele or, indeed, any other professor. She writes letters or looks over her note cards for the evening class in "Marriage and Family Life," which she despises. A committee of full professors said, in effect, "Take it or leave it," when they offered her this bread-and-butter course in order to meet her demands that she be given an upper-division class.

Adele had wanted her own course in learning theory, which was, after all, her research specialty. The possibility actually hung in balance for several weeks until the department gave it to a newly hired instructor who was finishing up his dissertation at the University of Wyoming. An older colleague explained to Adele that it was suitable for her to teach her course in an area of endeavor in which females played so large a role. The "Marriage . . ." course was popular among many older, part-time students who worked during the day.

Adele's version of the class met for seventy-five minutes on Monday and Wednesday evenings. Adele offered only a little straightforward sexual instruction and no mother-in-law jokes or cute-baby stories. Dr. Daheim's lectures were *theoretical,* and even her ad libs came increasingly to dwell on the historical victimization of those who bore most of the burden in marriage and the family. Once launched on feminism, she found the subject difficult to abandon. Her voice rose; she almost orated. Word passed to other members of the faculty. There was a ruckus when the local John Birch Society wrote anonymous letters with enclosed xeroxes of her prospectus to the regents of the state university system to inform them of Adele's requirement that the students read and report on a slender $3.95 paperback entitled *Marxist Lesbians Speak Out!* After a long meeting with the dean in which both started screaming thirty seconds after she entered his large office, Adele agreed to drop the book if he would promise to let her teach an upper-division course called "Women in Revolt." That was two years ago. "Women in Revolt" languished in committees, one of which required a change in title to "Women in a Changing World."

Adele lunches on Mondays at an off-campus vegetarian co-op, "The Marjoram Pot." There she meets three other professional women her age with whom she laughs a lot. Returning to El Dorado Hall for her official office hours from 4:00 to 5:30, she notices that, as usual, when they see her, almost all her colleagues duck into their offices or dip at the water fountain. And as usual, the only friendly one is tireless Milt, the old Marine with a brush cut, who, as he has for the past eight years, greets her with, "Hello, Adele, dear." Adele knew that when she was absent Milt Marback referred to her as "Tits-Adele." Milt believed that he was Adele's defender. His explanation for her edginess was that she did not screw often or well enough. Once three years ago, when Milt's wife was in the hospital for her hysterectomy, he left a message pinned to Adele's office door: "Please See Me! Milt!" When she entered his office, he blushed while remaining in his swivel chair and told her, "I'd stand up, dear, but my big hard-on forces me in modesty to stay seated. Can we sit close and talk awhile anyway?" Once in the hall she turned to kick his door after she slammed it.

Marback rubbed against most women who came near him. Occasionally he scored. Last spring Adele was thrown into a three-day depression when, after hearing hoarse laughter in Milt's office, she observed him exit with Rosie Russo, a part-time student whom Adele liked and envied. Rosie had been hanging around the department for years. She was tanned and the whites of her eyes were sharply defined from the blue irises. Unlike Adele, Rosie was large-hipped and small-busted. She sold twenty-dollar bags of grass and proselytized organic gardening to the younger psychology professors. For a few months Rosie Russo had been in one of Adele's consciousness-raising groups. Rosie loved a series of huge young men who were hairy and muscular. They were polite and attentive when in Rosie's company. Rosie talked with unaffected ease and remarkable precision about the sensual preferences and skills of her successive companions. Rosie never mentioned Milt Marback when Adele was around, but through intermediaries Adele learned that the pair went to the same Holiday Inn twice. The only further particulars she gleaned about the couplings were that Rosie had remarked they were "good for him" but "odd."

Adele uses her office hours to address folded-over and stapled 8½-by-11-inch sulfite paper sheets printed with invitations for a local conference of the National Organization of Women. She also does such tasks while at home in the evening with the kids. Her research has ceased. Over the previous two years she has let her subscriptions to three journals in experimental psychology lapse. Her few attempts as a graduate student to publish articles in these journals were returned with printed rejection slips, and the things they publish now have only a tangential relation to anything she teaches or is likely to teach. Aside from *Ms.* and *Signs: Journal of Women in Culture,* newly established by the University of Chicago Press, she reads no intellectuals' magazines. She purchases all her books at a female-owned bookstore near the UCLA campus which also sells feminist bumper stickers, feminist buttons for lapel wear, and non-sexist childrens' books. The store is open until 11:00 P.M., plays intricate eighteenth-century music on a good stereo, and serves free coffee or tea. Customers are often sitting on the shag-carpeted floor smoking furiously and planning future meetings. For a long time when Adele entered, someone always asked, "Well, Adele, how's it going?"

They were asking, of course, about Adele's campaign on all fronts —through lawyers, through the Department of Health, Education and Welfare, through the American Association of University Professors, through planted letters in local and feminist newspapers, through confrontations and petitions—to secure for Dr. Adele G. Daheim dignity and economic justice in the psychology department at East Palmyra State College. The war had begun in September 1972, after Adele had been awarded her Ph.D. and still was not given a job as an assistant professor but, instead, was rehired for the fifth time as a "temporary" instructor. Adele attacked, and the opposition delayed, diverted, and prevaricated. Adele, who had long been considered sweet-tempered, soured considerably.

Adele unconsciously picks at her cuticles—a habit conquered as a teenager, but which has returned—as 4:45 nears, and she smiles at her optimistic tension as she awaits the sound of the dull gray Volkswagen van that brings the daily mail. In learning-theory terms applicable to humans as well as rats and pigeons, Adele has the predicted visceral adjustment to a "partial reinforcement schedule" due, in her case, to the random receipt of good news.

The clattering van arrives and the side door slides shut. The old Chicano man leaves the large, string-bound packet at the secretary's desk. Adele meets her young colleagues at the mail slots before the secretary can distribute the stuff. Of course it is the same story. Notice of a general faculty meeting, which she will not attend, a ballot for new officials for the local chapter of the ACLU, the schedule of meetings for the Santa Monica rape crisis committee, her $37.25 bill at the neighborhood vegetable co-op, two textbook advertisements, a brochure announcing a new lesbian newsletter from Chicago, a revised edition of the campus parking regulations, apologies from the printing department of EPS for the lateness of the faculty manual, a dittoed invitation to hear a touring German Egyptologist give a slide lecture at 4:00 P.M. on December 12. Adele gathers the stuff and smiles at her mail-optimism as she detours to the coffee machine before returning to her office.

The ultimate good news of one's most colorful fantasies never arrives, but Adele had picked up a heavy dose of good news at her mail box last April 10. One marvelous mail delivery had (a) news of the sale for $1,000 of the Japanese rights for *Psychology for Nurses,* (b) one of the rare though long and kindly letters from Al, and (c) a curt note from the provost of the college stating that she had been promoted to assistant professor with tenure at a nine-month salary of $19,367 beginning the next fall quarter. The man was worn down by the shabby and incessant publicity arising out of Adele's campaign and ended it by an administrative fiat. The provost "carboned in" her chairman, the appropriate deans, and the personnel office.

Adele had considered holding out for associate professor rank. To be named an assistant after nine years of (the equivalent of) full-time teaching was an insult. However, the salary was almost at the top of the range that Sacramento allowed for an assistant and was more than she and the two kids could now spend gracefully unless she sharply increased her contributions.

On the evening that we see her, Adele downs a supper of overfried fish in the student cafeteria with a woman political scientist who has been frozen as assistant professor with tenure for six years at EPS. Then she walks to a distant building to lecture for seventy-five minutes to her twenty-five-member evening class on "Marriage and Family Life." Tonight she lectures sullenly on divorce—scarcely a cheerful topic under any circumstances.

She is haggard when the class ends at 9:15, and by 9:25 is in the Datsun on the graceful freeway. By 10:25 she is on the quiet side streets of Santa Monica and passes the Why Not Club, a notorious swingles bar. As always she considers and as always she drives on, since the place is only six blocks from her house. She has a good reputation to maintain. Both the kids—Margot, now fourteen, and Alex, now twelve—are before the television rather than in bed. She pulls each to her warm bosom and kisses them as her eyes well up with love. All jabber eagerly for a while about the day's small events and lights are out at the beach house by 11:30.

V

Getting the Job

A working assumption (and surely a hazardous one) throughout this chapter is that the academic industry will expand slowly, thus providing for some additional jobs. Except for a brief period in the 1960s when the industry grew fast, the system of professional preparation, the matching of candidate and position, the means of getting ahead have all remained remarkably stable for about seventy years. One who reads old critical literature on the training and hiring systems has an eerie feeling of *déjà vu* when comparing present hiring practices to them. The fortuitousness and circuitousness of the career of Joe Grantland as he seeks and eventually finds a professorial job in George Stewart's novel *Doctor's Oral,* published in 1939, are entirely believable for a desperate graduate student in English today. The pitiless discussions of Caplow and McGee in their *Academic Marketplace* (1958) of prestige and the obsession with it at our better universities seem remarkably apt when one regards the movements in and out, up and down in academia today.[1]

There will surely be changes in the hiring and promotion practices in the years ahead of us. For, as this is written, it seems certain that enrollments will stagnate and then decline, that the numbers of competent people seeking professorial employment will increase, and that the liberal world view (upon which our education policies have always been based) will continue to erode. Nevertheless, this chapter contains the social scientists' assumption that what was so for so long in the past will change but slightly in the near future. From the vantage point of late 1977, when many were convinced that the academic industry was approaching stagnation, no major changes in professorial preparation or in hiring practices could be foreseen. On the contrary, minor changes, making the process more complex, confounding honesty and efficiency, were producing new information screens and adding more and higher qualificatory hurdles and yet more trials of endurance for seekers of full-time academic jobs.

What kind of child grows up to be a professor? Almost overwhelmingly he is a good—indeed, almost a perfect—pupil in grade school and then, further, in prep school or high school. Book reading, the mastery of specialized knowledge, and, most especially, good grades bring lasting satisfactions to the child and to his family. Since in our schools good grades are rewards as well for dependability, inoffensiveness, conventional good manners, and exceptional hygiene, the good pupil destined to be a college teacher has these characteristics very early and to an unusual degree. The more physically active and mischievous kids in the neighborhood may single out the future academic by derisively naming him a "bookworm" or "the professor."

Academics tend to be raised in securely prosperous white-Anglo-Saxon-Episcopalian or Presbyterian families. The most numerous exceptions are the children of ambitious, protective Jews recently of European origin. Conservative Protestants and Jews show a remarkable propensity to brood about and plan future time and to praise and reward accomplishment as evidence of grace. Of course, in academic life there are some "late bloomers"—that is, brilliant men whose careers as pupils or students were speckled or mediocre, whose progress was unusually difficult, and whose eccentricities were especially resented by their fellows.

Almost all college professors attended conventional colleges that expected high standards of performance and reliability. Many were on scholarships. Their uncritical pursuit of A's caused them to avoid intercollegiate sports and idle partying. Such students rarely switch majors or voice skepticism about the assumptions or utility of the disciplines in which they have found spiritual rewards since they were ten years old or even younger. They go through college in the standard four years and along the way hang around those lively professors in their major department who are known to smile on their favorites. The helpful professors assure the continuation of financial help, if it is necessary, and urge that the student deepen his knowledge, perhaps going so far as to pursue the Ph.D. at the proper graduate school.

If the good student's college teachers have professorial common sense (and regarding the matter at hand, they almost always do), they will impress upon the apprentice of special knowledge the crucial necessity of going to the very best graduate school. The dedicated major professor will coldly list to his protectees the suitable graduate departments in the declining order of their excellence. His list of universities would verify the rankings offered in Chapter IV of this book. The rankings on the list of a geographer at the University of Oregon in Eugene will be just about identical with the list offered by an alert geographer at Davidson College in North Carolina. The professors with decent jobs know that the bigger, famous schools have more and better-paying fellowships and assistantships, that progress through the course work and dissertation (however long it takes) is less slow, and that a larger proportion of the other graduate students will have good minds and be willing to share them. At the famous universities the graduate professors know their stuff and have all the advantages in assisting the fledgling in that second great move in his career—obtaining his first full-time job.

Until recently (in the present context, until about twelve years ago) more than half of the Ph.D.'s who got jobs at respectable colleges and universities came from about ten great universities. Then the politics and fiscal policy of spreading excellence around led to the establishment or expansion of inferior, imitative graduate programs all over the place. As a consequence, the requirements for doctoral work in political science at the University of Nebraska or at Florida State University are described in their catalogs (a freely distributed description in book form of what the college or university has to offer) in terms reassuringly reminiscent of the catalogs of the University of Wisconsin or of Princeton. All the same, even if he is given lavish scholarship help and breezy promises, the ambitious opportunist with his eyes open enters these second-rank places only if he expects his career to remain local. Hiring and advancement in American academic life is rarely based on local standards. Besides, at the insubstantial graduate schools, many of the other students (from whom one learns most anyway) are apt to be psychologically crippled losers taken on in order to keep the rosters full. At graduate schools without an assured tradition, the students are far more likely to be pulled in and therefore damaged by interdepartmental squabbles. At an ambitious new graduate school, the requirements for course work or the dissertation are also likely to be inflexibly maintained or capriciously extended.

A useful aside here concerns careers for which the Ph.D. is valuable (in money terms) though so irrelevant for the job at hand that the substance devoted to its procurement is unlikely ever to be examined. The title of "doctor" and/or the appropriate letters after the name engender foolish respect in the upper levels of library administration, educational administration, the federal bureaucracy and even in the higher ranks of the Army, Navy, and Air Force. As emphasized above, it is perilous to assume that one can get a Ph.D. quickly at a school with no tradition of first-class graduate training. It is a fact that, the better the school, the less rigid the formal and informal requirements are. ("If we admitted him to the University of Chicago, he must be good. Why load the poor sonovabitch down with all those dumb requirements?" The converse goes: "If he came to the University of South Dakota, there must be something wrong with him. He'll have to show us that he has lots of stuff before we'll let him through.") If one *needs* a doctor's degree, he should go off to France, Italy, Argentina, or India, where there are to be had doctoral degrees that are recognized as such in North America which can be obtained for turning out a little piece of supervised writing.

The great graduate schools choose from among many applicants. The bases of selection are, in order of importance, (1) undergraduate grades, weighted for the prestige or assumed grading standards of the undergraduate college, (2) performance on the graduate record examinations (nationally administered, annual tests on specialized knowledge in the academic disciplines), and (3) professorial letters of recommendation. Not until they reach graduate school (usually when they are in their early twenties) are American students exposed to methods of learning that German university students, students at the French *grandes écoles,* and students at Oxford and Cambridge get when much younger. They are cast loose to master a body of special knowledge, to criticize research in some subspecialties within their discipline, and to prepare to do their own research. Though the graduate student working in plant physiology, motor learning, stochastic functions, organic compounds, astronomy, the pre-Socratics, or the Meiji period in Japan may have been reading and thinking about these subjects for years, few are as critical of their reading as the great professors believe they should be, and so the students must take some courses and pass comprehensive examinations before moving on. The remedial courses (though they are never called this) are usually the upper-division undergraduate lecture courses that the department offers at the great university. Graduate students at the better schools usually "audit" (that is, they attend class and take notes, but do not take the examinations) the undergraduate courses of the professors who will examine them in order to learn what the professor considers most worthwhile in his territory in the discipline. Wise students attach themselves to one or more professors who will require that they read special or professional literature in a language other than English. Departments or universities may require proof of language ability in the form of competence examinations before a student can progress very far. The language exams are dangerous qualifying hurdles and stop or delay many careers.

It is worth observing here that, since many universities have been overeager to turn out their products in the form of degrees, the language requirement, and indeed, respect for work in other languages has eroded at every level of American academic life. Naturally the amount of German or Russian required for a chemist or a mathematician to keep up to date is small. However, language knowledge is not of minimal importance if a researcher in early education is to remain informed about important new work in other industrial nations. The example of education research is worth considering because the dropping of the language requirement in the American graduate schools of education is a cause and a demonstration of the dismal and irresponsible level of "research" at these places. It is worth stating here that a convincing demonstration of a great graduate research department or a great graduate university is their hard line on language competence.

The distinctive activity at a graduate school is work in a reading seminar and, more particularly, the research seminar. A seminar is a professorially supervised discussion by advanced and presumably well-prepared students of research of their own and of others at the university or elsewhere. Typically the professor sits at the end of a long table with five to fifteen occupied chairs around it. Meetings are usually weekly for two hours separated by a coffee break. At the first two meetings of a seminar, the professor talks generally about the topic. Later he assigns special and highly technical reading or research assignments to each individual. The students describe and comment on what they learn and are questioned by their

student-colleagues. Some of the thirty-seven seminars offered in the
English department at Princeton University are:

502   Old English Poetry
507   Studies in the English Language: The Beginnings to 1400
510   Old Norse
511   Medieval Lyric and Dramatic Literature
512   Chaucer
521   Spenser
524   Jacobean and Caroline Literature
532   The Early Seventeenth Century (1600–1660)
533   Literature of the Restoration (1660–1700)
543   The Eighteenth Century (First Half)

At a large university with a solid (and presumably deserved) reputation for producing good work, seminars are immensely exciting.
They are the means by which dormant, superspecific intelligence
locked in the library or in the senior professors' head becomes
spoken, argued, and thus takes on new life. At the great universities,
the advanced graduate students may arrange, on their own, "seminars" at which they share the specialized stuff they have learned in
order to help each other get ready for the comprehensive examinations.

The discipline of attending lectures, preparing for seminars, reading at little tables in the library, or fiddling over equipment in the
laboratories goes on for years. New discoveries or theories must be
assimilated. An important professor may leave and be replaced by
one with different specialties. A piece of exquisitely adjusted apparatus may break down and make invalid the calibrations of the previous year. The critical examinations come to be dreaded as rites of
passage.

The examinations may, as in most European universities at all
levels, be furiously written over a three- to five-day period. The tendency at the leading research universities in North America is to sim-
plify things and make the comprehensive examinations a two-hour
oral performance wherein the individual is rapidly questioned by a
board of five professors. No matter how they are staged, these examinations are so feared that they may be repeatedly postponed and
then—far more often due to emotional clutching than to lack of
preparation—failed. Almost nobody performs well. Compulsive and
painful reveries common to every professor are the reliving of his
comprehensive examination. These undesired mental exercises cause

disgust at how stupid (in view of how well he *might* have performed) his answers were.

It is significant that in fields such as business administration, engineering, and chemistry, where there are professional alternatives to academic employment, the usual time "in residence" (that is, the period the student is doing course work at the university) before the examinations is two years. Sincere attempts, especially in recent boom years, to grant this brevity to such fields as English, history, philosophy, and sociology have always failed—usually because the keepers of the gates will not reduce the amount of formal preparation that has to be proven. Now, of course, standards are being kept high and the ways of satisfying them kept hazardous and devious in order to keep the number of resident students up and to minimize the number of degreed job seekers. It is not at all unusual to hear of classicists, art historians, or Sinologists who do advanced graduate work for eight years and then take eight more years to work on their dissertations. Such people, who have no alternatives to academic employment, are likely to refer to doctorates in chemistry or biology as "cheap" Ph.D.'s.

It is usually expected that the first year of all but a few graduate students will be financed by the student alone. For subsequent years, however, there are usually assistantships requiring the devotion of from five to twenty hours a week of the graduate student's time. The student assistant is a sort of novice professor and in general does responsible academic labor that needs no great expertise nor the professor's prestige. For this he or she earns roughly $2,500 per year. It is in the course of such work that the graduate student actually gets to know his professors, who, in turn, decide for themselves whether the student is indeed suitable for permanent academic employment.

All of the above sounds nicely figured out as well as dreary and stressful. In fact, life as a graduate student can be rather happy—especially in retrospect. The work may be long and the anguish considerable, but the company is exceptionally fine. One's companions are intensely alert, young, and ambitious people much like oneself. In the great graduate schools the professors may state what is to be done formally and guard the gates, but the students actually learn from one another. Incessantly, continuously, they are intense intellectuals with clear goals. High-strung, healthy, they create a fluid, extracurricular society where one rises or falls as he is witty and energetic. The graduate students form loving friendships that will occasion nostalgia many years later. The low pay of the assistants and the skimpy fellowships are the excuses for that delightful pastime of graduate students—the well-heeled as well as the poor—the poverty game. They transform slum apartments into warm nests by means of fresh paint and furniture from junk piles. The cleverest couple has a party for seventy-five and does it all for $17.58 with the help of filched lab alcohol, home-brewed beer, heavy-crusted pizza, and stolen cantaloupe. They drive fifteen-year-old panel trucks that need to be pushed to start. They make their own no-hassle clothes or buy them from the Salvation Army. They care for and adore each others' babies, and at the parties the nursing women pull out their milk-heavy breasts. They play charades. On long walks or across the table at a bar a graduate student may ask quite seriously whether his or her vis-à-vis has "read any good books lately."

All the while the graduate students are together educating themselves in a scholarly way, they are, of course, informing each other of what they have learned about the academic profession and, in particular, employment prospects in their chosen field of endeavor. They know well that even if they come out undamaged on the other side of the comprehensive examinations, they still have obstacles ahead.

The qualificatory trial that culminates in the award of the Ph.D. is the dissertation, which officially must be an "original contribution," but which might more realistically be viewed as a short book or long experiment that is technically competent and mediocre. Together, the student and a professor find or devise a subject worth investigating and solving that has not been done before. The student is cast free to locate sources or equipment and to do the job. And it is at this point that the odds in favor of the obedient, hygienic, "good" student break down. The assignments are general, not specific. To finish a dissertation demands a planning capacity, a cynical logic, and cold self-confidence that are all rare anywhere, but are especially rare among conventional good students. Dissertations in the sciences are often done in laboratories on the campus or on a campus elsewhere and are more or less monitored or supervised and so get done rather more commonly and quickly. However, dissertations in the humanistic disciplines often must be accomplished far from home and school. Removed from teachers who, until now, have been relentless reminders of scheduling and authority, as many as half of the "doctoral candidates" (for so a dissertation writer can be called) in English literature or history may take more than five years to finish.

Perhaps a third of the candidates never finish at all. This subject will reappear in the next chapter, but it is curious and almost paradoxical to observe that, despite the great rewards for finishing research in American academic life, the persons selected by the American system of graduate study (which is essentially based on research training) show a strange reluctance to do original research after the conclusion of the formal preparation for that research.

By hallowed agreement, the professor ignores the dissertation student and only observes his work. At a late stage the dissertation is examined by the other two to four members of the Ph.D. committee. Assuming that the student works along in a regular way, some slip-ups can be caused by laziness on the part of the dissertation "director" or by vendettas between the committee members that the student should have known about beforehand. Though anticipated with terror, the oral examination for the dissertation (in some places called the "thesis") is usually *pro forma*. By this time the student knows far more about the subject than his examiners do. Berkeley, the pace setter, has eliminated the thesis examination. Once news is out that the title page of the dissertation has been signed by all the committee members, everyone shakes the new Ph.D.'s hand.

Raymond J. Sontag, the late distinguished diplomatic historian, requested that students he was fond of who had finished their dissertation call on him at his low-ceilinged office on the top floor in the library at Berkeley. When the student entered with the glad news, Sontag pulled his great bulk out of the creaking chair behind 'his desk, rounded it, approached the initiate, reached out his enormous, dry hand, and awesomely intoned, "Well, Jim, we're colleagues now. You can call me 'Ray.'" One suitably intimidated student on such an occasion replied, "Gee, Professor Sontag. Do you suppose we could get there in stages?"

It used to be expected that the new Ph.D. did not attend graduation ceremonies, because he already had a job far from where he studied. His preparation for employment began early. He learned about job-hunting by talking to younger professors at the great university or to older Ph.D. candidates who were "futher along" than he was. Before the thesis was done, he knew how intricate it is to match candidates and jobs. More hurdles ahead.

An essential task of the man seeking his first full-time job is simply stated. He draws up a one-page schematic biography called a *curriculum vitae* or simply *vita* (Latin for "life") and gets it into the hands of as many people as he can. The vita gives the essential statistics about birth and marital status. It is brief regarding undergraduate education and expansive about courses taken in graduate school. The vita gives the topic and status of the dissertation and the names of professors prepared to write recommending letters. The job seeker also assigns himself a label that sounds like a two-semester, upper-division college course which he is prepared to teach. Examples are "French Literature in the Twentieth Century," "Invertebrate Embryology," "Symbolic Logic," "Algebraic Topology," "Business Cycles," "Portuguese America." He asks his major professor (that is, the director of his dissertation) to keep a stack of the vitas on hand. The major professor probably has a two-semester label like that of his dissertation student. A professor at a great university has as one of his major obligations to learn in advance of all openings in his and his students' field.

By tradition, the university departments that hire bright new men are autonomous. However, even in boom times it usually required considerable politicking by a chairman to get approval from the dean to hire. Do projections of enrollment in geography, art history, or mathematics call for a replacement or an addition? Should the department strengthen an area in which it is already strong, or should it branch out into newer areas that should no longer be ignored? Should it hire a "junior" man (that is, one at the assistant-professor level if his dissertation is finished, or at the instructor level if it has not been completed) or a "senior" man (that is, one with a proven reputation at the associate or full-professor level)? Furthermore, has the chairman co-operated with the dean in maintaining standards, in punishing people who make the university look bad, and in modestly rewarding those who make the university look good?

Once given the "line" (that is, a slot for which financing is assured in next year's budget) for a certain specialty at a certain rank, the members of the department search committee (consisting of professors working in related areas) write letters to experts at the big graduate schools for likely names. Vitas flow in. The committee makes a rough cut and asks for full dossiers (files of education records, photocopied letters of recommendation, and publications, if any) from the records office of the candidates' universities.

The narrow range of the salaries for professors and the *outward* similarity in working conditions all over America were emphasized earlier. Prestige is the critical variable. Ascertaining it, seeking it, enhancing it, preserving it are the primary purposes of the candidate seeking a job and of the department seeking a new colleague.[2] Matching the junior man to the junior position is, in the early stages, rather simple—or at least brutally stated: The department tries to get a candidate *from* the most prestigious department; the candidate employment *in* the most prestigious department.

Enthusiastic letters of recommendation from a famous professor at a great university have clout. Typical phrases that appear in the best letters of recommendation are: "an ornament to the profession," "brilliantly original," "altogether exceptional intelligence," "remarkable dependability." It adds that much more to the prestige of the famous professor and his great university if he can place his students very high up.

It has been claimed by outsiders that the big conventions for the academic specialties are shape-up yards where the jobless appear and are matched harum-scarum to bidding employers. The book-display hall (where the textbook manufacturers set up their offerings) at the annual meetings of the Modern Language Association and the American Sociological Association have been referred to as "meat racks." There was, indeed, some rapid hiring and job-switching arranged largely at conventions in the halcyon and atypical period that peaked about 1963–65. However, in normal times, the chairman or someone he trusts will use the convention to talk to and peer closely at candidates already deemed worthy in advance on the basis of vitas and dossiers. The hiring of a new colleague is too delicate a matter to rush. The established professors may have to live with a gross error the rest of their lives. So the department then invites two or three candidates to come to the campus at the university's expense.[3]

The candidate, if he is from a very great university and comes prestigiously recommended, and therefore might have some choice in where he will settle, has been investigating too. He calls about to verify that the institution is indeed as well regarded (or not) as he has heard. He may check median SAT scores for entering freshmen, the percentage of those who enter the institution who remain to graduate, the number of National Merit Scholars, etc. He inquires of third parties about feuds and their protagonists in the department. How many of his potential colleagues are disagreeable fools? He may ask knowledgeable friends of friends in the department as to the department's "AQ" (asshole quotient). For many years it was known that the foreign languages at the University of Toronto, the history department at the University of California at Santa Barbara and the philosophy department at Berkeley all had very high AQs.

Once on the scene, the visitor is led around the campus, narrated the standard anecdotes of local history, and told the price of nice new housing. Hard talk about admissions standards, class sizes, expectations and rewards for publication, the department's vendettas, and salary are deflected. The members of the department who chat, lunch, or drink with the candidate have already gauged how much prestige or (if he brings too much prestige and accomplishment) danger he will bring them. Now they must form predictions as to whether he will be a possible member of their camp or the enemies', a drone, a fool, or an asshole. Usually "departments would prefer to have somone who is 'comfortable' rather than a bubble-pricking eccentric."[4]

If it appears that the young man or woman (actually he or she will be from twenty-six to thirty-two years of age or even older) will be offered a job, there may be attempts to recruit him this early to one of the departmental factions. Curiously, the task for which the candidate is hired, that is, to teach, is almost never discussed. *A working assumption throughout academic life that is almost never stated is that anyone with a Ph.D. can teach well enough for any college students he might be required to face.*

The department brings in other candidates over a period of weeks early in the spring. Then the chairman either accepts or orders a consensus as to who is the fairest.[5] The chairman sends a formal letter that is the offer. It states the salary figure for the nine-month academic year, remarks that the university will pay moving expenses up to a certain amount, and gives a deadline by which the offer must be accepted. Offers for employment in public colleges or universities in California still warn, "You should be aware that the State of California requires all newly appointed personnel to sign an Oath of Allegiance prior to employment."

The task of matching man and job has been coarsely simplified above. It is far more complex administratively and very demanding of all who participate in it. In normal times a large department might hire from one to three new people a year, still this hiring task is a consuming, turbulent, and continually divisive operation. Hiring takes up hundreds of hours on the part of men who are highly skilled, but not in this line of work.

The task of hiring an experienced "senior" professor for a tenured slot is immeasurably more time-consuming and loaded with pitfalls for all. The factors for gauging his or her prestige are more varied, for one must also consider the national reputation of the place that is being raided and the presumed worth of the candidate's publications. Since a good or respectable department will only hire an experienced person who has some publications to his or her credit, any proven candidate is invariably an affront to the well-meaning losers on the faculty who never have gotten around to doing anything (that is, publishing). The emotional consequences are lacerating and some wounds never heal.

At the top fifteen or so universities, where the major concern of a department is to capture more prestige, there is some movement in and out at the full-professor level. The hiring process for junior faculty, however, may be a little simpler, since it is well known by everyone that the new assistant professors, if they do not publish a lot, quickly, and prominently, will be fired after three to five years. In the jargon, they do not have "tenure lines." However, these insecure positions are hotly sought after, since a pink slip from Yale or Princeton carries with it more prestige than a diploma from many lesser places. The rejectee usually still has a crack at a decent job in the provinces.

Job-switching at the senior levels of the great institutions is an operation of such extraordinary intricacy and relative rarity (considering academia as a whole) that it both scares off and scarcely merits discussion in a book that is about American academic life at all levels. In any case, job mobility, which has been declining, may soon cease at the senior ranks. Stability and fears of cuts have led to a "digging in" mentality, and that will make job-switching in academia yet more infrequent and complicated in the future.

The firing of a professor is still more complex than hiring is. The American Association of University Professors has devised an elaborate code of notification dates for ending employment that are designed to protect the professor and the institution. The college or university, it is felt, needs time to replace the essential departing one, and the rejectee needs time to find a new job—both of which, as we have noted above, are stressful, tedious operations. After the initial one-year appointment, it is recognized that the professor is to be given at least twelve months' notice before his job ends. In the tenured ranks (associate professor and full professor) dismissal is so difficult to accomplish that the deadwood is just permitted to stay around. Even subtle harassing is rather rare.

The fates of the "super" or "seed" professors who were so chic in the middle sixties deserve mention here. The stars arrived and picked up their pay checks on schedule but, since they had guaranteed themselves few specific duties, were rarely on hand for university functions of any sort. They did keep up their busy schedule lecturing (elsewhere) and wrote more of the polemics, memoirs, or novels that brought in real, vivid money in the form of royalties. Some, on the other hand, slipped deeper into depressions and self-indulgence. If other excellent men and women were indeed attracted to these bright lights (a dubious proposition from the beginning; truly excellent men and women who are able to choose are attracted to excellent institutions and excellent students), few were taken on, since shortly after the stars socked in during the years 1962–67, the job boom petered out. Most of the super professors hang on to good things at universities that have remained second and third rate. Probably the greatest damage they cause (besides soaking up finances that could be better employed elsewhere) is the deep jealousy of other professors who put in years of loyal service, who teach responsibly, and who earn much less.

We leave these reminders of the recent and atypical past to return to the *usual* practices in academic life wherein advancement occurs most often within the university that first hires the recent Ph.D. The new assistant professor's task is to acquire a *permanent* appointment, which usually occurs with his promotion to associate professor. Though tenure is most often combined with promotion to associate professor, it is, in fact, a separate decision and can be granted or withheld at any rank.

The official categories for judging a professor's competence are three: his teaching, his research, and his service. Since teaching competence by a long and apparently unassailable custom is almost never put to any kind of a test (there is much more on this in the next chapter), by default, the last two areas remain. Otherwise stated, once on the job, the professor can increase his prestige (a) outside the university and within his discipline by publication, and (b) inside the university by advising students, contributing to reform campaigns, or serving on committees. Immediately some clarifications are called for: Informally and in fact, a professor's stock goes up or down for reasons that are less easily specifiable. One can assume that the better (that is, the more famous or prestigious) the university, the more essential will be publication. The assistant professor at the University of Kansas, at Tulane University, or at the University of Washington at Seattle, all somewhat more than merely "respectable" institutions, must be some sort of cosmopolite. He probably will have to intrigue like a wizard to keep his job unless he has published the equivalent of a small book and otherwise appears to have a position, however narrowly defined, of national significance. Furthermore, the probationer at a great or good university who applies himself sincerely to committee work or (worse) advising or (worse yet) student affairs or (horrors!) radical student politics has to produce many, substantial, and unassailable publications to the faculty committee assigned to judge him in order to demonstrate that he is indeed "serious." And fame obtained through publication is the *only* way to move from one university to another of equivalent or higher rank.

Now it does indeed happen, particularly at middle-ranked schools where lip service is paid to the value of research and its proof, publication, that many who publish nothing do indeed become tenured. A previous writer has described these situations:

> Almost every department has a few distressing cases of weak or lazy colleagues whose incompetence at research and publication has been amply demonstrated, but who are nevertheless such nice chaps that one would like to see them promoted. Far and away the best method of doing so is to invoke their unproven, and happily, unprovable, excellence in the classroom.[6]

With the continuing tendency of American postsecondary educational institutions to resemble one another, lip service honoring research has extended to almost all colleges offering upper-division work. Nevertheless, the lower the quality of the place, the more necessary it is for the professor to show evidence of his "concern" or even "loyalty" by means, usually, of committee work or just hanging around and looking occupied. Formally this requires punctual attendance and inactivity (the best advice to a beginner at an inferior institution is, "A listener and not a talker be") at departmental committee meetings and the defending of departmental interests in college-wide committees. Less formally, the aspirant must dress appropriately (Sears' best is usually unassailable) for the president's and dean's receptions, omit no senior professor in the department from the invitation lists for his large parties, and unfailingly assume an attitude of charming decorum with the departmental secretaries. He who wishes to stick around must never write sardonic letters in reply to the local rag's editorial opposing détente or knock the custom of including howitzers from the army base in all the local parades. A treasured skill in provincial academies is the ability gracefully to intercede and patiently to soothe tempers, attributing noble objectives to all the parties in an especially petty or vicious dispute. If the beginner in an inferior, low-keyed school publishes little things, fine. But it is advisable not to risk being praised as "brilliant" (the death word in academic Siberia) or (worse) attract national attention. The lazy intriguers who dominate half the American campuses will put knives in the back of men or women whose manifested energy exposes their lack of it.

There is another sort of judgment that enters into all deliberations to hire, to keep, or to promote. The question asked is: "Is he a shit?" When the departmental committee on promotions and tenure meets and later the full and associate professors meet to vote on the individuals, the talk is cautious and vague about research, service, and (more cautious and vaguer still) teaching, but the professors know if the person is or is not a shit. The perception of shittiness and of determining who manifests it are the same as they would be in any comparable organization with from ten to forty members who see one another a lot. As everywhere else, the judgments are anecdotally corroborated by means of gossip that becomes a body of lore growing outside the formal communication network.

In any case, one enforcer of the up-or-out system is the aforementioned departmental promotions and tenure committee. In the spring of the assistant professor's fourth or fifth year the committee, not without trepidation, hands up to the dean and those above him recommendations to hold or let go. If the departmental committee is overruled by deans, vice-presidents, or provosts, it is usually an act of clemency rather than the ax—except in the case of ideological radicals, almost all of whom, by now, have been eliminated from American campuses.

The loser will receive a letter announcing that he will be allowed to eke it out another year. When times were good a young man, especially if he was not a shit or could suppress indication of this trait, could find employment at a place a couple of rungs down the ladder. If considered dependable, not vengeful, and not a shit, the loser might settle in a minor job in the university administration or in the library. However, the looseness of professorial job-discipline makes later adjustment to the forty-hour week, fifty-week year, difficult. Many discharged professors become quiet drunks or drifters.

The tenured associate professor now begins his campaign to be a full professor. This, the final step up, brings little besides a small raise in pay and the right to judge the promotion of other associate professors. However, if the associate stays "in rank" for more than five years, this relegation is considered a slap at his (research) productivity, university service, ability to attract students, and particularly his popularity among the full professors. At a great university treasuring energetic cosmopolites, it is expected that a man cannot become a full professor without publishing a second book. This feat should be buttressed with proof that the individual does not repel students—particularly graduate students—and claims of an attention to university governance that was not expected when he was younger. At lesser places and even more so in Siberia, the license to put "professor" alone after one's name at the bottom of letters often comes as the result of keeping one's nose clean and putting in about seven years. At colleges that make no pretense of courting national fame or that are frightened by energetic teachers who may attract more than their share of the rare bright students or who demonstrate large enrollments at the expense of others, the final promotion may be withheld from an overachiever or a crochety boat-rocker as a punishment to get him (or, in the case of a noisy feminist, her) to resign in a temper.

How unfortunate that the American colleges and universities have not come up with more ranks or higher ranks! The military services have done much better. They have provided for more minute gradations of rank and have, besides, devised promotion criteria that offer realizable and institutionally beneficial channels for the performance orientation and competitiveness that swell within us all. Any large university, particularly one that got large quickly, has hundreds of full professors aged thirty-five to sixty-five of widely varying abilities and potential. With the prospect of the cessation of job mobility in academia at the upper levels, even in the competitive great universities, a stasis condition perilous to morale has begun to set in. It is, in fact, the stolid condition of no movement that causes some energetic men to move up into the administration *faute de mieux*.

A schematized scenario could go like this: Young Henry Zwingli's dissertation on "Sartre's German Sources for Absurdity" was published by the University of Missouri Press and he was duly promoted to associate professor in 1963 when he was only thirty-three years old. His next book, a five-hundred-pager, was an explanation of the nineteenth-century sources of existentialism and was published by a minor New York press. The reviewers agreed that it offered little that was new, that it had stylistic inconsistencies, and that it seemed to have been hastily written. Nevertheless, the second book fulfilled a major requirement for forty-year-old Zwingli's promotion to full professor at the number-two state university near the northwest Pacific coast. What the hell is Zwingli, a healthy man who now hates teaching the ever-more-torpid undergraduates but dares not utter a word of this to a person other than his wife when both have been drinking, going to do now? The Zwinglis have three kids, the oldest of whom is about to enter college.

Almost without knowing it Henry gathers support as the heir-apparent of bumbling old Schneider, who is sickly and hints that he wants out of his job as chairman. However, Zwingli is opposed by those who fear that he may post on the department bulletin board precise evaluation standards for merit raises—a project he brought up five years ago. Nevertheless, the same future time perspective and methodical gauging of the characters of his superiors that carried him in an orderly fashion through graduate school and the academic ranks bring Zwingli the prize when he is forty-four. As a chairman, he gets a sharp raise to $29,000, which, however, requires that he work the eleven-month year. In order to "keep his hand in teaching," the new chairman offers one course every other semester. He also publishes an occasional book review. Like all wise chairmen who prize harmony above all qualities, he does not distribute or even bring up the subject of precise evaluation standards for merit raises.

Three years pass. Listening to the tedious and clumsy narratives of imagined slights endured by his now-obsequious colleagues, the whining pleas for firm intervention by "State's" wretchedly insecure graduate students, and the burden of elemental paperwork have caused Zwingli to give up teaching "for a while" and to put all his writing projects "on a back burner." Tuition for his children at the good little liberal-arts colleges is eating up his savings. In one week the roofing contractor's bid for new composition shingles and gutters is $1,300. His wife tells him her depressions are getting worse since the last kid went away and demands that she see a psychiatrist. By a curious coincidence, on Friday of that same week, Zwingli lunches with Arch Himmel, Dean of the College of Arts and Sciences, who has lately become much less subtle in expressing his loathing of the university's "do-nothing" president and the "Neanderthal" board of regents. Himmel, late in the large meal, leans over the coffee to whisper ("For God's sake, Hank, keep this under your hat for a few weeks yet!") that he is dickering over the details of his new job as an academic vice-president somewhere in Texas. Zwingli rubs his chin for a while and asks what the dean's present job pays. When Arch replies that it is $38,700, Zwingli decides it is time for him to move up. And so it goes.

If Zwingli (or anyone else) takes a job in the upper levels of university administration, he enters a world of tough men. Administrators are almost always short of clear indications of just what they are supposed to do besides keep the peace. They lack the time, knowledge, or expertise to do even that. Much of an administrator's time is spent urgently working on plans for a reorganization of the university that will be far more effective than the last two. It is a curious world quite taken up with travel, committee meetings, and listening to grievances. The higher the position of an administrator, the more he is viewed with incomprehension and contempt by the professors. All administrative jobs, from that of the president to those of the assistant deans are frighteningly insecure since the next reorganization might eliminate or demote them.[7] Though the return to normal conditions (that is, an oversupply of job applicants) has slowed job-switching among the professors at all levels, there are more jobs available than ever before all over North America for college and university administrators at all ranks. The most difficult job to hold on to gracefully is now the presidency. In February 1975, seventy-eight four-year institutions were without chief executives. Administration is and will very likely remain a power vacuum offering attractive prospects for the bored and ruthless.

Thus far in this narrative a heuristic assumption that surely has become obvious is that college professors are white, Anglo-Saxon males. Though progress all the way up our educational ladder, from kindergarten to university president, is most regular for this dominant type, others also avoid the pitfalls and go over the hurdles to become professors.

In introducing the excursions that follow, it is necessary to refer again to the claim made in Chapter II that a deep cause for the great university expansion of the 1960s was an especially aggressive and optimistic surge of ideological liberalism, now waning. But for a period that lasted long enough to build our present splendid academic facilities, governments at all levels assumed much of the responsibility for the environment that builds character and skill by providing and indeed making higher education so attractive as almost to constitute enforcement. Aspects of education in the primary and secondary schools were reformed or at least strikingly altered in some places. On the other hand, as liberal philosophy more or less climaxed, the colleges and universities were scarcely reformed at all. They were merely expanded. Almost nobody—students, professors, parents, or state and local politicians—opposed the extraordinary growth along familiar lines until very recently.

Now the universities were, it is true, expected to take on a few additional tasks. Since it has always been the case that any modestly prepared American who knew how colleges worked could find an institution that would accept and then harbor him or her, access to college had to be made yet easier in order to fill those dorm rooms and classroom seats. Local junior colleges with minimal or no requirements for preparation and with so-called "practical" programs have now made nonattendance for almost all children of higher than underclass status at some kind of postsecondary school a social gaffe or a character failing that requires explanation. Those recalcitrant colleges and universities in the South that were lily white were (rather gracefully, as it turned out) integrated by a few dozen heroic black children in a federally supported campaign. The access of blacks to what between 1930 and 1960 worked as instruments of white upward mobility, the nearly all-white universities, was assisted by federal grants and federally urged exemptions to admission requirements.

Since universities give people jobs, their practices regarding minority employment, particularly that of minority professorial candidates, have also come under federal scrutiny. Federal grand administrators have informed the administrators of schools dependent upon federal subsidies that discriminatory hiring must end or the subsidies will dry up. On the other hand, sacrosanct tradition, dating from the medieval times, determines that university teachers alone have the right to renew their ranks—which in the modern university means that the critical decisions for hiring are concentrated at the departmental level. Professors insist that hiring remain insulated from administrative controls. This has produced an impasse in the universities at present. Administrators fear that certain money wells may actually dry up and are frightened, since the professors refuse to recognize that these threats are serious.

A joke is going around the faculty clubs and lounges: Three senior professors are drinking sherry just after the dean has warned in a faculty senate meeting that an official in the Department of Health, Education and Welfare (in Washington—not at the college) has objected to their thirty-man (that is, all male), WASP department:

> Slaunwhit: What we have to find and quickly is a Jewish, Black dyke named Martinez . . .
>
> Blanchard: . . . whose father is a Sioux Indian and whose mother is a Sicilian Catholic . . .
>
> Lilly: . . . and who is a Vietnam veteran confined to a wheelchair.[8]

There are various kinds of discrimination in academic employment that do indeed deserve examination in order to exonerate as well as to reprove.

The recent efforts of the American professors to integrate their ranks racially has produced some comic results. Almost everyone would like to have at least one black face in the occasional departmental photograph in order to demonstrate their atonement for the most notorious failure of American liberal democracy. Many professors have long been regular contributors to the NAACP. Even in the South, though few professors of fifteen or twenty years ago risked immediate (and illegal) dismissal for effectively promoting racially integrated enrollments, almost none resisted integration once it was under way. When it was seen to be safe, professors accepted (rarely welcomed) black-studies programs and closed their eyes to exceptional (that is, in this case, lowered) entrance requirements and remedial (that is, in this case, tutorial) programs for "disadvantaged" (that is, government-subsidized and black) students. Many professors, particularly younger ones in the humanistic and social disciplines, shade their grading criteria in favor of black students. The self-assumed guilt of academic liberals has eased the way for the increasing number (though still few) of blacks who have made their way into the respectable graduate schools. One very good reason for pushing black graduate students ahead is that, since the passage of various equal opportunity laws, there are now jobs for them, including jobs in academic departments.

However, the outside society and the mass educational systems derailed or screened out intellectually endowed blacks from the routes to academic employment long ago. Those who finish their Ph.D. theses and put themselves on the market are rare and choice birds indeed. Their integration into the faculties is necessary not only to demonstrate liberal commitment but also to satisfy certain federal guidelines. And there are not enough to go around. The case of Kenneth Ian Leighton Mills is instructive here.

Professor Mills was born in Trinidad and was educated at London University and at Oxford before taking a job in the philosophy department at Yale. During the time of troubles in 1969 and 1970 at Yale, Mills deftly maintained his position as the great university's most prominent faculty radical while working with President Kingman Brewster to maintain the disturbances at manageable proportions. He was a tall, graceful man and a popular teacher. His "imposing presence, British accent, quick mind, high-piled Afro and sartorial inclination to blue jeans" made Mills popular with his colleagues, too.[9] Then in February 1972 Kingman Brewster learned that, since September 1971, Professor Mills had been successfully meeting the requirements of a full-time teaching job not only at Yale but also at the State University of New York at Stony Brook, which was across Long Island Sound. Mills taught two courses at each campus. Yale paid him $13,000 a year; Stony Brook had stretched to $26,000 a year. Since he was untenured at both places, both could fire him.[10] The Mills case should illustrate the chic among classy liberals for credentialed, bright black males with good diction, as well as a certain (to employ a kind, equivocal word) flexibility in the statutory requirements of academic employment.

Though blacks are about 11 per cent of the total population, they are about 3 per cent of the academics, and most of those are in the black colleges. The search for exemplary black professors who will fit in at the better and respectable schools goes on. Ads in various publications that advertise job openings often state, "Minorities preferred," or say that minority members are "urged to apply." The black colleges have already been raided, thus causing *their* administrators and trustees to whine that the rich white schools are irreparably damaging black higher education.

It turns out, of course, that few of the professors at the black colleges can fit in. At the black schools that survive, the professors are not at all discipline-oriented (that is, they are not scholarly cosmopolites). As they prepared for their careers, they left the academic mainstream. At these little sectarian schools, most of which are just getting by financially, the instruction is moralistic. The real purpose of the colleges is to keep black youths with little sophistication off the job market for a few years and to prepare them for bourgeois life as preachers, as grade- and high-school teachers, and as low-grade, dependable bureaucrats. Howard and Fisk and a couple of other places have the usual academic programs and the usual academic standards. However, at almost all the other black schools one finds a religious and social atmosphere that is reminiscent of the usual American college of a century ago.

When writing about homosexuals in American academia, one must guess, just as he would if he were to write about them in the publishing industry, in medicine, or in long-distance trucking. Although gay liberationists urge all to "come out of the closets," those established professionals in any field of endeavor who do declare themselves are few.

One of the rare ones is Richard Aumiller of the theater department of the University of Delaware. The Wilmington Sunday *News-Journal,* in an article on campus homosexuality, quoted Mr. Aumiller as saying, "There's no need to go around denying you're a homosexual for your entire life. It's a fact. There are millions of homosexuals." At the time, Richard Aumiller was advisor to an eighty-member student group known as the "Gay Community." Contrary to the rules of the American Association of University Professors, the president of the University of Delaware, E. A. Trabant, informed Mr. Aumiller in January of 1976 that his contract would not be renewed for September 1976. Mr. Trabant claimed he was not challenging Mr. Aumiller's right to be homosexual but rather his advocacy of that life style. Significantly the theater department and the college of which he was part favored Mr. Aumiller's retention. According to the AAUP rules and the Faculty Manual of the university, Mr. Trabant should have given Mr. Aumiller more warning. In the fall of 1976 Mr. Aumiller was no longer advisor to the "Gay Community" because he was out of a job. However, he was still directing the theater department's production of Leonard Bernstein's *Candide* and was awaiting a favorable outcome from a suit against the University of Delaware for back pay, costs, and damages.

A couple of groups of organized gay academics have surfaced, held press conferences, and published the addresses of their headquarters, but none have been responsive to requests for statistical information. The few vocal academic gays are mere subsections of the larger gay-lib movement. The scary rhetoric of the militant gays annoys most professors, but gay-lib agitation especially frightens the academic homosexuals, who, overwhelmingly, are sweet-tempered, responsible, and usually fair.

Most professors would not challenge the claim that gays are more than twice as prevalent in academic employment as they are in the general population. They are likely to settle in the social sciences, but even more in the humanities. They are usually of the superdiscreet, "closet" type. If they band together, it is likely to be for bridge parties or trips, later described to others in vague, enthusiastic terms, to Provincetown, San Francisco, Sylt, or Mikonos. If a sort of "homintern" exists on a university campus, it does little besides provide shoulders for its members to cry on. By a tacit agreement nowhere stated and everywhere in force, the gays are tolerated unless they become topics of general discussion. In one large university in Montana a trustee merely commented (though caustically) to an academic vice-president that a certain department consisted almost entirely of bachelors. The next hiring season (this was in the early sixties) the chairman hired three married men with children, and two bachelors already in the department were ordered to marry the women they had been seeing or someone else.

The possibility of blackmail cannot be dismissed. This may be why few gays work in the administration, where hatreds can get hot and vengeful and where, in the absence of tenure, one can be suddenly forced from his job. Anyone who cares to listen to drunk gossips knows which professors frequently trick. The notoriously comprehensive and precisely informed gay gossip network includes some gay students who confide to nongays who confide further and so on. Athletes, particularly the swimmers and divers, play up to susceptible professors shamelessly. Hilarious vignettes are those surreptitiously observed playlets wherein a smooth-skinned gymnast in a tank shirt moves gracefully from one exquisite attitude to another as he chats in the corridor to a blushing, boggle-eyed professor about his progress in the course.

Many campuses have at least one clean little man who on rare occasions gets plastered and then wanders along the town's cruising street or through the cruising park, clumsily trying to strike up conversations. The patrolling cop approaches him and says gently and firmly, "It's very late. You better get along home now, Dr. Adams." If Adams seems incapable of ambling that far, the polite cop will put him in a police car and deliver him to the door of his apartment.

The gentle tolerance of men who prefer men does not extend to women who prefer women. Even the accusation of lesbianism draws the vengeful hatred of most academic men. Lesbians must be abnormally circumspect and use diversionary tactics, such as dating men who repel them, to sidetrack suspicions. Accusations plus the slimmest of evidence can lead swiftly to the wreckage of their careers. Lesbians are a small minority within the larger minority of academic women, who are unwilling or unable to protect them.

Thirty or forty years ago anti-Semitism was enforced throughout academia by means of informal quotas. Thus the proportion of clambering Jews was kept small in the quality undergraduate colleges. From about 1927 to 1945, Harvard's quota for Jews was about 15 per cent, Yale's 10 per cent, and Princeton's less than 4 per cent.[11] The medical schools, dental schools, and law schools of the Big Ten kept their proportion below 20 per cent. It should be noted here that almost any time and anywhere and at almost all universities, including those of Czarist Russia and Weimar Germany, notoriously anti-Semitic professors have been able to make exceptions for Jewish students who were outstanding and co-operative. The delight of intelligent men and women in other intelligent men and women has almost always overcome prejudice—particularly in the arts and sciences. However, this delight did not extend to the acceptance of Jews as colleagues. At their conventions in the early 1950s historians with more than a few Jewish colleagues had to think of ripostes against remarks that their departments were becoming "Jerusalems." All this has passed with the triumph of the excellence orientation in American academic life.

Once again, the pace setter was Berkeley, which in the 1930s welcomed refugee German-Jewish intellectuals and later extended full status to a disproportionate number of Jewish professors who had been languishing elsewhere. In order to remain number-one, Harvard had to hire more Jews—including some who got their big break at Berkeley. Harvard gave up on quotas for Jewish undergraduates, too. Yale (but not Princeton, which succumbed late) and all the elite bastions fell. By the mid-sixties smart Jews who had worked in the best graduate programs earlier had ready access to the best jobs going. There were simply not enough correct WASPs to go around.

There were holdouts. Some Southern universities and denominational colleges everywhere delayed until the late sixties their establishment of sociology and anthropology departments because there was no way to do so without hiring whole phalanxes of New York and New Jersey Hebrews. In some colleges, departments of economics (which are largely Jewish) are merged in schools of business administration (which are more likely to be gentile) to prevent Jews from having a base of operations. For a few years in the dynamic sixties only a few members of the psychology department of a huge midwestern university would reveal where they worked when they attended the August convention of the American Psychological Association. Their old chairman stolidly continued to reject Jewish job applicants, and the derision these innocent men faced at the convention was based on the assumption of Jews and gentiles alike that those who remained in a Jew-free department were badly educated, milksops, and poor psychologists besides.

All this has passed. As one rises in the prestige scale in American universities, the more heinous is the crime of anti-Semitism.[12] It is conceivable that in his lectures at some rural denominational college, a professor of the old school could allude to "international conspiracies" and the propensity of Jews for both banking and its opposite, political radicalism, but not in the mainstream. In departments of the social sciences in most good American universities, it is not unwise for professors whose Anglo-Saxonism is so pure as to make them vulnerable, to erect defenses. One amusing technique is for a WASP professor to let a *soupçon* of New York inflection come into his speech—particularly when he is arguing. Or one can incorporate for infrequent use at large social gatherings certain Yiddish words like "nebbish" (fool), "schlock" (damaged goods), "measkite" (ugly person), "kitsch" (trash), "dreck" (crap), "touchas" (fanny), and "maven" (expert).

Some observations about Jews hold for Catholics. Long ago, when almost all academics came from the same families that Protestant clergymen and bankers came from, ambitious Catholic academics, like Jews, ran into suspicious obstacles. No more. The boom and the excellence orientation evened opportunity out. All the same, except in the Catholic colleges, Catholics are not numerous or well placed.[13] But slurs against them, as against the Jews, are not allowed.

Except in English-speaking Canada. American academics have flocked to the booming Canadian campuses to be delighted with the well-prepared students, an even shorter academic year, and yet more perquisites. However, Americans are often unpleasantly astonished at the sheeny and mackerel-snapper jokes that are passable in the conception of good manners in the faculty commons (Canadian faculty clubs) and at cocktail parties in the far North. In Canadian academic life, the preference given to native Canadians is open and unapologetic and so is the discouragement to Jews and Catholics—whatever their origins.

A last remark here: Academic Catholics and, more so, academic Jews, are not pious observants.[14] Their second and third marriages, even more than their first ones, are likely to be mixed. The secular religion of liberalism will not allow the demonstration of piety with heathen (that is, nonliberal) symbols and rites. Just as the academic black must not have field-hand diction and the academic gay should, if at all possible, play on the departmental softball team, the academic Jew must be on deck for his lectures and office hours during the high holidays.

There is one form of academic discrimination that is so long-standing, so nasty, and so pervasive that it must put into doubt the authenticity of the professors' supposed impartial quest for excellence, their devotion to democratic service, and their objective quest for truth. The enduring insults to women in academic life are vastly more damaging to the pose of impartiality than the cases given above combined.

Of course, the larger society, which includes electricians and cops, bankers and architects, also discriminates against competent women. But these occupations have never posed as especially moralistic or as democratic equalizers. And there is a peculiar obstinacy about academic antifeminism. Caplow and McGee have observed in their discussion of hiring practices of major universities that:

> . . . women tend to be discriminated against in the academic profession, not because they have low prestige, but because they are outside the prestige system entirely and for this reason are of no use to a department in future recruitment.[15]

This famous quotation makes a terse statement, but fails to explain why women are outside the prestige system. Academics may resent women for the same historical and psychosexual reasons that some men in the larger society do, but, as mentioned above, they seem more stubborn in enforcing this antipathy. It may be that academics are afraid of women, just as they were afraid of Jews forty years ago.

It is well known that girls outnumber boys and get better grades in the primary and, more so, in the secondary schools. In colleges and universities they are about 40 per cent of the enrollment and also get better grades. Conventional attitudes toward women's roles lessen the percentage of females in the graduate schools sharply, where their percentage varies greatly in the disciplines and professions. Women graduate students encounter obstacles in the form of male attitudes toward them that are discouraging. Ann Sutherland Harris, an art historian at Columbian University, collected a series of professors' remarks at the University of California at Berkeley that reveal both overt and covert discriminations. Some of them follow:

> The admissions committee didn't do their job. There is not one pretty girl in the entering class.

> You're so cute. I can't see you as a professor of anything.

> (Professor to student looking for a job) You've no business looking for work with a child that age.

> Why don't you find a rich husband and give all this up?

> Our general policy has been, if the body is warm and male, take it; if it's female, make sure it's an A—from Bryn Mawr.

> (To a young widow who had a five-year-old child and who needed a fellowship to continue at graduate school) You're very attractive. You'll get married again. We have to give fellowships to people who really need them.[16]

There are mere handfuls of women in graduate schools of dentistry, engineering, and business administration. They make up the majority in enrollments (but not in faculties—a telling point) in graduate schools of librarianship, social work, and education. Those women who make it to the comprehensive exams and dissertation stages at the major graduate schools have already shown remarkable determination. It is in the later stages of graduate work, when a woman makes clear her preference for a permanent academic career, that the male professors become inflexible and cruel.[17] Many professors, reminiscent of the old-time anti-Semites who were delighted to harbor brilliant Jews in their seminars, enjoy the minds of exceptionally intelligent women and then do nothing to help them find dignified employment once the degrees are finished.

Nevertheless, these women do present themselves to departments for jobs. Since they are somewhat aside from the prestige system, they work from feeble bargaining positions. They may arrive on the campus appropriately experienced as teaching assistants and impeccably degreed, but, alas, married to a man who was just hired by the customary process. Or they pursue the Ph.D., in the course of having children while the old man labors for tenure at the same university. In any case, the vitas of all women, unless there is some compelling reason (such as threats of legal action backed up by imminent use of the federal antidiscrimination laws), go to the bottom of the pile and are taken up for action only in emergencies. Some schematic scenarios:

I. At a university in Pittsburgh a male professor quits late in April and cannot be replaced in the conventional, leisurely fashion. The chairman calls in Alice, the wife of Topping of pharmacy, who got her Ph.D. at Ohio State seven years ago, as a "temporary" assistant professor. Since she does the job faultlessly and gets good ratings on the student evaluations and even publishes an occasional article besides, they keep her on year after year "temporarily."

II. All members of the regular staff of a large English department in Indiana were reluctant to teach the (low-prestige, sometimes called "dummy") remedial course to the "equal opportunity" students. All the new Ph.D.'s interviewed balked at the prospect of what was really low-level high-school teaching. September neared. The chairman hired sweet Edna Schumann, whose husband teaches at the "good little college" thirty miles away. Edna's last child has just entered grade school. She got her doctorate ten years ago at Radcliffe-Harvard. She has translated Italian short stories and has published some of her shorter poems. She commuted and took the first of a long series of yearly appointments as a "visiting" assistant professor.

III. Allgutt, the famous environmentalist and courageous chairman of the Faculty Welfare Committee spends way too much money and so is financially strapped, though his salary is at the top of the scale for full professors. The chairman of the sociology department reluctantly agrees to hire Sandra Allgutt, who got her Ph.D. in his department two years ago. She will teach two courses a semester (that is, two thirds of a full "load") on a part-time (that is, half-pay) basis computed from the bottom of the scale for assistant professors.

Even the few females who make it through the intricate hiring process for permanent appointments are often stuck with the low-

174   THE PROFESSOR GAME

prestige elementary courses or channeled (much as the blacks are) into women's courses with ephemeral (everyone knows it) popularity—for example, "Women in Colonial Times," "Women in Classical Literature," "Sex-role Stereotypes." Their promotions come slowly or never.

A never-acknowledged principle in academia that nevertheless has been proven by various investigations is that women must be paid about 15 per cent less than men doing the same work. There are many male professors married to female professors who accept (unwillingly) permanent and substantial salary reductions as well.

Since the sexist cutting procedures in the graduate schools have guaranteed that those tough women who finish are more competent than the average male, the professoriat grabs at feeble excuses for discrimination. For example: Menstrual disturbances make them erratic. Childbirth would (or even should) remove them from the classroom for months. They really want to marry and be housewives who hum and dust. It costs too much to add separate toilet facilities for faculty women too. All these so-called "reasons" of course indicate psychosexual phobias and suggest that there are knotty and sickly reasons for sexism in academia.

Whatever the reasons, the passionate identification of many female intellectuals with potentially disrupting aspects of the liberation movement has led to the far-reaching (though far from total) solidarity of academic women. There are blanket organizations of academic women and organizations within the disciplines; for example, the Women's Caucus of the American Association for the Advancement of Science, the Committee on the Status of Women of the Association of Asian Studies, and Women in Cell Biology of the Society for Cell Biology. The irresponsible promises of some judges and federal bureaucrats that they would, by means of various enforcement powers, end female discrimination in academic employment roused and solidified the militants by raising hopes that could not and would not be met. The dashed hopes were not attributable to cynicism from Washington but were due more to the incapacity of legal enforcers to act on even a small fraction of the enormous number of obvious, open-and-shut cases.

The women's movement among members of the larger upper-bourgeois society has nurtured new academic types. The brave, bitter, and noisy female professor is not alone. Some academic women are of a sort that the professors view with near incredulity and fear.

Everyone knows them. They have lunch in widely interdisciplinary quartets in the faculty club, where they smoke intensely and laugh gutturally. They stalk into the dean's office and, while he sits and they stand, poke fingers almost into his puffy face demanding to know what happened at that crucial committee meeting on promotions from which they were excluded. (He, of course, lies and they both know it.) They deflect the drowsy progress of faculty senate meetings to introduce, loudly and clearly, motions for equal pay for equal work. They walk three abreast and arm-in-arm in the hallways. The female students, particularly graduate students, adore them.

The graduate students set up a little section of the department's bulletin board to hold "The Sexist Remark of the Week." The male faculty members suppress it at once, because they do not want their "confidential" conversations "monitored." Those who do not join the activists are openly sneered at as the "queen bees." The activists stop shaving their legs, they carry their research materials in canvas bags stamped, "Never Underestimate the Power of a Woman." Their office door contains a placard (often stolen from them): "Uppity Women Unite!" Their car bumpers, in addition to the faculty-parking-lot stickers, have slogans: "Sexism is a Social Disease," "Adam was a Rough Draft." They are seen reading newsletters from NOW and sometimes clumsily printed sheets with titles like *The Amazon Quarterly, Sister,* or *Majority Report.*

Of course, all this, while raising consciousness and being fun, has produced slim gains.[18] Women whose consciousness has been raised are merely another irritant or a disrupting force in the colleges and universities. Academic women remain the class most consistently discriminated against in the job market and, since the key decisions for hiring in the colleges and universities still are made at the departmental level, are likely to remain so.

Illustration D:

AL KORPER OF HOWIE COLLEGE

He washes down a frosted jelly doughnut with sugared, sour coffee from the faculty club's urn. He glances up often from the Detroit *Free Press* to catch anyone who might come into the lounge. Al Korper's spot is the big armchair facing the door. When the door opens, he lowers the sports pages that inspire his conversational bids:

"Hi, George! I didn't see you at the game last Saturday."

"Why can't 'Bo' [He means Schembecher—the football coach at Michigan] hold those guys back?"

"I guess that ape [meaning Ali] is going to beat the crap out of some other ape for *three* million now."

"Freddie! What did *you* think of that fight?"

Each of these openers puts those whom Al addresses on the defensive, for no one at Howie is better informed about televised or reported sport than he is. And, if persons elsewhere in the large room might settle on the good old days, the weather, miscellaneous grumbling, or Howie College's continuing efforts to delay bankruptcy, Al interrupts them all to bring conversation back to his fief. Al's spirited blustering about intercollegiate and professional sport provides a basis for camaraderie and allows him to be indignant, vigorous, or joyous without touching on any subject that might bring forth discussions of the real world or the dismal future.

The younger and more hopeful members of Howie's faculty avoid the lounge with its maroon carpets, mohair, and dust motes. The lounge seems like a dry warehouse for the college's deadwood. Al himself is a large piece of academic flotsam. Long ago he had played a lot of college basketball and, though now bent a little, is still tall. However, he had steadily thickened after he began coaching. Now he is merely huge, with an extended paunch, colossal hands (his enveloping handshake is still reassuring), and a big nose with large pores and some broken veins.

Though only sixty-two, Al Korper shuffles as he moves about his few stations on Howie's pretty campus. It would require someone well acquainted with Howie's recent history or someone with access to the college's balance sheets to know on this Wednesday morning in October that the red and orange maples, golden sunlight, and cold dews all beautify a scene of dubious health. Al could notice that the density of the students on the curved walks and in the halls of the Georgian-style brick buildings is not much more than half what it was when Howie's enrollment peaked at 2,613 in 1968. After that, enrollment leveled and fell slowly. Then Howie's real troubles began when the trustees imposed that risky jump in yearly tuition to $2,900 in 1973. The "huckstering" (and Al was one of those who called it that) of sending recruiters who were paid commissions to the high schools in Detroit's suburbs, of making chapel optional, of abandoning the old dress codes (Howie's girls used to be forbidden to wear any kind of trousers; the boys could not wear sandals, and their shirts had always to be tucked in), of allowing dormitory visitation (it meant that teenagers from good families were screwing each other at all times of the day or night), and of lowering the minimum verbal-math-combined SAT to 700 had not stopped a decline in applications. And along the way, the school was transformed from a haven for clean-cut children from responsible Christian families into a resting place for a smaller number of very young, spoiled hippies.

As Al walks the quarter mile from the faculty club to his office in the physical education building, he carries a green and gold (Howie's colors) plastic sports-equipment bag with loop handles on either side of the zipper. He kicks up oak leaves on the sidewalk before fraternity row. A couple of the big houses are closed now, but from the others, where tattered sports cars are still parked on the tattered lawns, he is assaulted as usual by the racket from the stereos. It was these sounds that old Fornehm of English in his harangue four years ago in the faculty senate called "nigger-fuck" music.

Just inside the B. T. Sand Memorial Building Al perfunctorily checks the mailbox. He gets no personal letters, because he writes none. He even resists writing the letters of recommendation that former students ask to have sent to prospective employers. He eventually dictates enthusiastic ones only after boys or girls desperate for some teaching job phone him from Saginaw or Bay City person-to-person. The charming textbook salesmen have ceased their personal visits to little Howie. Al rarely receives book advertisements either. In order to save paper the college-wide and departmental memos are no longer placed in each faculty member's mailbox but on a green-backed bulletin board marked off by vertical pieces of string into five sections representing the work days. Everyone is expected to read the memos of the day. This last was one of the recent in a long series of economy measures. Since Al feels guilty for not attending emergency meetings of certain faculty committees and of the campus AAUP chapter, he merely glances at the bulletin board, which contains notices of little else.

Myrna, the old secretary, says, respectfully as always, "Good morning, Coach Korper," and thus she brightens Al's day by acknowledging his long service for Howie's basketball, track, and wrestling teams. "Coach" also masks the fact that, unlike almost all of Howie's younger faculty members, Al lacks the degree that would allow "Doctor." The young "Doctors" themselves sometimes greet Al mock-cheerily with, "Hi, Coach," on the campus walks. But when they say it, it sounds disrespectful or an easy way to shrug off their responsibility to learn his last name.

In 1964 the new, dynamic chairman appropriated Al's old pine-paneled office near the gyms in order to enlarge the chairman's "suite." Al had to move up to the third floor. For a few years he had two officemates. One was a sinewy, bull-voiced woman who taught several sports "methods" classes for the girls. The other, a jittery birdlike lady, was a scandal, for, though she taught classes in health education, she could not stop herself from smoking three packs a day. The new, dynamic chairman harassed all three in his campaign to get their resignations. The women finally left. He boasted of his success in "getting rid of deadwood" as he started sending his vita out for a dean's job beginning in 1970.

Al remained impervious and even stood up to the purger. One afternoon the new, dynamic chairman suggested to Al that if he was unhappy with the way things were progressing at Howie he might go elsewhere. He would even give Al "a good letter of recommendation." This meeting in the inner office of the suite ended with the following lines of dialogue:

"I've committed nineteen years to this college."

"We don't want deadwood around here."

"You dirty Jew son-of-a-bitch, you better start guarding your wife and kids."

The chairman was one of the first to perceive that Howie could not avoid financial calamity and began afterward to lower his sights for the next step up and away. In the fall of 1972 he took a job as dean of education at a branch of the University of Wisconsin. Al passed two rather serene years alone in his new office under the temporary chairmanship of an old and trusted friend until the old man retired. The next chairman, a young, nice fellow, at least agonized aloud to everyone before he made "tough decisions." Al was one of the last to learn that the trustees had been using the faculty retirement fund to procure the federal matching grants that were the basis for Howie's building expansion throughout the sixties. Howie's administrators built, among other things, new dormitory space for 650, a white marble conference center, and an Olympic-size swimming pool that regularly piped in light classical music and the Tijuana Brass. All of those buildings, indeed Howie's whole plant, are becoming shabby due to a lack of preventive maintenance.

Howie's administrators wish to be rid of Al and others like him because these old people are about to make demands on the retirement fund that cannot be met. Some chunks of the retirement fund had also gone in intricately circuitous ways to finance the expansion of the plants of some auto-parts manufacturers who were Howie's trustees. The retirement-fund scandal (news of it appeared in the Detroit and Lansing newspapers) and harassment were not enough to dislodge Al from his job. Now, more than ever, he needs his wages ($11,150 for the nine-month year after the 15 per cent cut in 1975) until he is eligible for social security, the anticipated monthly check for which will be $460 for him and Agnes.

Several trustees have urged that Al be "let go" in staff reduction campaigns. However, those pleading for clemency overrode those who felt not only that he was expensive but that his "teaching" has also hurt the reputation of the institution. For two years now, when Al sits alone in his office, he compulsively doodles figures that are his guesses as to what his financial condition might be in 1979, when the mandatory retirement age will surely be enforced in his case. He and Agnes will have to raise the rents on the old people who live in the other three units of the four-family flat they own in East Detroit. It all might work out, if the inflation remains modest. In any case, he has to hang on at Howie until he gets Medicare and the social security checks.

Promptly at noon, Al pulls the quart-sized old thermos from his athletic bag and spoons in some steaming stew made with a sharply spiced Polish sausage. He also eats some chunky slices of rye bread that Agnes wrapped in wax paper. To take his leak, Al strolls down the terrazzoed stairs to the row of shoulder-high urinals next to the showers in the locker rooms. He usually manages one or two trips to this area between noon and one o'clock, for here his old heart leaps up. He watches the shower- or sweat-glistening boys skip about as they flick clean-laundered towels at each other's high buttocks. They are all vigorously in motion and superoxygenated. They greet Al loudly, but perfunctorily with "Hi, Coach!" as they rush by. Al is stung to sweet nostalgia by the acid, earthy smells from their damp gym clothes, their innocently healthy feet, armpits, and crotches. These are the sights and sounds and smells of what were his happiest years.

His great size, grace, and eagerness to please signaled him out early. He had played baseball as a child and then, when he shot up to a gangly six feet seven inches when only fifteen, he guessed correctly that his future was in basketball. In 1930 he went from Detroit's Southeastern High School to the University of Michigan to enjoy one of the first athletic scholarships that great institution gave to someone other than a football player. The Depression therefore touched Al lightly, and he even sent a little money home to his parents and three sisters in 1932 and 1933. He was, of course, enrolled in the university's school of education, and so study or even class attendance were tangential concerns. Al graduated with the B.S. in education in June 1935 and in September began graduate work at the University of Minnesota, where he was also a part-time assistant basketball coach. Here again his studies were not demanding, and Al got A's and B's. In 1938 he married Agnes, a chubby, sweet girl who had a fellowship to learn sign language so she could help deaf children. Al had been desultorily collecting dissertation data on the psychological trauma due to basketball knee injuries when he was drafted in 1941.

His first four years in the army were even more exciting than the college years. The army intensified his patriotism and permitted (indeed demanded) that he impose peak physical performance on large numbers of healthy young Americans. He was a basic-training sergeant. However, Al and Agnes spent a bleak eight months in 1945 when Al endured a court martial following the deaths by drowning of three trainees, two of them Negroes, whom Al forced at gunpoint to swim a muddy river in Georgia. Hostile witnesses claimed that they and many others had pleaded exhaustion after spending ten hours repeatedly negotiating an obstacle course of which that river was the final section. They said that Sergeant Korper's satisfaction in imposing tasks seemed to increase with the pain that others endured performing them. Al was eventually cleared, but the army gave him office work until his honorable discharge late in 1946.

Helped by the GI Bill, he picked up again at the University of Minnesota. However, during his first semester back, a young professor learned and talked too much to his young colleagues about Al's secret which his previous professors and the army had kept. Al read about as well as the average American with an eighth-grade education. Minnesota was, at the time, well into a campaign to "upgrade" all its graduate programs, and the senior coaches and some old friends could not save him. Still wholesome and handsome at age thirty-four, Al now had two daughters ("Just like Jack Dempsey," he joked) and needed those GI checks. The department let Al hang around until they found him a job, paying $4,200 a year, at Howie, a private, coeducational Lutheran college outside Detroit. He became basketball and baseball coach and taught courses in the same subjects.

Al's teams occasionally made it to the eliminations for the regional championships. Besides his "methods" courses, he occasionally, and after 1959 regularly, taught courses in "The Philosophy of Physical Education" and "The History of Physical Education," both of which were remarkably similar. He quickly established himself as a "character," for he demanded that male students in his lecture classes shine their shoes and wear ties and white shirts. His athletes gathered in a circle for interdenominational prayers and saluted the flag before their games—even away games. Al was the faculty sponsor for the Fellowship of Christian Athletes. His moralism, though it might have been excessive at other places, still harmonized with the old Howie until about 1963, when, as part of the building program that brought with it a scheme to double enrollment, the trustees agreed to "bring Howie into the mainstream." In general the reforms of 1963 and later "brought the modern world to Howie," and so commenced Al's decline. In November of 1965 the president himself called Al in to ask him to ease up on the fingernail inspections and the distribution of anticommunist tracts in class. Al stuck with his demands for good manners and patriotism. He had strikes by his basketball team and in one of his classes in 1968. He continued to organize little rallies to support the crusade in Viet Nam. Shaggy, jeans-clad students pointed at him on campus and snickered. He began to drink beer compulsively at night. His teams had a few shameful seasons. In 1970 Al's teams were given to a cheerful young black man writing a dissertation at Springfield College. Al was assigned to coach girl's baseball, basketball, and tennis.

On the Wednesday that we observe him, Al has two classes in "Basketball Methods" for boys and one for girls. The basketball classes merely require that Al check out some equipment, throw the balls into the gym, and blow the whistle forty-two minutes later so the boys and girls have time to shower and change. His two History and Philosophy of Physical Education courses meet late on Monday, Wednesday, and Friday afternoon. Except for the first two meetings, during which he repeatedly stressed to the students that their mission was to "reform the American body," the lectures are done by the students themselves. Al assigns them "topics" and "research areas," which they are required to "share" with their young colleagues. Actually they know enough to lift paragraphs from old textbooks or files in the fraternity and to read these old reports. Like many of the students, Al himself sometimes dozes. The material for the final examinations comes entirely from Coach Korper's first two lectures.

He might have combined the "History . . ." and the "Philosophy . . ." classes and halved the work of himself and of the students who read their "research" reports, but the present chairman, who, despite everything, is a "nice guy," feels it is best for Al to give the appearance of teaching *two* lecture courses. Tuesday and Thursday mornings Al teaches two more baseball and basketball courses for boys which merely require the checking out and in of equipment to see that it is not stolen and blowing the whistle a few times. His five two-hour sports methods classes and his two three-hour lecture classes give him a full "load" of sixteen hours.

Al is listed as a member of the departmental Guest Speaker Committee, which never meets. For years now he has been kept off university committees, since he compulsively interrupted his colleagues in order to talk about the losing records of the athletic teams and the dangers of leftist subversion in our colleges. He quoted J. Edgar

Hoover. Almost everyone agrees it is best to keep big Al Korper under wraps.

Al's two o'clock and three o'clock classes pass slowly for everyone, even though he keeps the students only forty minutes. The few students who bother to appear flee when he releases them. Al looks in on the happy boys in the gym before locking his office and checking the afternoon mail. He throws the Red Cross appeal into the "round file" (one of his little jokes), gives to old Myrna the request for a character reference for some student of whom he has no slight recollection and no written records. He takes the weekly eight-page student newspaper with him as he strolls, his head bent down, to the faculty lounge in the administration building.

Today Coach Al is lucky. On hand at four o'clock are three friends: Bonwright, the old chaplain, who now does some office work and teaches small classes in "The Bible as Literature"; Fress, the manager of the dormitory food services, who, according to the never-enforced faculty-club rules, should not be allowed in the place; and eighty-year-old Saleeby, the emeritus English professor, who taught at Howie from 1926 to 1971. The old companions talk about televised sport almost exclusively.

An aged custodian locks them out at 6:20 and Al walks into a graveled parking lot to climb in the '66 maroon Chrysler that starts reluctantly. As usual at this time of night, the expressways into Detroit are clear so that the driving is pleasurable. Alas, Al has to fill up the gas tank. Even at the serve-yourself, discount station, the tally comes to $9.67.

As he enters the living room of their neat apartment, he hears Agnes, who has long been obese, wheezing in the kitchen. The big meal is finished at 7:55. Al is in the green corduroy easy chair before the excellent color set almost at once. Agnes tidies up quickly and begins her nightly nagging to get him to bed at a reasonable hour rather than allowing him to doze on and off until very late as he watches sports programs and the contests.

VI

What Professors Are Supposed to Do and How They Try to Do It

What follows are some official statements that describe professors' duties. First a paragraph from the University of Georgia's "Guidelines for Promotions and Appointment" (1973 edition, page 1).

The raison d'être of The University of Georgia is to provide superior quality in the performance of three major functions of a modern state university, viz., (1) the communication of knowledge to students, the development in them of the comprehension and skills necessary to continue the quest for knowledge and the training of students for entry into the professions and scholarly disciplines (teaching and practice); (2) the discovery and communication of significant new knowledge (research and scholarly publications); (3) the outreach to the society which sustains the institution through the application of knowledge to the solution of public problems (public service programs).

A recent dittoed memorandum from the History Department of the University of Nebraska states:

Criteria to be considered in deciding tenure and promotion shall include:
(a) research, publication, and other scholarly activities.
(b) teaching ability.
(c) service to the Department, College, University and community.

A recent instructional manual for new academic employees states:

As a faculty member you will be held responsible for three areas of endeavor: teaching, research and service. The emphasis varies with the institution and the field.[1]

Professors are supposed to be continually examining each other and themselves as "teachers, scholars and as colleagues." These three activities are the major divisions for this chapter.

Teaching is, of course, what outsiders assume the college professor gets paid for. And most outsiders believe that (like a grade school teacher) this is all that he does or is supposed to do. Simply described, teaching in North American colleges or universities usually means that the professor talks to a group of people about a subject that he knows very much better than they do.

In a word, most often, and typically, a college or university teacher lectures. He stands before a narrow box of about chest height, the top of which slants toward him in order to hold the written reminders of what he has planned to say. The classroom is longer than it is wide and has rows of movable seats placed in a grid arrangement. Each seat has an extended arm for holding the student's writing materials. Roughly three quarters of the formal instruction that takes place in American universities and colleges varies little from this pattern.

The lecture hall may be a sloped auditorium in which the 2,000 seats are filled for a lecture-demonstration course in introductory physics or it may be a small room in which only one fourth of the twenty-four seats are occupied for the semester's forty lectures on "The Comic Spirit in English Literature." However, in almost all cases, and almost all the time, the professor is entirely in command.

The momentum of traditional obedience, the examination schedule, the credit system—all conspire to affirm the professor's control. The room's shape, its lighting, the characterless, solid furniture and even the thermostat (often set low in order to accommodate the professors who exercise off some calories because they are the only persons allowed to move during the fifty minutes) all establish the professor in the central role. By a never-questioned tradition, a college classroom has no pictures, no decorations, no warm colors, no pleasing surfaces of any kind, and is coolly fluorescent lit. The professor even demands that, before he arrives to perform, the blackboard be devoid of any trace of any other professor's performance.

A characteristic enmity has its origins as follows: The names are invented. The playlet could take place anywhere. Geography's Karter forgot five times in a row to wipe the board clean for geology's Erder, whose lecture began promptly at 11:00 A.M. Erder wiped away Karter's "mess" four times with the dusty felt eraser and then after the fifth time, waited outside the big lecture hall in "Old East" and ran in to shout at Karter as his class of 175 filed out at 10:51 on March 10, 1973. Karter analogously overreacted two weeks later in the faculty senate after Erder's overlong speech opposing restoration of the old grading scale; he called Erder a "stuffy, pompous ass." The two department chairmen and mutual friends have been unable to smooth things over these past four years.

The grading system which rests on frequent, compulsory examinations is a foundation for the professors' control. Professors will usually have a statutory requirement for supporting or "outside" reading in one or more textbooks, but in North America almost all of a course's subject matter, mastery of which is asked for in the tests, comes from the professors' lectures. Similarly, many courses, most often in the specialized areas of subjects a college student takes in the junior and senior years, require outside, written reports or "research" papers. But the attention most professors give to these "term papers" is perfunctory. When not purchased or plagiarized (in the aggregate, rather uncommon occurrences), the term papers are so sloppily done that they are, particularly when regarded all together as a pile of work on the professor's desk, so discouraging that professors are rarely capable of summoning up some personal stake in them. On the other hand, the sweet, living sap of his individuality is in the lectures, and he wants mastery of their content demonstrated on the snap quizzes (usually ten minutes of questions—posed without warning and delivered from the lectern) that require brief written answers, midterm exams (occupying a whole class session), and final exams (two to three hours during "exam week" following the ten—in the case of "quarters"—or fifteen—in the case of "semesters"—weeks of lectures).

Variations from the lecture are possible. The distinctive instructional form for postbachelor's students is (or should be) the seminar. The giant universities use subprofessional "section leaders" or "teaching assistants," almost always graduate students, to manage small seminarlike "discussion" classes of ten to fifteen students. At the small, quality liberal arts colleges, the undergraduate "seminars" (this usage is permissible) are run by professors earning professors' wages—which is why these places are considered good and why the tuition is so high.

Up-to-date academic reformism and some token dollars-and-cents wisdom requires that the students be put ever more on a do-it-yourself basis. The sciences and several branches of engineering have long required that students learn by doing in laboratories. They titrate, dissect, calibrate, and record. Studio art students draw, paint, sculpt, and move mud around on the potter's wheels. Similarly, the dynamic professors of journalism help students make their own newspaper and let the photographers make their own pictures. Aspiring programmers fiddle with real computers—which may be reasons why all these fields are so very popular lately. Earphoned modern-language students now mumble sample, model sentences in new tongues in the pauses after the sentences are impeccably and slowly stated by a disembodied native speaker. The students put their hours in at "language labs," where tape recorders distribute sound to seats arranged in grids of rows and aisles just like the lecture classrooms are. Analogously, students of art history in some well-equipped places in the provinces can all by themselves look at twenty-minute films or TV tape cassettes while famous professors in accompaniment dilate on the refinement of the *kuoros* in classical Greek sculpture, the classical elements in Romanesque sculpture, or the distinction of Giotto's frescoes.

Many sensible men have done the obvious and clever and have organized and struggled to keep alive companies which manufacture these and similar "instructional aids." Professors almost everywhere receive attractive prospectuses in their mailboxes describing premade transparencies for an overhead projector that demonstrate lucidly in graphs or tables almost all the problems likely to come up for discussion in macro- and microeconomics courses. Geographers keep on hand dozens of catalogs, each listing thousands of slides that illustrate and make more exact and vivid the points their disciplines require that they make. Nursing professors can purchase or rent strip films or movies showing procedures the students will later encounter in hospitals. It is possible in most universities now for a professor to "can" his lectures on TV tapes so that for certain subjects that are regularly offered to large numbers (departmental chairmen call them "our bread-and-butter courses") a professor need not appear in person. An underling can merely flick a switch. One can also buy or rent recorded or canned lectures by such authorities as Arnold Toynbee, Thomas Mann, and other intellectual titans.

All the same, the conventional curriculum and course content have changed little in twenty years. Nor has there been much alteration in the habit of compulsory, frequent tests or in the credit system. That these audio-visual techniques offer even the most conventional material more skillfully and attractively than the average lecturer is beyond dispute. The students usually prefer them. Yet these supplemental materials have made small inroads into traditional practice. They do indeed require of the professors some preview of the materials, the mastery of elementary machines for their installation and transmission, some rearranging of the usual semester-long scenario around them. Audio-visual aids require some fetching and returning —in short, more work than a row of droning lectures from old five-by-eight note cards. The real reasons for the meagerness of their success is that the professor by employing them gives up some control of his course to others and that professors are lazy.

Professors who relinquish even a part of their act to others, besides admitting their own imperfections, open themselves to accusations of charlatanry or even incompetence from their more timid and even lazier colleagues. A well-trained and conscientious assistant professor at a university in New England quite correctly recognized that Kenneth Clark's *Civilization* movies, though opinionated, were immeasurably richer and more attractive than most of the lectures she would come up with on comparable topics for her "Western Civilization" course. So the young woman reserved the thirteen films for use in her eighty-session, two-semester course. As she was setting up the camera and loudspeakers for the eighth in the series, a full professor, known to be vocally sardonic at meetings of the department's promotion and tenure committee, approached her and acidly remarked, "Say, Shirley, I wonder if you'd give me the popcorn concession?" He then walked off chuckling himself hoarse with satisfaction at the little joke. Shirley canceled her reservations for the remaining five films.

No one who has attended an American college or university needs to be reminded that most lectures are wretchedly boring. Some are scarcely endurable. There are many reasons why the teaching is bad. Some blame can be placed on the professors: their exclusively research training in graduate school, their timidity and laziness. Some faults are due to conditions in the profession itself: the lack of performance criteria, tenure. Perhaps a fundamental reason that teaching is bad is the never-questioned assumption that the divisions of arts and sciences and professional schools and the subdivisions within them are somehow in harmony with the cosmos and also with what the students deserve or desire.[2] Claims might be made that teaching is poor only in comparison with other, more accessible entertainment. However, few professors are courageous enough to attribute much of the bad teaching to the disinterest of those who show up to be taught or to employers who require that, before an American can be considered for a decent job, he or she must be defensively credentialed with (minimally) a bachelor's degree.

Earlier chapters have shown that graduate training is directed toward mastering the content of a particular discipline and, more particularly, toward the production of research findings in that discipline. The graduate student is scarcely ever encouraged to question the social, moral, or entertainment value of his studies. The only training in dramatic presentation he gets is by watching his professor or, on the job, by his (invariably unsupervised) work as a teaching assistant. Professors are, perhaps, intrinsically no lazier than other humans. But the statutory workyear of less than eight months and a workweek of less than ten hours is sheltered by an obscurantist bureaucracy and a social organization that is overwhelmingly authoritarian, mutually protective, and sealed from almost any scrutiny that might be skeptical. Aside from a few general requirements such as that he be prepared to start talking when the bell rings and that he not fail too many of the better athletes, a professor's teaching is likely to remain isolated from any sort of performance criteria. Somewhere along the way he may have been told about the "three f's" ("Be friendly, firm, and fair") and that each point he considers important must be repeated three times. But he need not earn a profit or commission or show any substantial product whatever—not even a demonstrable rating on an applausometer. In North American universities and colleges, the teacher's earnings are quite independent of what his clients gain from his work or what they think of him.

Reform waves wash lightly over academia. Persistent ripples bring the professors the message that theirs is—or should be—a "performing art." The teacher should "inspire," "dramatize," or, at the very least, "hold the students' interest." These goals can indeed be approached by the employment of good language, breath control, and lots of modulation—in short, the techniques of a stage actor. It is difficult to make abnormal psychology, the French Revolution, or the Russian novel dull. Opportunists who dwell on the lives of the poets (rather than poetry) and the Kennedy brothers' sex lives (rather than what they were and are up to politically) will have large followings. Most of the performances students do endure are so unappealing that they appreciate any gesture that might be interpreted to mean that the professors care about the students more than about the subject. Their gratitude is touching for the man who offers some of his lectures on Early Modern Europe in costume, or who changes his voice to take character parts in Plato's *Dialogues*. They keep warm memories of the professor with a lovely smile who bothers to learn their names or who invites them to his backyard on a Saturday late in April to drink beer and eat sandwiches from a ham his wife baked. These or similar efforts to bring wit, energy, or affection into the college or university do not require any diminution of the intellectual content in the course offerings.[3]

Alas, there are subjects that cannot be made much more appealing by costumes or by concern, and, as it turns out, these are irreducible elements for the induction of young people into high culture and admission to the technical professions. And, as it turns out further, these same subjects are those of the traditional college curriculum which have in the past fifteen years steadily lost ground. The essential languages such as Greek, Latin, and German and French are now studied by isolated, defensive small groups. Life drawing, theoretical mathematics, econometrics, grammar, historiography, theology—each of these critically important subjects accumulated by mankind over millennia and laboriously communicated from generation to generation appeals now to a pathetically small minority of college students. Artistic performances or adherence to the three f's on the part of their propagators cannot increase their appeal much, for they demand a vigorous commitment from the students almost exclusively.

Furthermore, almost any of the lectures that occupy some ten to fifteen hours of the thirty weeks a year that classes are in session have to be inferior to the performances (as performances) the student encounters during the average of thirty hours per week the year round he or she surrenders slack-jawed to television or the movies. It may be the case (as many suspect) that the average lecture, rather than decreasing in quality or relevance, has been moving in the other direction and becoming better, since the lecture system became the norm in our universities some three quarters of a century ago. At the same time, however, the quality (that is, the appeal quite apart from content) of alternative forms of entertainment has increased much faster.

A basis for the professors' pathetic performances—and one which in turn determines much of the quality of American education, is that *the great majority of students do not want conventional, structured higher education*. It is necessary to refer yet again to the prestige ratings here. At the great institutions since about 1930 the demand for their degrees permits these places to admit only those who present statistical probabilities (SAT scores, high-school grades, etc.) that suggest preparedness and even proven enthusiasm for disciplined intellectual work. At Amherst College, Bowdoin College, Dartmouth College, Haverford College, Radcliffe College and at Cal Tech, MIT, Johns Hopkins, Princeton, and Yale only a few sluggards and anti-intellectuals slip through the admissions hurdles. Even at many slightly less selective and slightly less prestigious places the 10 to 20 per cent of the students who in their hearts reject high culture and intellectual discipline are carried along by the atmosphere and peer-group pressure and shape up or leave quietly. However, at almost all the "respectable" places, the state universities and other institutions that need and seek out students, the atmosphere on the campus is that of the culture at large. Most American college and university students have already rejected conventions and disciplined work in the high schools. They wish to avoid hard work and the determined structuring of time and have alluring alternatives to these pursuits on or near the college campuses. Many professors at the merely respectable or worse campuses nobly maintain and attempt to demonstrate their partaking in the grand academic tradition and their intellectual integrity. However, many, perhaps most, students see them as curious wraiths, annoyances, specimens of a bygone age or reminders of quaint, harmless life styles that, for ecology's sake, should not be allowed to become extinct.

The professors (and this includes about two thirds of their number) are more or less aware of their superfluity. The dedicated teacher who always honestly demands of himself that he accomplish *something* in the classroom progressively simplifies his presentations and lowers the performance expectations until he shames himself by the banality of what he says and performances he gets. As noted above, some lecture with forensic intensity or dramatize in order to keep their subject before their captives—those who do, in fact, pay their wages. But most professors after a few years at the same place accept the perquisites and come to assume in the classroom a take-it-or-leave-it attitude. Those students who take notes as he talks, are most often playing the game of guessing what he will ask for on the quizzes. Or they doodle, doze, or watch him with benign contempt. They are there because they need the grade which enters the credits that add up to a degree.

Discussions in earlier chapters passed over, callously perhaps, a most distressing aspect of professorial work. A fifty-minute class may be painful work, because the professor cannot avoid it. He knows he is a failure as a teacher and is racked with terror that he may be found out and denounced. Even though this never happens, the demoralized poor teacher still regards his academic specialty of vital importance in his life and would have his subject assume some significance in the lives of all others. He must endure sorrow because the beautiful boys and girls all about him have rejected his devotion to Ichthyology, Industrial Safety, Music from the Baroque Era, Milton, Analytic Philosophy, The German Novelle, African Culture, or Sociological Theory.[4]

There is a dubious assumption built into all formal education for which tuition is charged. The assumption is that the acquisition of knowledge requires the physical presence of a credentialed teacher. This may have been so in Plato's Academy. In the medieval universities lecturing scholars were economically justifiable because their services were so cheap and because books were so dear. However, this association

> began to lose force at some time between the middle of the fifteenth century and the early decades of the sixteenth. During that period, pedagogues discovered that the process of printing had made books so cheap that students could buy them, and that if they bought them and used them under appropriate conditions, and with appropriate sanctions for failure to read and master their contents, *they learned things without actually having been told them.*[5]

It might indeed be the case that almost everything now presented in classrooms in our colleges and universities could be learned in some better way, yet all of these better ways would still require a self-mastery that few of our youths possess.[6] And such education would call for relatively few professors, whose jobs would consist of assigning tasks, asking questions, and listening. This is hardly a description of American higher education.

Though it is often very frustrating for those who do it, college teaching cannot be considered exhausting work. It would be, of course, if professors had to teach forty hours a week, fifty weeks a year. But even where teaching requirements are most onerous—in the quality liberal-arts colleges and in the community colleges—teaching loads rarely exceed fifteen hours a week, thirty weeks a year. Such a lot of time devoted to teaching is justified at these places because there are no (or few) demands for research. In American universities the twelve-, nine-, or most especially, six-hour teaching load is officially justified by the need of the professor to "stay abreast of his field" and, more specifically, to produce publishable research. Thus the attention moves to a subject shrouded in myths and shielded by mysteries.

Most of our college teachers are trained and credentialed at a few giant universities. Their graduate training was set up to make the trainees critics of research and to turn them into researchers themselves. Once on the job, almost any four-year college provides the libraries, laboratories, additional financing, and time for research. A little domestic belt-tightening gives the professor a financial cushion to do away with the need for summer-school teaching and gives him almost four uninterrupted months to pursue new truth. At the great universities the teaching demands are less, the facilities so fine as to be (or appear) irresistible, and the rewards for research (in terms of promotion, prestige, or even capital value[7]) are extraordinary. At certain institutions all the time and at certain others at certain times in certain departments published research findings are required to obtain a permanent job. It would seem that many things—not the least of which is the professor's self-respect as an intellectual, a scientist, a professional, or a worker—would induce American professors to think hard and creatively, to investigate new things, and to present to narrow or broad audiences of peers their conclusions. Why, then, is the output of the 400,000 or so college professors so mediocre in quality and so small in quantity?

As some evidence of the mediocrity of published research, we might have added an appendix to this book consisting of the photocopied tables of contents of the second-ranking American scholarly journals in the fields of theories of history, sport history, Renaissance studies, librarianship, sociology, economics, classical philology, and Romance linguistics; but, considering the book's intended audience, they would appear to be lists of gibberish—as they are, incidentally, to many of the people who specialize in those very fields. The reader interested in an odd voyage might drive on a Saturday (when nobody is around and parking places are to be had) to the nearest campus (one is always within reach) and browse in the main library's room for scholarly periodicals. Or one can look through the catalogs of the presses of the universities of Missouri, Colorado, Kansas, or Southern Illinois. Or one can look at the annual list of topics that win Guggenheim fellowships.

Professors who do publish the results of their research do so almost entirely in the subsidized journals or presses and in near isolation not only from pop culture but from what is generously conceded to be general intellectual culture. Despite an entirely normal love of gain, the substantial amounts of time to use as they wish, and their research facilities, they rarely even attempt to score with a good New York press. They rarely get by-lines in the solid periodicals such as the New York *Times Magazine, Harper's,* or the *Atlantic.* A few professors—almost always Jewish and living in or near New York City—are used by *The New York Review of Books,* and *Commentary. Psychology Today* and *Natural History* publish a lot of professorial findings, but the editorial policy of both magazines is almost always to rewrite the professors' articles completely.

American *belles lettres* have been created on the campuses, but not by persons trained as professors. In order to appear lively and relevant, some campuses have installed nonacademics in their English departments as "writers in residence." The Writer's Program at the University of Iowa has, at various times, sheltered Phillip Roth, William Price Fox, Kurt Vonnegut, John Cheever, Robert Coover, and others. Joseph Heller teaches at City College in New York. Archibald Macleish has worked at Harvard. Saul Bellow has decorated the University of Chicago. Reynolds Price gets a salary from Duke. Joyce Carol Oates resides at the University of Windsor in Ontario. These *real* creative, publishing intellectuals may or may not be expected to offer courses in creative writing or to give occasional public lectures. All are well paid for the "exposure" they bring their hosts. They may be called "professors," but they are a minuscule proportion of the total number of literature professors.

The American universities shelter thousands of painters and sculptors; hundreds of photographers, film makers, and composers. No more than a few dozen of these indulged professors establish reputations outside their own departments. Professorial studio artists intellectualize and timidly imitate what is done in the dog-eat-dog art worlds of New York, London, and Rome. Professorial composers

write short musical works that amuse or make envious other professorial composers and are greeted by tolerant boredom or derision
when and if they are performed by working musicians before a
broadly cultured public.

The sort of publication encouraged and awaited varies in the
different fields. Productive mathematicians and chemists should publish frequent two- or three-page articles consisting largely of symbols.
Philosophers, psychologists, and geologists write articles that are
longer. Sociologists and linguists publish articles and books. The political scientists and the historians of art, politics, and many other
areas also publish long articles, but they are really "book fields"—
that is, professors are expected to make their mark among their peers
with something one can hold between his hands in hard covers.

Those twenty or thirty American universities that supposedly hold
a "hard line" on publication (and provide the light teaching loads to
encourage it) may set vague guidelines for production such as the
entirely unenforceable one that a historian should try to publish an
article a year and a book every five years. Such or analogous performance criteria terrify the troops anywhere in academia and are,
even in the hard-line universities, impossible to enforce due to
tenure.

The article-a-year-book-every-five paradigm merits some examination. Making generous assumptions that articles are twenty pages
long and that a book is four hundred pages long, this totals five hundred pages or one hundred pages of finished prose a year.[8] Otherwise
examined, it is two pages a week or, alternatively, twenty-five pages
for each month of the professor's free summers. This is not much,
but a very tiny number of the Ph.D.'d historians (usually less than
5 per cent) maintain this pace in the course of their thirty-year careers. A far, far larger percentage of historians may require that their
undergraduate seniors write twenty-page term papers in five weeks.
This example applies only to "book fields." But comparable and
rather gentle performance criteria would show up the pathetic standards of production in other areas of academic research.

"Publish or perish," a phrase used within academia to frighten laggards and outside academia to explain that professors are too busy
researching to do a good job teaching, is, then, a paper tiger outside
the great universities where "greatness" is attributable to the demand
for solid evidence of scholarly engagement.[9] If flatly asked, most academics would subscribe to the notion that their colleagues should

demonstrate, if even in the exquisite criteria of their chosen discipline—that they are intellectually alive.

However, even though their professional preparation was almost exclusively training for research, many, perhaps more than a third, of the graduate students who start dissertations never finish them. Roughly half of the professors now in place have never published anything—not even a two-page book review, a pasted-together chapter in a textbook, an edited document, an anecdote for a genealogical journal. Another twenty-five per cent never publish anything of substance that was not originally in their doctoral dissertations.[10] Roughly 15 per cent of the professors labor along, perhaps publishing a second book (or its equivalent in a nonbook field) requiring ten or more years of work. Fewer than 5 per cent of the professors who have been on the job five or more years are indeed strenuously engaged in scholarly work. Those few labor to maintain their self-respect as intellectuals by rationing their summer-school teaching, by circumscribing their golf, television, lushing, fretting, procrastinating, and companionable analyzing of colleagues that absorbs the discretionary time of almost all of their associates.

A truer phrase to apply to the upper reaches of the academic world might be "publish and flourish." For only the working scholars have access to the glittering world of the name universities, where the wages are higher, the fringe benefits better, and where the students are bright and dependable as well as lovely. A producing professor at a merely respectable school is also likely to flourish in that he may be promoted faster. However, at almost any university, even Columbia or Chicago, that professor whose output exceeds a norm—which is approximately the average rate of scholarly production for the department's full professors—thereby endangers himself, for he has bared a fearsome, slimy truth. Professors are lazy.

The naive professor who devotedly or (worse) successfully battles at the frontiers of knowledge risks ambush within the ranks. His jealous colleagues will pump unhappy students for stories demonstrating that he makes factual errors in his lectures and that he has temper tantrums in his seminars. They watch his comings and goings to trap him appearing late or not at all for his classes. They may ask students to see if his comments on blue books are sufficiently voluminous. He must hold more office hours than others. The drones set for themselves the task of proving that the scholar maintains his position only by neglecting teaching, which, they loudly insist, demands and gets their last reserves of energy.

In fact, rate-busting scholars are usually rate-busting teachers who do far more than the minimum on all counts.[11] Still, in order to maintain their morale, the lazzaroni must damage the rate-buster. They do so by setting afloat stories (which might be true) that the worker-scholar-teacher plagiarizes, exploits his graduate students, neglects his wife and children, uses amphetamines, or disposes of his sexual needs speedily in the bathrooms of the bus station.[12]

Thomas C. Reeves, a history professor at the University of Wisconsin—Parkside, offers an explanation for the dismal quality and quantity of academic research. In a comment on the Ladd-Lipset survey, he observes:

> The great majority of us toil in obscure institutions that passively if not actively discourage the labor related to research and publication.
>
> Rewards are distributed to those who, regardless of means, win student popularity and maintain high enrollments. Moreover, college teaching is much less demanding than the production of articles and books—as any honest professor will admit. To be increasingly rewarded for doing little is almost irresistibly attractive. The wonder is that 25 percent of the professors polled could stubbornly cling to their professional ideals by proclaiming themselves committed to the work of scholars. Surely masochism is involved.

A professor risks a lot by consulting or writing for the general public. The danger is yet greater if his services or his books earn money. By all accounts Erich Segal was a decent classist and a conscientious teacher, yet his position at Yale became miserable there after he made a fortune on *Love Story*. A professor may never afterward be able to shake the epithet "popularizer" if one of his books makes it to the general book stores. The level of exposition will be incomparably more lucid, thoughtful, and intricate than what his colleagues (and, indeed he himself!) employ in their lectures to college students. The logic of the "scholar's scholar" pursues the successful writer and goes like this: "My book is good and did not sell. Yours sells. Therefore it cannot be any good."[13]

The most frequent explanation for the pathetic quality and quantity of academic research—that the professors lack time due to their crushing teaching and committee duties—must be dismissed. Another claim—that the professors, particularly beginners, do not know how to publish—deserves consideration, but can be disposed of too. Their graduate training was research oriented. If their graduate professors did not hammer home the fact that research is in fact a public activity subsidized by public funds, the directing professors were grossly negligent. There are, in fact, good manuals on how to publish.[14] Beginners or laggards could call with respectful mien on their campus's "heavy producers" (almost every college or university with a faculty of two hundred or more has a couple) and ask how they do it. The genuine scholar would be effusive, for he yearns to talk intimately about one of his life's sustaining forces. The producer would describe with relish his strategies for hooking editors and might even lean forward in his chair to tell of useful articles or book topics that he knows could and should be carried off but that he just cannot get to. Similarly, editors of lesser journals, the lesser intellectuals' magazines, and the commercial presses have their own lists of topics that deserve skilled attention, hard work, and publication and have not yet received them.

Another explanation for measly scholarly output is hypothetical-statistical and proves conclusively that the editors of the several hundred scholarly journals and the nearly hundred scholarly presses would be inundated if each professor wrote the equivalent of an article a year and a book every five years. Therefore, out of consideration, most professors modestly hold back. The argument must remain hypothetical, for the professors do not write or research at this rate. The obvious journals such as the *American Historical Review*, *The Annals of the Association of American Geographers*, *The American Economic Review*, the *Psychological Review*, the *PMLA* (*Publications of the Modern Language Association*), *The American Sociological Review*, and editors of the Princeton and Harvard University presses are indeed swamped with workmanlike stuff that could appeal to a readership of 100 to 500 specialists. Alas, the editors at these places have to keep in mind a minimum paying public of about 1,500. Still, after the first cut, at these or comparable presses, numerous good things are excluded that might be published, if given to the right, but less obvious editors. Many editors at commercial as well as scholarly journals yearn for responsible, timely, well-written research findings that rarely get to their desks.

The cruel but true explanation for the meager scholarship on the campuses is that the professors just will not think hard and consecutively, pull their chairs up to their desks, return to their quiet laboratories after supper or during the summer vacation. Nor do many of them read with care the newer journals in their fields or attend scholarly congresses for the purpose of finding out where the exciting problems in their fields are likely to be in the years ahead.

Some of the blame for the dismal level of American professorial creativity may lie in ancient and narrow prejudices. Ever since Johns Hopkins University established the first scholarly journals in the 1870s and 1880s, status has been most emphatically acquired by specialized publication. The more specialized, the better. However, many universities now eager for fame would prefer that their professors publish trash rather than nothing at all. Opportunities for noble contributions to the intellectual ecumene are, however, plentiful. Professors who could do so, do not write book reviews or articles on local affairs for local newspapers or magazines. Perhaps they fear exposure close to home. All professors object to the texts they, all the same, require their students to read, but hold back from writing their own because they assure themselves that textbooks do not "count" much in the weight given to a vita.

A sort of exalted drudgery, scorned by American scholars, is that of translation, which, if the subjects were judiciously chosen, would enrich the American intellectual community far more than almost any equivalent expenditure of professorial work hours. It is sad and perhaps stupid that so few American intellectuals or professionals in many specialties have access to the work of the best French historians, the most daring German sociologists, the leading Russian educationalists, the liveliest South American novelists and poets, the smartest Czech and Hungarian mathematicians.[15]

Though official statements accommodate research and many professors claim to be doing research, relatively few professors are in fact, researching, and since this book is about all the professors, there is a justification for going lightly over professional endeavors showing such paltry results. And it is difficult to encompass well the variety of academic research the results of which take such forms as the historian's book, the anthropologist's description, the sociologist's correlation, the mathematician's proof, the painter's show, the sexologist's revelation, the literary scholar's annotated text; the archeologist's report, the criminologist's proposals, the economist's policy evaluation, the educationalist's sermon. However, in all these categories not much is produced.

If so few professors are capable of the sustained discipline necessary to bring forth the scholarship that, officially, their job descriptions require, how do they stay on—as indeed they do? There are a couple of sorts of scholarly drones who are recognizable on most campuses who need to be presented briefly here: One is the old gaffer hired God-knows-when and tenured shortly afterward who simply cannot be moved. He needs to do nothing and knows it and so does nothing except attempt desultorily to appear busy and to attack scholarship as useless and a sham. Such persons are immovable and still vote as they please on the promotion and tenure of their younger colleagues. Such deadwood most determinedly seeks to punish those colleagues ambitious to make reputations away from the local scene.

Another common type is the jittery man who is "working on" an eight-hundred-page book (or its equivalent in a nonbook field). He is always "working on" it and will describe to good friends how he tosses in his bed sleeplessly due to worry over the knotty problems in an analytical chapter at the beginning of volume two. The dedicated scholar may indeed at rare intervals publish an article indicating that, if the book were to appear, it would be more than creditable. The articles and his wickedly ironic, long book reviews and the promises of publication "soon" got the man tenure.

The fictive case finds factual analogues most often in the major research universities, where pressure for scholarly production can be most emphatically perceived. The great researcher may even be operated on for ulcers after a few years. He may see a psychiatrist briefly about his "block." Again and again the handing over to a publisher is delayed. In his will he leaves his notes, all seven shoe boxes full of them, to the university library.

A common type of nonscholar who flourishes is the "good" (sometimes "excellent" or even "superb") teacher. His prosperity is best assured in a giant institution where admission standards for students are loose and where the coaches care for the academic survival of their charges. The man is likely to be an amiable buffoon before very large numbers of students, a disproportionate number of whom are football players. The serious parts of his lectures are those parts near the end of the class sessions (which he regularly cuts short by five minutes) wherein he tells the students exactly what the questions will be on his short-answer examinations. He fails students rarely—athletes never. The coaches send him free tickets to the home basketball games, where he always appears. He spends much of his time in the stands in a nearly rabid state of passion.

This great teacher serves the essential departmental function of keeping high the "count" of students who register for the department's courses. When he encounters other professors on the campus paths, he deftly offers to exchange meteorological commonplaces or sagely predicts the imminent success of the intercollegiate teams. If some chairman or dean were to attempt to deny him raises, tenure, or promotion, he would encounter the wrath of the athletic department's magnates, who would apply pressure where it is effective—on the trustees. Sanctions for the teacher's doing no research whatever —particularly something as drastic as the threat of termination— rouse alumni whom he amused years ago and other professors of his sort, who with grand assurance (for accusations of slipshod, opportunistic "teaching" are unprovable) state that he is a "superb" teacher.

In sum then, regarding the performance of all American college professors, it seems clear that teaching adequacy is incapable of being proven and that per-capita scholarship is sparse. This leaves the third category suggested at the beginning of the chapter, service— which is a broad one. It is useful to recall here that universities are supposed to govern themselves. "Service" as applied to professors in a modern university most often means the energy they devote to self-governance. Modern universities are so diffuse, so rich, and so large as to be ungovernable by any means, but all subscribe to a myth of self-governance. What "self-governance" and "service" actually require is committee work.

Committees are of several kinds: university-wide committees, committees for various large, administrative divisions, and departmental committees. The universitywide committees of a good private university near Chicago are listed below, with the membership of each committee in parentheses:

Chancellor's Administrative Council (32)
General Faculty Committee (15)
Faculty Committee on Educational Policies (10)
Admission and Financial Aid (undergraduate) (18)
Animal Care Committee (10)
Architecture, Aesthetics and Physical Plant (10)
Board of Religion (8)
Board of Student Publications (7)

Budget and Resources Advisory Committee (7)
Computing Center (17)
Curriculum and Teaching Committee (8)
Environmental Studies Council (9)
Faculty Planning Committee (8)
Fulbright Scholarships (8)
Harris Lecture Committee (8)
University Appeals Board (6 faculty, 3 student)
University Hearing Board (6 student, 3 faculty)
Honorary Degree Committee (9)
Human Relations Committee (7)
Human Subjects Review Committee (16)
Intercollegiate Athletics (11)
International Studies Council (12)
Klopsteg Lecture Committee (6)
Naval Science Department (9)
Community Council (9 faculty, 9 student)
Administration (3)
Parking and Traffic Committee (10)
Advisory Committee on Public Safety (5)
Radiation Safety Committee (8)
Research Committee (18)
Science and Technology Interdisciplinary Center (12)
Senate Steering Committee (6)
Shaffer Lectures Committee (8)
Student Facilities Planning Committee (10 faculty, 4 student)
Student Health Services Advisory Committee (6 faculty, 6 student)
Teacher Education (10)
University Academic Committee (12)
University Press (11)

The college of arts and sciences of that same university has fifteen committees. Each of the eighteen departments in the college of arts and sciences has from eight to fifteen committees.

A university may have appointed or self-designated temporary committees for special purposes, such as those to establish a program for women's studies, a search committee to find a new dean for the engineering school, a committee to consider the best employment of an unrestricted gift of $1,200. A provost or a president may assemble by means of a few telephone calls an *ad hoc* committee to act on matters for which a decision must be made but for which he eschews responsibility. There can be ephemeral *ad hoc* committees to amend the rules for admission to the swimming pools and tennis courts, to meet with architects to save the trees and gardens menaced by the library expansion, to meet with student-government representatives to design an "equitable" teacher-evaluation questionnaire, to draw up a statement explaining why the libraries should stay open until 11:30 at night, to change the school symbol from an Indian brave to a comet. Committees usually gather every two weeks, late in the afternoon, and often work under a "gag rule" that requires that they dissolve after fifty to seventy-five minutes.

At their most useful, the committees may warn certain administrators who can, in fact, act decisively if they think the faculty's recommendations are correct. And, the obverse of the above, committees do permit some curious faculty members to learn what is going on or what is likely to occur. A committee works most effectively if it has stated purposes, the chairman prepares an agenda, and it is run according to *Roberts' Rules of Order;* it works most smoothly if it justifies policies already set. Athletic committees are the best examples of the last category.

There is a danger, from which persons approaching retirement seem to be exempt: that of taking committee duties seriously and of behaving determinedly on what seem to be urgent matters. The young man who knows his *Rules* and who has definite ideas which he expresses around the conference table risks being referred to behind his back as a "smart ass" by the administrators and the deadwood. He is likely to suffer for his cheek when his teaching and research are subjected to unusual scrutiny.

A corollary of the myth of self-governance requires that everyone serve on some committee or other. Actually, a little less than half of the faculty members do much committee work. For promotion, tenure, and raises it is prudent and indeed sometimes necessary to "serve" on a committee, but there is no requirement that anyone do anything while there. Many, perhaps most, members of committees inexplicably succumb to the temptation to talk. Some do worse and make dogmatic speeches or, worst of all, propose specific actions. The wise young professor always appears cleaned and pressed and on time, but heeds the old hands who advise quiet circumspection.

The embrace of "service" can reach far. The good academic citizen can be a faculty advisor for fraternities and sororities, Phi Beta Kappa, the 4-H, the bicycle racing club, the Rugby team (which flourishes apart from the athletic department), the Sierra Club, the Socialists' League (in which case the professor must wear business

suits commonly thought to symbolize right-wing Republicanism) or
the Young Americans for Freedom (in which case he should wear
jeans and affect some hippie jargon). These only suggest possibilities.
The duties of a faculty advisor to student groups often go no further
than signing their request for a little funding from the university's
student-activities budget. In any case, advisor's duties (if indeed they
are that) bring few plus points to a faculty member and are usually
assumed to be as harmless and as useless as the hobbies pursued in
the professors' homes.

Clean-cut and genial professors in provincial universities and colleges learn after a while that they must keep on hand a few forty-
minute after-dinner speeches that can be pulled out on short notice.
They need them for the Kiwanis clubs and chambers of commerce in
towns thirty miles away, the high-school assemblies, and the local
Hadassah. Professors of theology or philosophy whose courses or
research emit hints of a high moral tone are invited often to talk to
the Newman and Hillel clubs and to the youth organizations of the
Episcopal church and the Reform Jewish congregation. One can
plead indisposition or prior commitments or otherwise evade some of
these invitations, but not all of them. If a luncheon group of bank
vice-presidents invites a professor of computer science to show them
his slides of a trip taken eight years ago in Yucatan, he is on hand at
12:15 on Tuesday at the Marriot, bright and shiny and carrying the
department's carousel projector.

A professor is wise to state in his vita if he is chairman of the faculty club or the secretary of the faculty senate. To show that he is a
good liberal, he might list that he is on the advising board of the
NAACP, Planned Parenthood, the Cherry Hill Drug Crisis Center,
the zoo, the Mayor's Select Committee to Consider a Mall for Main
Street. In most places one gains luster rather than loses it if he
knocks on neighborhood doors for the Democratic party. In a few
other places, the Republican party is to be preferred.

Most official descriptions of faculty obligations state that service
ranks below teaching and research. At most institutions, particularly those ranking below the great universities and the good colleges
—service (broadly described) is, in fact, of much greater importance
in determining the professor's local prestige and, therefore, in determining his belongingness and his material rewards as well. "Service"
here, however, must be generously expanded to encompass what a
professor of physics in San Diego aptly calls "leverage"—the mani-

festations of which are quite impossible to suggest on a vita or which may leave but little documentary evidence. This point must be illuminated by four lightly fictionalized examples:

I. Two years before the tenure decision, Assistant Professor Leonard Fowle faces up and realizes that he has neither the energy, the wit, nor the vulgarity to become a popular teacher at the college. His case of writer's block is so grim that last summer he almost vomited from terror each of those few mornings he sat before his typewriter to rewrite (My God, yet again!) his dissertation for the University of Florida Press, whose editor three years ago expressed casual interest in the subject. Fowle was widely and accurately quoted after a party at which he referred to one full professor in his closely knit department as a "horse's ass" and to another as a "chicken hawk."

Fowle volunteers to take on the jobs of class scheduling, preregistration, and book ordering for the department, which he does adequately for two years. At tenure decision time the vote of the full and associate professors is too close, seven for—six against. However, the chairman carries the day with his two-page letter to the deans and vice-presidents which, though oddly lacking in particulars, praises his lackey's "exemplary teaching" and "scholarly promise" and which dwells on Fowle's "altogether devoted, energetic, precise, and selfless service."

II. Whenever possible (that is, about four days a week) Klorning eats lunch in the faculty club of the big state university. His wife plays bridge with the wives of elderly professors in the law and medical schools. Though Klorning teaches in international studies, he is the shortstop for the English-classics-art baseball team and drinks beer with them after the biweekly games. He is on the phone a lot, both local and long distance. He listens mostly. He is known to nod and wince empathetically with students who tell tales about unfair professors in Klorning's own and in all other departments. He and his wife are often the confidants of all the aggrieved parties of the especially squalid divorces.

Klorning will call on anyone with information that can prompt action. He keeps the dean informed of the efforts of the chairman of the anthropology department to get the chairman of the chemistry department to hire his possibly alcoholic nephew who is about to be fired under not-so-mysterious circumstances by a teachers college in Louisiana. Klorning tells the secretary of the board of trustees that not only has the university architect been demanding 5 per cent of all contracts, but details of his methods and his successes have just become cocktail-party gossip among the more established bankers and lawyers of the town. The architect is released three weeks later with a warm letter of recommendation. Klorning knows how much everybody paid for their houses and how much of the total price was down payment. He knows how much Kaminski of automotive engineering will inherit when his sickly mother-in-law finally dies. He knows the figures before and after inheritance taxes. Klorning knows which departmental secretaries put out.

However, Klorning releases only innocuous information to those who demonstrate no legitimate (in his eyes) need to know. He is always busy. Who cares if he fails to show up for many of his classes, if his lectures are disorderly and bumbling, and if he never reads (much less writes) anything whatever?

III. Old Crax has taught constitutional law for twenty-five years. He wears clean, old suits, black oxfords, and small rimless glasses. His paunch is large enough to inspire gentle jokes, some of them made by Crax himself. He is president of the local chapter of the American Association of University Professors. He sometimes takes the university president and a couple of the vice-presidents to lunch. Three years ago when organizers of the National Education Association started visiting the campus, he made vigorous speeches on the need in the "troubled years ahead" for faculty solidarity—under AAUP guidance. However, Crax quit this saber-rattling when the NEA organizers left. When Crax learned that one energetic trustee despised his next-door neighbor, Hobble of chemistry, and that the trustee expressed a determination to turn the university upside down in order to prevent Hobble's third wife from getting an assistant professorship in statistics, Crax advised certain members of the faculty, including Dr. (Mrs.) Hobble's intended chairman that, alas, the nepotism rule installed in the faculty manual in 1953 was, in this case, still enforceable.

Crax tells the president and the trustees that the business professors were quite livid upon learning that their new building will have vinyl-tile floors and windows that will not open. They are meeting in the evening about it. One accounting professor is even threatening to examine the contractor's profit-and-loss sheets. The architects revise the plans so that the business professors have wall-to-wall and fresh air.

IV. Leona Reine is one of the university's three female full professors. By all accounts she teaches her classes responsibly. She gives occasional papers at the regional conferences. She is dainty and wears rouge. Her dresses are a little out of date and are still a little too young for her. Her voice is musical and she flirts incessantly and harmlessly.

Until three years ago Leona was as unapologetically ignored as any woman on the campus and she too was angry, though terror of being suddenly discharged and a visceral revulsion kept her from the assertive younger women on the campus. Then, all at once, Leona got a bigger office of her own and her salary jumped $5,000 from the bottom of the associate-professor range to the precise middle of the range for full professors. Now she asserts that any woman who is competent and who keeps her nose out of other people's affairs will be recognized at the proper time. Hence, those women who are badly treated are, in all likelihood, bad professors. She is invited now to a remarkable number of official functions and to more parties thrown by university administrators than her husband, a modest highway engineer, would really like to attend.

Leona is on the university's Affirmative Action Committee, the committee for women's studies, and the faculty welfare committee. These committees have various functions, but Leona's special function is always the same: to urge caution. When other women claim (or prove) callous discrimination, Leona points to herself and says, "Look at me! I'm not being discriminated against." And the deans and chairmen also point to "sweet Leona" as proof of the university's fairness in dealing with "truly qualified" women.

The militant women on the campus refer to Professor Reine as "our queen bee."

Several matters in the pages above have touched on disputes within the universities that revolve around "service" and "leverage." Since these disputes also occupy professors' time on the job, they merit coverage even though the incessant stirring up of these cans of worms brings no one gain of any sort. Gathering these matters under an additional classification called "bitching" allows the covering of much more of what officially and unofficially can be considered as professors' work.

The usual *general* complaint or bitch consuming lots of time and conversational energy (though little application or precision) is against "the administration." This entity, briefly described, is a staff, numbering roughly 10 per cent of the number of professors. Along with their clerical workers, these bureaucrats inhabit a centrally located building also called, conveniently, "the administration." Academic deans, particularly in small colleges, might not be included in the bitching against the administration, but all officials above them are. Most administrators are former faculty members. They are well-paid, well-meaning, undertrained, and grossly overloaded with responsibilities. Since the academic bureaucrats know quite well how breezily professors are able to fashion their working and living conditions, the administrators rarely let themselves become harried.

Administrators expand, contract, and maintain the university. All these are more difficult to accomplish than running a city or a large corporation. As usually perceived by professors, the administrators' duties seem to be to welcome the schemes of enemies of the professor in question and to thwart the plans of the professor himself. The administration cannot accede to the demands of the "Ad Hoc Committee on Economic Justice" because to employ more female professors and to raise the pay of those few on hand would be leaping across the principle that hiring responsibility rests with the academic departments. Administrators in such states as New Jersey, New York, Georgia, Alabama, and Wisconsin cannot let ambitious, interdisciplinary groups of professors start a Doctor of Humanities program because there just will be no more state or even federal funding for new graduate programs.

The perfect parking place is under a solid roof and empty except when the professor's six-cylinder station wagon occupies it. The perfect parking place is five feet from the elevators leading to the professor's office. At no time is the arrogance of the professors more blatantly displayed than when their parking committee finally gets the vice-president in charge of campus facilities and planning to appear before them. The roster of the committee is complete and additional interested professors have been allowed to participate in the show. The following are quotes gleaned via long-distance telephone from friendly professors who overheard them: "I hunted for thirty-five minutes and got so damned upset that my headaches came back. So I drove right home and had to cancel my classes for two days" (Wayne University, Detroit). "I had to walk a mile, yes, at least a mile to get to our building!" (Northwestern University). "I absolutely *demand* that my students be on time and then *I* was seven minutes late for my ten o'clock class!" (University of California at

Irvine). "I was wet clear through and my shoes were muddy because I forgot my galoshes. It was hellish!" (Kansas State University at Manhattan). "Well, why don't you *tow* the students' jalopies away, instead of just giving them tickets?" (University of North Carolina at Chapel Hill). "That's tough, Adelman, I had to grab the Health Service physician's reserved space, because I absolutely could not miss another meeting of the graduate council. You can double that five-dollar fine every two weeks until it equals the book value of this madhouse. I simply won't pay it" (University of Michigan at Ann Arbor).

Nowhere is it officially stated that the title of professor relieves its holder from the need to walk a short distance in good or in bad weather to his job. However, almost no professor with four rubber-tired wheels at his command doubts that his employer must assure that the passage from residence to job will take place without annoyance or effort.

Professors find it both elating and easy to bitch about the library. This category of bitching is eschewed by those educated abroad or who have researched abroad. For these know that library collections and services available at respectable North American universities are far superior to what alert and richly productive scholars employ usefully elsewhere. Still, the supine librarians are maligned in their presence or otherwise. Some misogynists shout at the overworked, sallow catalogers or reference librarians so that they will weep. A medievalist who but seldom will crack one of them open may demand to keep all 221 volumes of Migne's *Patrologia* . . . or the more than 500 volumes of the *Monumenta germaniae historica* . . . in his office, claiming, "No one else in this dump would ever crack one of these open." A professor of Spanish literature learns that the library's copy of the book he published eleven years ago on Unamuno is missing from the stacks and concludes that it has been stolen. He loudly expresses his indignation in the faculty senate. Actually he is flattered that at least one reader wants his work badly enough to steal it. Another professor in Minnesota, on the verge of retirement, pesters the academic vice-president to fire the acquisitions librarian. Since the library possesses them already in photocopied reprints, she refuses to pay the $10,000 he demands (the sum had long been anticipated as part of the purchase price of a cottage in Cuernavaca) for the unbroken runs of mathematics journals in the old gaffer's office.

The libraries are, like the universities, imperfect. Things get lost, they stray or, more often now, are stolen. The demands to acquire are far more urgent than the pressure to process and maintain properly. Scholars who are working (always a tiny minority) know they will be frustrated in any library at hand and have options—such as purchasing printed or photocopied materials they need for their research. They may buy a lot of books. The shrillest bitching ("How can I possibly finish my article if that dizzy flit doesn't replace the missing concordance to Horace?") is done by men who would do nothing, if the New York Public Library were a stroll away.

The symbiotic cohabitation of the teaching, research, and service college and university with the intercollegiate athletic program troubles many moralists. A few young and idealistic faculty members go through a three- or four-year crusading phase in the course of which they delude themselves that changes are possible. Some acknowledged working intellectuals quietly tell them to "keep up the good work." Some frightened distance runners or baseball players, begging the preservation of their anonymity, may call on the crusaders to reveal the similarity to prison life of their incarceration in the athletic dorms. The crusader may even shame the chairman of the athletic committee or the president of the university into sadly agreeing that the athletic program wastes years in the lives of good young men, that the publicized balance sheets of the athletic director show losses that are a fraction of the real deficits.

The crusaders give up, always. Nothing can be done. Once the athletic programs have been solidly established (something that occurred, in many cases, fifty or more years ago) almost no public and few private institutions have been able to place them in a position of respectful subservience to a college or university's purposes, that is, teaching, research and service. Athletics is a quietly corrosive issue causing far more damage to the professors' self-respect than others might expect, for it shows that their employers are dishonest. The responsibility of professors to query, examine, criticize, and publicize meets a solid wall regarding athletics. Here the professors are without influence. Any changes in the athletic programs are arranged by the coaches.

But reasonable professors who reluctantly acquiesce in the preservation of a large and costly, victory-oriented athletic program may be forced to do so because professors alone are unable to produce any unequivocal, comprehensible, or vivid evidence for the taxpayers, their student-clients, or the general public of the legitimacy of the professors' labors. Indeed, if large numbers of the taxpaying, tuition-paying public were to want, devise, and apply performance criteria to the professors, would the professors be able to show that their teaching, research, and service are demonstrably worth what is paid for them?

Leaving questions of values, ethics, and morals aside (as one must in such a case), at the football or basketball games—or in the replays on television or in the newspapers—the students, alumni, and taxpayers viscerally experience and emotionally perceive their institution. Even when the teams lose, the perception is vivid, substantial, sympathetic, and therefore favorable. A young, powerful, clever, and winning quarterback is a far more satisfying representative of "State" than any dozen professors. The cheerleaders appeal at once and more often to deeper, more substantial desires than some buffoon occasionally called a "superb" teacher, or a thin book whose appearance caused rejoicing by only two hundred other, dry professors, all of them far away. A stadium with its green infield, the homecoming queen, the drawling baseball coach, and the team's tiger or mule or bear are vastly more energizing and indelible symbols than the university's Latin motto, its unsingable "Alma Mater," and the outrageously expensive and laboriously assembled library collection. All this may be vulgar, but these are the facts. It is sometimes claimed by noble professors that their less noble colleagues abdicate moral and economic responsibility by accepting the status quo, that is by continuing to let the academic university legitimize the illegitimate and costly sports university. It may be the other way around.

As a summary here: The job of a professor encompasses a variety of duties which are classifiable under the official headings of teaching, research, and service, to which might be added the important but unofficial one of leverage and the useless, time-consuming one of bitching. The proportions of expenditure devoted by departments and especially individuals varies a great deal, but in general we can say that professors see themselves essentially as teachers.[16]

It is generally known that professorial existence is characterized by hazy divisions between life on the job and life off of it.[17] Some professors at least attempt to do their jobs well. Many do not. An adjective that is often applied by his associates to a comfortable colleague is "collegial." "Collegiality" is, in fact, the best quality a professor can have. Below is a fictive sketch of an Ideal Colleague:

Ideal Colleague is short and a little portly and wears his hair in the style that was usual among graduate students when he was writing his dissertation at Harvard. I.C. knows that his degree (while adding luster to his department) might be held against him, so he eschews the Brooks, J. Press, or Chipp clothes he used to wear and could easily afford. He wears brown suits and some conservative polyester knits purchased locally. He also labors to be cleanshaven and well-pressed before his lectures, which he regards, though he never says it, as difficult, semisacred performances.

I.C. always lectures. He uses no films or premanufactured illustrative materials, or, indeed, any sort of supplementary material aside from a seven-phrase-long outline of his lecture, which he chalks on the blackboard behind him before the class begins. He invites no guest lecturers nor does he let his teaching assistants lecture, confining them to grading the examinations for his large classes. His students are asked to read only a standard textbook. He awards few A's and therefore ambitious students avoid him. His failure rate is quite low, but not quite as low as that of the frightened lush who gives a notorious "crib" course. I.C. has been called a "good teacher" for so long that no one ever questions the accuracy of the appellation.

I.C. always teaches the statutory nine hours, never requesting the six that many of his colleagues scheme for. He passively discourages graduate students from taking his rare seminars, but when he does give a seminar, his declared standards are very high and his grades astonishingly generous. He knows that graduate students are builders and destroyers of reputations. He muses modestly aloud to his friends about the need for a new lecture course that only he could teach, but never begins the campaign (troublesome to everyone) to get it listed in the university catalog.

Long ago, a leading journal in his field published a chapter from his Ph.D. thesis. The twenty-six-page article had seven long footnotes per page. Publishing scholars in his field elsewhere know him because he enthusiastically praises every book he reviews, though the reviews are submitted very late. Due to his special kind of scholarly fame, he is asked to review two or more books a year. Each book review is about a page or four hundred words long. If asked if it is indeed so, he will not deny that he himself is "working along" on a large book that is a "major extension" of certain problems first posed in his dissertation.

I.C. is often seen walking rapidly in or out of the central library carrying under his left arm paper-clipped sheets of yellow, legal-sized paper, xeroxes of printed material in several languages, and tiny boxes of microfilms. When he is anywhere near the library, he is frowning and is difficult to distract. Elsewhere, however, his "Hi!" is cheery in an exemplary way. Though obviously a consecrated scholar, I.C. never asks for research funds. He applies for no fellowships nor even sabbatical leave. Obviously his is lonely work. However, he progresses steadily on his important project. It is always clear to the department's nonresearchers that his major publication is so far off in the future that it threatens them scarcely at all. Still, his devotion to research requires that he spend many hours in his lockable carrell in the library. For the whole academic year 1973–74 a vengeful librarian he once scolded before other librarians regularly used a master key to check his carrell. The librarian knew that I.C.'s principal occupations while so isolate were to suck wintergreen Life Savers and to read the complete works of George Meredith.

I.C.'s university committees are those on commencement, honorary degrees, long-range planning, and academic standards. This last committee has the job of readmitting (or not) those undergraduates who were once suspended. I.C. is a pushover for a sad story. In the department he is on the library committee and the undergraduate teaching committee. These last committees rarely meet. In none of the committees is it necessary for I.C. to speak and I.C. always votes for the most generous course of action. He is also the department's fund-raiser for the Red Cross and the Community Chest, to each of which he himself gives a hundred dollars yearly. His organizational obligations for these charities require him to put the local offices' appeals and pledge cards in the mailboxes of the members of his department and to keep track of the contributions that trickle in. He refuses invitations to speak to community groups, because the topics he is best prepared to talk on as an expert are of interest only to a few dull scholars—and many of these are not even Americans.

I.C. seeks no leverage. The president and the various vice-presidents and deans know him only as a dependable man who works very hard to maintain the highest standards at the university, yet who never causes any trouble whatever and who is friendly to everyone. I.C. has no friends in other departments. In the department his friendships are not close. He listens intently and with great forbearance to those of his colleagues whose feelings have been hurt, but says nothing while deftly encouraging them to tell all. He knows a great deal more about old scandals than he lets on, yet he keeps all entirely to himself. The chairman is wrong in believing that I.C. keeps him up-to-date. I.C. resolutely shuns any crusader who is notorious and is particularly standoffish to those assistant professors who, it seems clear, are likely to be let go.

His wife (who has some money of her own) demands that they have two parties a year, for their house is large, faultlessly maintained, and comfortably furnished. The first floor looks rather like a Christian Science reading room. One party is from 5:00 to 7:00 on the last day of fall registration; the other is from 8:30 onwards on the Friday just before the Christmas vacation. She sends out engraved cards that have at the bottom, "Regrets only, please." She invites the whole department plus spouses and all the line administrators between I.C. and the president. She also invites the chairmen of several other departments.

She hires two bartenders, a cook, and three serving maids. At both parties the drinks are inexhaustible and the manna includes three varieties of Harvey's and three varieties of Cockburn's sherries. For the Christmas parties her specialty is little quiches served very hot. I.C. and his wife wrangle before every party over the caviar. And she wins, but is allowed to put out only a small dish. I.C. apologizes to some professors for its appearance and to others when it is quickly gone.

I.C. fears always that his WASP origins, his expensive education, his hygiene, and his coolness may offend his colleagues—almost all of whom have one or more traits associated with Jews and blacks, as well as poufs, lushes, bankrupts, and several sorts of psychological cripples. Over the years his conversational speech has become slovenly, though his diction while lecturing is consistently impeccable. He kept his children in the public schools after the imposition of busing. He teaches summer school, explaining that he would otherwise miss the "stimulation" of teaching and that he "could use the money." Every three years or so he drinks too much scotch at another professor's party, dances with a faculty wife rumored to be loose, says "fuck" a few times, and after a brief, loud argument, lets his wife drive him home in the Chrysler Newport. In the course of the next week he confesses to the department's gossip that he vomited the whole following night. Stories of such antics suffice to characterize I.C. as "a lively guy, if you can only get a few drinks into him."

If we could follow I.C.'s career to its end, we would see that the raises and promotions come in an orderly fashion. His good health will hold. He will be allowed two year-long extensions to teach after the mandatory retirement age of sixty-five. He then will garden and work along on his major scholarly contribution. Elderly and then ancient, I.C. will appear, his robe trimmed with Harvard's scarlet, at every fall and spring commencement. At the enormous funeral the Episcopal priest will be instructed to make a statement about how disappointed scholars "over the entire globe" are that the emeritus professor did not live to complete his great book and will praise the corpse strenuously and repeatedly as an "Ideal Colleague."

Illustration E:

WYLIE LOGAN
OF THE SATELLITE CAMPUSES
OF LOUGIASEE STATE UNIVERSITY

Wylie Logan squirms his small behind well into the driver's seat of the ten-year-old Karmann-Ghia, nicks with a long fingernail some crust from the inner corner of each eye, and buckles up. Today, a Tuesday, is one of his long driving days. The two-lane road to Paris, in the northern part of the state, goes through rolling farm country, now bright green and pink in early spring. Wylie's natural optimism is buoyed up by his usual visit to the Park and Chat, a drive-in diner where he flirts with Lu Ann, a pale waitress, who, though still young, wears a black wig and has beige teeth. Wylie downs three cups of bad, weak coffee. They joke, as always, about how both of them are too busy to "get together sometime."

Wylie needs response to his flirting and gets it. He is sallow and is just starting to lose his short brown hair. But Wylie has nice blue eyes that wet easily when he is being appreciated and a swooping Tartar mustache planted beneath his nose, which is almost too small. His red lips part easily to show his little, perfect teeth. He moves about almost incessantly but gracefully.

Today Wylie is dressed in his "straight" costume, composed of low J. C. Penney work shoes with translucent soles, J. C. Penney chino tans, a pale blue dress shirt, an old striped tie, and a tweed sports jacket with the label of the best men's store in Louisville. Wylie bought the jacket for $3.75 at a Salvation Army nearly two years ago, immediately upon learning that he would be teaching as "adjunct" faculty at the satellite campuses.

At home on the main campus and when he teaches in Grandee on Monday, Wednesday, and Friday, he wears his preferred outfit: L. L. Bean moccasins, gray T shirts stolen from the athletic department, Lee Rider jeans, and a much-patched Levi's jacket.

One hundred twenty miles from the bustling capital there is no parking problem at the Paris campus, which is of new, one-story, red-brick construction in a spacious scrub pine tract at the edge of an enormous shopping center. Just before 9:30 Wylie has set up the two screens and the two carousel projectors, each containing forty slides. These materials are essential for almost all the meetings of Art 7471, "The Triumph of Art in Modern Times." In subject matter and even in the slides he uses, Wylie's course is a near duplicate of the one Professor Louis Canning teaches at the main campus. Indeed, Wylie prepares for his 7471 lectures by closely reviewing the notes that Lorna, his girl friend, takes in Canning's classes the week before. Canning likes Wylie and readily gives him his lists of slides—which consist almost entirely of avant-garde painting since that genius Picasso first dazzled Paris (France) with his incandescent brilliance. Wylie further prepares for his lectures by reading an art-history textbook other than the one he and Canning assign and also employs some of the rhetoric he picks up from the magazines that cover the New York, Chicago, Houston, and Atlanta gallery scenes.

At first the Paris students—a mixed bag of six teenagers without jobs, an equal number of smart children too poor or too timid to leave home, and four jittery housewives—had an I-dare-you-to-teach-me attitude. But Wylie won them over. He is especially heated and convincing when a student, confronted with a color slide of something that appears indisputably nonsensical, asks, "Do you really like that, Dr. Logan?" The words "beauty" and "beautiful" gush from Wylie on such occasions and he buttresses his enthusiasm with phrases he first heard from the lips of painting professors at the University of Dayton as well as from professors at the great state university. Wylie knows well that the best policy when one is required to teach something about which one knows little is to praise without restraint those things that are acknowledged by all to be praiseworthy.

Wylie's class examinations—based on slide identification and recall of Wylie's descriptive phrases—are also similar to Canning's. However, Wylie knows that the standards of the main campus cannot be applied way out here in Paris. His grading is generous. He gives A's to those who show up and appear to be trying, C's to those who do not show up, and B's to the rest. Since Wylie began adjunct teaching, he has never heard a murmur of discontent with any aspect of his performance. He has no supervisors and, happily, all of the courses he has taught so far have no prerequisites and are prerequisites for no other courses.

Wylie gives his 7471 class a five-minute break after forty minutes of volubility and slides. They assemble again for another twenty-five minutes, and Wylie releases them a little early at 10:40.

For several months last year Wylie Logan had a few of his own canvases in progress set up in the corner of the painters' studio at the Paris campus. But the paintings progressed scarcely at all, since he was only in Paris on Tuesdays and Thursdays and he had to leave so soon for the base. Now Wylie usually drinks coffee and eats lightly in the Paris cafeteria, reads the Houston *Chronicle* and chats warily with some resident full-time members of the Paris faculty.

At 12:45 he draws back the patched top of the Karmann-Ghia and drives in a southwest direction. He chuckles the last half hour of the ninety-mile drive after drawing close to read the bumper sticker, "Put Your Money on Jesus!" one he had never seen before, on a dusty Ford pickup in front of him. He suppresses as always the laugh that wells up within when the MP at the gate salutes him after a hard inspection of Wylie's special pass. The base had a contract with the university to offer twenty courses a semester from at least ten different arts and science departments.

Art 7471 for the twenty noncommissioned and commissioned officers is the same as in Paris, but the atmosphere is not so nice. The men devotedly take notes when Wylie speaks. Their responses to Wylie's performance almost always have as their object to get their teacher to repeat a phrase or a sentence—an act that is difficult for Wylie to perform, since he has no prepared script but is inspired almost entirely by what is praiseworthy in the slides. All these men are being relieved from other duties to take courses for which they get transferable college credits at the state university. The neatly creased men do not like bouncy little Wylie, and the atmosphere is tense, almost eerie. They endure him. Sometimes, when a few of the men snicker or snort, Wylie stammers helplessly in the semidarkness and the backs of his hands prickle with strange sweat.

During the fifty-mile drive back to the main campus in the capital, Wylie begins at once to anticipate with pleasure his Art 1001 class, "The Expression of Basic Design," which meets Mondays, Wednesdays, and Fridays from 9:00 to 11:00 at the Grandee branch of the university. At Grandee almost all the students are amiable, handsome, eager-to-please black teenagers whose college educations are being paid for by federally funded scholarships. Wylie's "Basic Design" requires that he get the forty-five children to "trust" him, "to loosen up visually," and to "express themselves" "sincerely" in "assignments" or "projects" covering line, light, color, texture, mass, spatial relationships, and volume. There are no tests. Sincerity and attendance (declared mandatory by the grant supervisor at Grandee) get the kids an A. It is all fun, and happily the Grandee campus is only thirty-five miles from Wylie's apartment.

Actually the compensation of fourteen cents a mile for driving 750 miles a week contributes to Wylie's prosperity, since the "VW" costs far less to operate. The bulk of his income, of course, comes from the adjunct teaching, for which he gets $765 per course. Therefore, his income for teaching a nine-hour load for the academic year is $4,590 plus the profit of about sixty dollars a week out of the mileage allowance for the thirty weeks a year he drives. From this money Wylie lives well. At the sprawling apartment on the edge of the campus, the windows rattle in the wind, but rent is only ninety-five dollars per month, including water and heat. When Lorna, also a painting student, finally moved in last winter, she brought with her a six-hundred-dollar stereo, a five-foot shelf of soul and soft rock music, and a three-hundred-dollar-a-month allowance from her mother. They drink little. Indeed, in no way are they gluttons and can make an ounce of good grass last two or three weeks. Wylie also has a big, dark blue Kawasaki and flies to Atlanta when he feels like it. A nice life.

All the same, Wylie is restless and sometimes complains that this life is not rich enough for him. He has always been nervously in motion. As a senior at the University of Dayton he began sending color slides of the oddly tinted, fuzzy, watercolor nudes of himself to noted graduate art departments. In the paintings his ordinary glans penis was clearly lined in colors of fuchsia or orange and stood out glowingly, much like the women's bandanas in Corot's landscapes. Several state universities offered Wylie Logan exemptions from tuition and measly graduate fellowships to work for the degree of Master of Fine Arts—which, for someone in the studio arts, is the highest degree and the essential qualification to become a college professor of painting. Lougiasee State offered the best deal: $2,600 per year in addition to the tuition exemption.

Wylie, who was then twenty-five, began graduate work in the fall of 1971. The M.F.A. program at the university required lots of art history. During the lectures Wylie took few notes, but whenever possible he deftly flattered old professor Canning. He worked most devotedly with the resident painters, both of whom were abstract expressionists and each of whom hated the other's guts. Both courted Wylie, however, and helped him through his stylistic periods. For a while it was desecrations of the American flag—the montages actually included pieces of dirty old American flags. Then it was wildflowers painted on long sheets of silver Mylar. Then portraits of people who were clearly old, but who had no faces. For almost a year Wylie painted immense pastel canvases covered with overlapping tiny *w*'s. For these works the expense of the chipboard, canvas, and oils in tubes briefly brought him to a condition where his outgo was more than his income.

A gallery owner in Atlanta invariably greeted Wylie with puppy-like happiness when Wylie dropped by dressed in his Lee Rider and Levi's jacket outfit. Wylie could have his own show (the gallery owner would take a 40 per cent commission) as soon as he could gather twenty or thirty paintings in a style that Wylie, his two painting professors, and the gallery owner all felt was "really, sincerely, Wylie Logan." The show would also be acceptable as a "creative thesis" and would thus round off the formal requirements for Wylie's M.F.A.

The degree, the slides of the paintings, the verbose reviews, Wylie's teaching experience, and (not least) Wylie himself would all together make a neat package, a desirable prospect, even in these difficult times. As assistant professorship would pay double his present earnings for no more work and, naturally, far less driving. He would have a studio of his own, and the professorship would give him various other advantages to offset the principal disadvantage, committee work. All in all, a cheering prospect.

But somehow, Wylie just could not "get it all together." He had periods lasting four or five weeks during which he painted ecstatically, like a man possessed. But then Canning or another professor or even another graduate student would remark:

"Pollock did that in 1949."

"Somehow, Logan, those chopped-up stars and stripes don't *speak* to me."

"Castelli said last week that from now on, big canvases like that are *out*."

"I don't know, Wy. Those chunks of art are dynamite. But are they really, I mean really, *you?*"

He got depressed and waited for another inspiration.

Since Wylie began work as an adjunct instructor in the fall of 1975, the jolts of inspiration have been distressingly infrequent and brief. During the summer of 1976, he and Lorna went into a frenzy and in three weeks turned the apartment's shabby living room into a sleek, perfectly outfitted and lighted studio. But the driving and teaching take away pizazz as well as time and render it impossible for Wylie to set aside blocks of days for the creative concentration a great artist needs. Lorna does not paint much either. They find that when they are alone, slight movements, sometimes the most ordinary gestures of affection, ignite them both and they eagerly go off hand in hand to make love desperately and ingeniously until they arrive at a state of adoration and satisfaction so complete as to make any activity other than the one just reveled in seem paltry, egotistical, and ridiculous in comparison. A good life, remarkably free of hassles.

Now it is quite true that Professor Orville O'Connell, the art department's director of graduate studies (and the only member of the department Wylie fears) has been threatening to send ultimatums to M.F.A. candidates who have been "hanging around too long." The good reputation of the department has to be maintained and they need to admit "fresh-blooded," "younger" graduate students. Wylie is sending out his curriculum vitae along with two slides of paintings done in each of his periods in attempts to find some kind of job if O'Connell's ultimatum should be imposed. The replies from the little colleges are always that, if they had a position, they would hire only someone whose degree was completed.

Another looming worry for Wylie is Lorna, who is only twenty-three. She has whined lately that she wants to "learn more about life" and seems to be ever more aware, as Wylie long has been, of the predictable consequences of flirting, which she indulges in with obvious relish. Her most recent targets were some professors in other departments at the university and a few other mature men who showed up and stayed long at their parties.

But it is still a delicious life. Since Wylie has finished his course work and since his teaching is under no supervision whatever, he spends most of his free time at the apartment. Lorna is a plant freak and Wylie loves, just as she does, the sprawling greenery. All their friends are funny, generous, and sincerely interested in Wylie's and Lorna's futures. The magnificent stereo faultlessly and incessantly plays the young electronic music of love and yearning spirituality. Everything would be just fine, if Wylie could only get the paintings out and did not have to drive so much.

VII

Students and Professors in the Late Seventies

The present preoccupations and fears of the professors are occupationally specific. However, the professors' unease is attributable to a weakening faith in our economic health and a decline in optimism generally. The debacle in Viet Nam, the exposures of grotesqueries in the highest levels of government (and the general acknowledgment that irresponsibility antedates and will follow Richard Nixon), a mistrust of growth—all these matters have effects or corollaries among those professionals who have been especially well nurtured by the American higher-education system.

Academic liberals are naturally chagrined that the architecture, the enrollments, and the nicer working conditions that their old professors yearned for have not brought about an appreciably better society or a more elevated level of American culture. Twenty years after the conversion of national and local politicians of all parties to the task of expanding higher education, we face embarrassing disclosures and the likelihood of constraints on the occupation of college professors.

In fact, the professors' glorious days which were at their best about 1965 or so have not ended at all. Only the hardest pessimists are preparing for reversions to those earlier times when men now sixty or so had to teach fifteen to twenty hours a week and when the acceptance of an academic post meant that one resigned himself to a life of genteel crust wiping. The professors foresee no sudden decimation of their numbers. Financing for higher education has continued at generous levels. The diffuse but effective education lobby in Washington seems unassailable. In addition, state legislatures appropriated $12.5 billion for higher education for the academic year 1975–76—an increase of 28 per cent over the year 1973–74.[1] It is only when the professors project recent trends into the future that their collective paranoia is aroused and their volatile morale tends to evaporate more quickly.

Within their own ranks, the prosperous professors have not themselves responded with disclosures or self-abnegation before the larger society. The requirements under federal laws conveniently summed up as "Title Nine" that require an end to sex discrimination in higher education cannot be met without major erosions of departmental autonomy, which the professors have stubbornly resisted. The professors (really some researchers among them) now endure humiliations when the national magazines publish the titles and costs of some of their federally subsidized projects.

Increasingly governors and state legislators are requesting explanations of how professors spend their time to determine how they earn (if indeed they do) their salaries and perquisites. Several governors facing urgent demands for inadequate revenues have not been prevented from learning that the nine-hour teaching load refers to a weekly burden, not a daily one. Productivity (a word that makes professors bristle with defensive arrogance) has certainly declined at the state universities. In Nebraska, Governor J. James Exon noted that, despite nearly static enrollments since 1969–70, the college and university teaching faculty had increased 29 per cent, administration 120 per cent, and total university employment 44 per cent.[2] Michigan's governor, William G. Milliken, said in his state-of-the-state address in January 1976 that though outlays in higher education had increased 148 per cent in the past ten years, enrollments had risen 43 per cent and the consumer price index 71 per cent. Sherman W. Tribbitt, governor of Delaware, noted that higher education now took ten cents of each tax dollar and commented, "Intelligent support is one thing; aimless subsidizing is another."[3]

Public officials at all levels are questioning a custom that allows professors who are state employees to charge two hundred dollars a day for consulting, plus expenses (and this includes Ramada Inns, $4.75 breakfasts, and lots of taxis), for advising state agencies. One might list a lot of sensitive indicators suggesting that, while the lives of few professors now working have been badly altered, things will get worse. It is psychically disheartening for working professors to *feel* that their palmiest days were some ten years ago. Peering into the future gives rise to gloomy foreboding or itchy paranoia. These are the new and dominant moods in the academic lounges, offices, and committee meeting rooms and these are all background for the incessant, informal gossip sessions.

A piece of bad news for everyone was the widely publicized acknowledgment by the College Entrance Board in September 1975 that average scores of high-school students on the Scholastic Aptitude Tests (SATs) had fallen sharply. These scores had been decreasing slowly since 1963, but after 1974 they had declined ten points in the verbal section (to 434) and eight points (to 472) on the mathematical section. The other important body that statistically appraises high-school students' preparation for college work, The American College Testing Program, revealed comparable declines in the ACT scores. The declines, particularly in the number of scores in the upper ranges, were absolute and not attributable to the much larger numbers of high-school students who now take these tests. Educators have been mystified, but have tried to explain the declines as due to the poorer quality of high-school education or really (as one might expect of public-school educators) the lack of adequate financial support for public education.[4]

The deterioration in beginning students' precollege preparation has been noticed by professors everywhere. Academic administrators responded variously to the news:

"The truly brilliant scholar is an ever-decreasing commodity, especially for the expensive, selective college."

"If there are 20 percent fewer students scoring above 600 (on either the verbal S.A.T. or the mathematical S.A.T.), some colleges will have to recruit more of the lower-scoring students."

"The most logical explanation is the advent of a 'new student' in higher education—the type who would not have considered going to college because he lacked traditional skills. Now . . . students such as these can find programs designed for them in college."

"In most general terms, the decline presents colleges with a difficult instructional challenge."[5]

Ever since the foundation of those hundreds of little colleges early in nineteenth-century America, the teachers in those places and, later, those in the larger institutions that grew out of them have worked with the raw material of their calling. Their clients and reasons for employment have been, for the most part, ignorant youths. At present, the jobs of the "new" (that is, rigorously and expensively trained) professors depend ever more on meeting the "difficult instructional challenge" of "new" (that is, worse-prepared than ever before) students. Though enrollments doubled between 1962 and 1972, demographers have predicted a declining pool of high-school graduates (whatever their skills might be) to draw college enrollments from. All this suggests that the expanded professoriat, in order to hang on to the high enrollments that are the without-which-nothing of the occupation will indeed confront some difficult instructional challenges.

The great numbers of new students have, in fact, been altering the professors' occupational lives for a while now. The irrelevance (and conceivably incompatibility) of the traditional liberal-arts curriculum to the amiably ignorant has long been obvious enough so that the curriculum's constituent parts are in advanced disarray. Enrollments for courses in history, government, philosophy, and mathematics, most particularly at the upper-division level (that is, for juniors and seniors), where they are not required but "elected," are declining. Professors with vested interests in these and related subjects have been losing a long battle to keep as mandatory graduation requirements courses in these areas at the lower-division (that is, freshmen and sophomore) level. The irreversible decline in foreign-language study in America is indicative here. In the four years preceding 1974, when college enrollments were still increasing, enrollments in foreign-language courses decreased 15 per cent. The sharpest decreases were in German and French.[6] At the same time, the proportion of institutions requiring foreign languages for graduation declined from 46.8 per cent to 23.3 per cent.[7]

Even at the colleges and universities resisting recent trends students flock to courses that are interesting or easy or that can pose successfully as "vocational." It has become obvious to the clear-eyed that the survival of the college and university professors (at least in something like their present numbers) will depend on their devising market strategies based on an educational product that is some fetching combination of the easy, the interesting, and the purportedly useful.

The booming departments on the campuses now are those of journalism and speech, which may be combined as "communications," a word and an area with envied drawing power. Some journalism professors believe that their heightened desirability is due to the brave persistence of a few hero-reporters in exposing the Watergate horrors. Some appeal for these chic areas of study might be due to the intellectually slight, but exciting, up-to-date reading imposed by the professors, who also depart rather frequently from the lecture method. Traditional professors in old disciplines gnash their teeth at news of the enrollment gains in journalism and speech because the educationalists' slovenly rhetoric and their gentle performance standards have also infected these newer "disciplines," which are not disciplines at all.

Sociology, anthropology, and psychology have not declined as the humanities have. Most subsections of these areas are immediately interesting, and some promise a little kinky fun. The professors in these areas, especially the younger ones, are so appealingly unprofessor like. To undergraduates these courses, particularly those in clinical or abnormal psychology, hint at supplying scientific implements for revelatory introspection—an obsession of our age. It also seems obvious to those students with employment in mind that we cannot possibly have too many people to assist others in their own constructive introspection or therapy. And so psychology departments promise to offer degrees that many think will be marketable.

The wise department chairmen in most departments actually encourage the devising of deftly labeled courses that promise solid titillation. Examples are these courses taken from a recent undergraduate catalog of the University of Texas at Arlington:

Architecture 2346, "Communication Skills"
Art 3316, "Fashion"
Communication 4320, "Radio, Television, Film and Society"
Education 1131, "College Adjustment"
English 2334, "Technical Writing"
Military Science 0180, "Leadership Laboratory"
Sociology 2308, "Women in the Modern World"

Similarly, a dean of pharmacy seeking splendid enrollment figures offers classes for "nonmajors" at the popular time of 10:00 A.M. Monday, Wednesday, and Friday in the biggest auditorium on the campus on "Drug Abuse in Modern Industrial Society." The kids see lots of movies and read some sober stuff that assures them that they can safely blow all the grass they want and even trip once in a while if they arrange the atmosphere carefully. Avoid coke, and no smack ever, please. And everybody gets an A or a B. The English department tries to counter hemorrhaging enrollments of its courses in poetry and the novel and so fills rows of upholstered seats in new

auditoriums with the many hundreds of students who watch flicker-
ing old movies. *The Battleship Potemkin, The Triumph of the Will,*
and *The Children of Paradise* may be murky in parts, but in the
darkness one may doze without fear of exposure, and in sum the
courses on "The Film as Art" are vastly more appealing than any of
the courses in criticism. Attractive professors teach the movie
courses, and their own appearances in the flesh are mercifully infrequent and/or brief. Similarly, chairmen try to have their younger and
more toothsome male or female professors teach courses in science
fiction, criminology, sexual stereotypes, or fitness.

A pathetic reforming trend in the old departments is the vogue to
rename and to advertise courses. The political scientists attempt now
to make their offerings more appealing by inserting "violence" and
"dissent" into their course titles. Reluctantly, old-time historians will
rename their "France: 1789–1815" as "Revolution, War, and Napo-
leon" or "The United States: 1865–1914" as "The Transformation
of Our Society in Modern Times." The lectures, of course, remain
the same. Art historians advertise their renamed course listings with
pretty posters placed on all the campus bulletin boards. The posters
contain Callot or Picasso vignettes.

The bidding for enrollments can take some curious forms. *Esquire*
in September 1976 listed a selection of our universities' most appealingly named courses. One is not much astonished to learn that
fundamentalist Bob Jones University, sometimes called "the buckle
on the Bible Belt," offers Church Administration 401, "The Minister's Wife," for two credits or that the University of Florida offers a
three-credit course, Ornamental Horticulture 463, "Physiology of
Closely Clipped Grasses." But, it is odd to learn that the University
of Wisconsin offers Physical Education 740069, "Carnival Acro-
batics," that Cal. at Berkeley offers Extension Course EDP 014381,
"Cartooning and the Comic Strip," that Harvard University in its
catalog lists Afro-American Studies 124, "The Black Preacher as
Teacher," and Brown offers Afro-American Studies 113, "Sound
Awareness Brother Ahh."

Departments and, more particularly, the professors within them
struggle to maintain their F.T.E.'s. These letters are much used in
the colleges and universities now. They stand for "Full Time Equivalent" and are a statistical tool that indicates drawing power by dividing the department's or professor's enrollments by the average study
load—usually fifteen—of the full-time students. Departments and

professors compete with others for F.T.E.'s by easing up on the less appealing aspects of college life over which they have control. The professor known to require written work in the form of term papers or even essay (that is, written) examinations rather than the multiple choice, fill-in-the-slot-with-a-soft-lead-pencil variety is likely to discover after registration that masses of students turned him down in favor of those professors who have adapted better to the times. Ever fewer students are willing (able?) to devote their time to assigned reading.[8] In order to indicate respect, textbooks may indeed be assigned, purchased, and carried from class to class, to the student union, and back to the dorms. However, professors at other than the most selective colleges dare not apply sanctions if the "outside" reading or written work is not done, for they would have to fail from half to three quarters of their students, which would be very bad for their reputations and, consequently, their enrollments, and their F.T.E.'s.

"Grade inflation" has been under way for some years in academia. Part of the chic for consenting to a student "voice" in university policy in the late sixties was the trend to eliminate the D and/or not to penalize a student's unsatisfactory performance in a course but simply to substitute "NC" (for "no credit") for F (which everyone knows is "failure"). So now in the colleges and universities, ever lower performance criteria are combined with much higher average grades. In June of 1975, 70 per cent of Harvard's graduates were in Phi Beta Kappa. In 1965, 14 per cent of the grades given in the history department at Northwestern University were A's; in 1975, the figure for A's was 49 per cent. In fact, the average grade in American institutions has increased a full grade over the past fifteen years just as the caliber of student work has been falling. Some educators explain grade inflation as the individual professor's humane adaption to ever higher criteria for college transcripts that are set by employers of college graduates and by admissions officers at the better graduate and professional schools. Some possibly sincere professors claim they give A's to all or almost all the applicants for the insufficient seats in their classrooms in order to protest against the "punitive" or "infantile" grading system. But these same professors also know that, due to methodological problems and the sacredness of their classrooms, teaching effectiveness cannot and will not be measured. The sole indication of effective teaching that an administration can employ and the one most susceptible to corruption (particularly when students seek entertainment and high grades) is class enrollment.[9]

It is increasingly common for high administrators to threaten the cancellation of classes and the removal from the university catalogs of courses which do not "draw" a minimum enrollment of, say, twelve for a lower-division class, eight for an upper-division class, and four for a graduate class. So, good professorial "drawers" are essential in order to maintain departmental and college-wide "counts" of enrollees—who, all the projections tell us, are going to be a scarcer commodity in the near and distant future. The bidding for enrollments has produced ominous results. Professorial morale is wretched in the language and mathematics departments and, to a slightly lesser extent, in the science departments, because the already low performance requirements simply cannot be further compromised.

Many professors in all departments have capitulated to demands for eased requirements and good grades. Some make a practice of flatly informing students what the answers to their examination questions will be in order to be able to give a locally acceptable number of passing grades. Early in the semester some may actually inform the students of the days when their "review" sessions will be so that they need not appear for regular lectures.

One outcome (if not a direct result) of the "disturbances" by ideologized and energized students in the late sixties was that most young professors surrendered a traditional means of control of the classroom by ceasing to take daily attendance for what were claimed to be adults answerable to themselves alone. At the merely respectable and worse institutions, half or more of the students may stay away from classes in government or philosophy unless the classroom performances are remarkable. Opportunistic professors are able to come up with techniques that satisfy almost everybody. Geographers or sociologists in four-year colleges may promise to "give" lots of "cuts" of scheduled class sessions for which the students are not required to appear and, of course, the professors do not appear either. Another recruiting and holding technique is to shorten class meeting times. It is well known that certain professors in certain departments, even though they still take attendance, let their seventy-five-minute classes go about fifteen minutes early. Indeed, the professor with such a reputation may find that after about fifty-five minutes of his talk the book shutting, chair creaking, and foot shuffling of those seated before him have become so intrusive as to indicate to him that indeed his lecture is about to end.

A professor of gerontology at a branch of the University of Maryland has evolved an imitable method of maintaining enrollments and attendance. He gives A's to those few students who meet what might be called modest requirements for both his introductory and his advanced courses. Minimum performance merits a B except for those students who cut more than ten of the forty-three scheduled meetings or who fail to appear for the scheduled examinations. These last mentioned get C's. As a result, this professor has high enrollments, good attendance, and consequently feels secure in his position. An unfortunate aspect of his job, however, is the almost palpable resentment of the sullen B students who appear regularly before him only for the good grade.

Unless the professors can come up with some better indication of teaching effectiveness, the brutal focusing of his higher-ups on enrollments is going to become worse. To bureaucrats in H.E.W., state legislators, trustees, and deans, enrollment figures signify (*faute de mieux*) success or failure and are auguries of the future. Leaving aside the question of whether there is or is not value in academic residence and the degree ending it, real substance in the form of guaranteed loans and various other federal subsidies, both to the students and to the institutions, depend on enrollments almost exclusively.

The institutions recruit material to demonstrate enrollments in several ways. A few private colleges advertise the pleasures of existence on their pretty campuses in the *Wall Street Journal,* and the *National Geographic.*

The following ad headings in block letters could be found in the "Spring Survey of Education" supplement in the New York *Times* of April 25, 1976:

New Yorkers Grow at the New School

Antioch is . . . Wherever You are, and Whatever you Want to Be

There's only one YU [Yeshiva University]

Come Ski With Us [Weber State College in Ogden, Utah]

Regis College Measures up for Today's Woman

College Bound? There's room at the Top [New York Institute of Technology]

The readers are asked to request catalogs. Many of the larger ads list the special programs or some courses the schools offer. In the provinces, many universities send out recruiters to high-school assemblies assembled so that sixteen- and seventeen-year-olds can hear declaimed from yet another source the advantage of (from the point of view of the recruiter, a particular) college education. Some recruiters are paid bonuses for each enrollee in a private school who actually appears on the scene in early September to pay the tuition.

Southern public colleges and universities are now particularly eager to attract capable blacks, many of whom bring not only special, federally provided tuition grants but a federal bonus per student for the institution itself. The classics department of a huge state university may send out announcements to the state's scattered high-school Latin teachers for the university's annual "Greek and Latin Saturday" early in April. The mathematics professors might also ask help from high-school math teachers for participants in *their* Saturday a week later. After the kids are bussed into campus, they get a couple of light lectures from young professors. They see the newer dorms, the cleanest cafeteria (where they enjoy a roast-beef lunch on the house), and the football stadium. The potential majors are presented rosy views of the job opportunities for classicists or mathematicians four years hence.

Chairman of government and political-science departments in New England now send out their more appealing assistant professors, male and female, to provincial high schools to give talks on "After Watergate, What?" or "Assassination and Our Time." The recruiters are expected to weave in a pitch for tentative majors. Naturally the best catches are the capable students, but incapable ones cannot be scorned. And the pitch to the last mentioned can be justified by many state universities' "remedial" programs.

The remedial wave is a recent one. Administrators are more aware than professors are of the importance not only of recruiting material, but of keeping it around once it arrives on the scene. Hustlers from the education schools have done nicely by obtaining government grants and institutional go-aheads to assemble teachers and workers of subaltern rank to teach "basic skills" in labor-intensive (and therefore expensive) "reading labs," "writing labs," or "study labs." These functions may be grafted onto the existing administrative structure (possibly in "institutes") and apart from the academic departments. Though expectations of student performance have plummeted the past five years, departments still take on responsibility for these (secretly called "dummy") courses most reluctantly, which, in view of the new emphasis on enrollment, is not prudent. However, Alan M. Hollingsworth, the chairman of the English department at Michigan State University, has learned that if one attempts, as he and his troops have, to teach reading to college students using methods in accord with modern linguistic theory and therefore not approved by the education schools' theorists, they get sniped at by the educationalists as well as by the mandarins in the usual disciplines.[10]

A promising way to keep up the "count" is to record as enrolled those young persons elsewhere and not studying. Little Antioch College in Yellow Springs, Ohio, pioneered in devising programs in which work or travel apprenticeships were integrated with the traditional intellectual training that took place at the college. Now many, if not most, large colleges and universities will grant, after the shuffling of petitions and the gathering of signatures, a semester of credits to juniors and seniors who take jobs as various and as uncollegiate as working for six months in a Venezuelan mental hospital (Spanish, psychology, and history), a German bakery (German, business administration, and home economics), or an Israeli newspaper (Modern Hebrew, journalism, and political science). The students, of course, pay tuition at the home place. More than 150 colleges also give college "credit" for "life experience," such as study in a Franciscan seminary, army service in Tokyo, and police work in the Public Morals Division, to students *before* they begin course work at the college itself.[11]

As in the larger society, the distrust of ideology and the creeping pessimism can have a brighter obverse, which on the campuses is a languid live-and-let-live milieu for which the luxurious parks are suitable settings. Of course, the honor systems are now only nostalgically recalled. Years ago, say as late as the mid-fifties and especially in the South, students used to maintain among themselves systems to guard against cheating and to punish those who were caught. But the only campus in the University of California system with the honor system now is the one at Davis, where it is believed to be "ineffective" or a "farce." At Johns Hopkins, which has kept a small and very selective undergraduate college, the students voted to end their fifty-one-year-old honor system after a poll revealed that 30 per cent of the students admitted cheating and that 70 per cent had seen cheating and refused to "rat."[12] The cheating scandal at West Point was mentioned earlier. Plagiarism is so common now in respectable and worse colleges that most professors no longer attempt to prove obvious cases. It is easiest to fail the student if the professor is certain the work was done by someone else and to tell the criminal that he will change the grade if the student can prove that the work is his alone. The student is asked to present his notes and earlier drafts of the paper. In some freshman composition sections almost half of the papers are plagiarized. Helplessness in combatting plagiarism is another reason for the decreasing demands that even conscientious professors set for courses. Some professors in second-class, but larger schools are so dismayed by plagiarism that their graduate students do annotated bibliographies and not "original" papers.[13]

Despite the innovation of enforcers similar to supermarket checkout clerks at the university library exits, enormous numbers of books are stolen anyway. Sheltered in their study carrells, graduate students and, one suspects, a few callous faculty members razor out of the scholarly journals the articles they desire free of cost and for their own use exclusively. The head librarian at the Virginia Military Institute was recently arrested for stealing books from the Institute's library. Police said they found a large number of books at the home of Lt. Col. George B. Davis. Mr. Davis had shortly before announced his plans to retire and to open a rare-book store in Millbrook, New York.[14]

Unlike high-school teachers, whose work their labors (however brief they may be) come increasingly to resemble, professors outside the big cities rarely encounter boorish disrespect. The professors, even those who are martinets in their classes and who demand old-time standards of student performance, are still treated with generous forbearance. On the other hand, about 60 per cent of the professors now in place were hired after 1965 and are likely to be tolerant of dirty toes at the end of bare feet in the front row, the slurping of iced Cokes from styrofoam cups, the ever-so-slightly embarrassed 20 per cent or so of their students who trickle in during the fifteen minutes after the lecture has begun. It is as though the students and the professors alike long ago gave a subliminal wink to each other to acknowledge that the loosely structured life at the university is preferable to any conceivable alternative and that it is senseless on the part of anyone to set or to meet unreasonable requirements.

The students, more of them than ever before, have never looked better. One result of the turbulent late sixties, the end of style in dress, has been an effulgent, endlessly contemplable variety of costumes. The fact that most of the new students are surely yet more healthy than those who preceded them, and are more assured and ignorant besides, perversely increases their erotic appeal—for they engage the nervous intellects of the professors less than ever before. The professors ravish them with their eyes.

It is difficult to offer proof, but one could suspect that there may be some further erosion of the taboo regarding sex between professors and students. Two recent novels, Richard G. Stern's *Other Men's Daughters* and Alison Lurie's *The War Between the Tates,* deal with affairs between professors and graduate students. The young women cause severe dislocations in the personal lives of professors of biological and political science respectively, but, significantly, the affairs do not threaten the professors' professorial reputations.[15]

Comparable to the published schedule of attractions at a very large, very expensive and well-run resort, the ringing of bells, the examination schedule, and the degree requirements indicate to those paying for it all that there is at the universities a program and a goal. Conventional learning is expected and is still likely to be accomplished by most of the enrollees at the famous, elite schools. Most students at the urban universities and at the junior colleges commute, and so their lives are rooted in their homes or their work. But elsewhere the students are most sincerely devoted to enjoying themselves or one another in their dorms or shared apartments. If a professor should drop in on the students in such places (an event that scarcely ever occurs), he or she would be astonished at the unspeakable pleasures suggested by the whiffs of mystical incense covering the nutty aroma of stale cannabis, the insipid or slamming rock music, the dark nooks to sleep long and alone or playfully and experimentally with beautiful friends. The professor would smell the shot semen, the anguished sweat, the experimental perfumes, the sloughed-away fat of young Americans growing up apart from, though tolerant of, the professor's educational intentions.

The professors may have ever less control of their own fates as well. The threats of the federal government to require the hiring of women and minorities have been mentioned. That the professors are not teaching successfully or researching much cannot help but become more widely known. There are threats that work may increase.

Wages may fall—or at least fail to rise as the price level does. Still, careers in college professoring are immensely attractive to thousands of people who have been prepared or are being prepared by the graduate schools for just such careers and who have or will have the hard-earned credentials and every other qualification for such employment. Except, of course, the offer of a job.

It seems unlikely that professors now working will remain exempt forever from performance criteria or, at the very least, an examination of just what they do to earn their substantial salaries. Even now, many institutions are beginning certain "faculty development" programs intended to improve the effectiveness of their teaching. The Lilly Endowment finances some of these programs. The federal government's Fund for the Improvement of Postsecondary Education subsidizes others. These programs, which now exist in over four hundred (mostly small) schools consist of seminars and (yes!) lectures for faculty members on how to teach better. In some cases the object of a program is humane—for example, to retrain black professors of agriculture at Florida's A. and M. (formerly all-black) University. Some blacks who might have enrolled there for agriculture courses now go to the formerly all-white University of Florida. Almost everywhere, participation in the development programs is voluntary. Still, by their very existence, the courses in how to teach better challenge a ruling assumption in the academy—the one that any Ph.D. can teach. The day may not be far off when a professor must prove that he is concerned about how he can best impart his knowledge of his subject matter to his students as well as the value to the students of this knowledge once they have it.[16] The most frightening assumption that may be built into the "faculty development" programs is the one that unsuccessful teaching might be attributable to the teacher and not alone to stupidity or laziness on the parts of those who appear to be taught. On the other hand, it has not occurred to many who labor to raise the quality of college teaching that the students for whom the improved product is designed might be disinterested or incapable of absorbing any significant part of the traditional curriculum however seductively it might be presented to meet the "new" students' presumed (to use an educationalists' phrase) "learning needs."

Whether teachers or students are to blame for faulty teaching, there is widespread awareness among the administrators of America's two-year colleges of the lack of training in teaching given

in the graduate schools. Mr. Robert J. Leo, director of special services of the Dallas County College district, set up some courses for
English teachers in the Dallas–Fort Worth area because of a general
"feeling that the universities were turning out people who were too
theoretical, faculty who knew English, but didn't know how to teach
it." A survey made by Robert McCabe and Cynthia M. Smith of
seventy-two community-college administrators in the Miami area
revealed that in considering a teacher for employment, most administrators opposed "strong preparation in a single discipline" and favored "multidisciplinary preparation." Skills and attitudes rated
highly were a commitment to "the open-door philosophy and to
working with a more complex student body" and "good interper-
sonal skills."

Like any up-to-date program launched by a trained social scientist,
business administrator, or educationalist, "faculty development"
brings with it subsequent evaluation procedures. Evaluation of college and university teaching requires that professors submit to examination (by others, in most cases) of their stated course objectives,
their organization, their rhetoric, their employment of audio-visual
supplements, their use of the fifty- to seventy-five-minute periods,
their actual supervision of outside work, the clarity of the problems
posed on examinations. And a chilling accompaniment of all this is
the imposition of "visitation"—that the professors must submit to
having supposed teaching "experts" or, worse, their own colleagues,
or, worst of all, administrators sit in on their lectures to pass judgment
on their professorial performances.[17] Evaluation of teaching customarily also requires that students fill in machine-readable forms
that allow them to record anonymously their judgments of professors' adequacies.

A machine-gradable form with seven gradations from "highest" to
"lowest" plus an "X" for "don't know" is used at the University of
Kentucky. Each student is asked to grade his or her professors on
the basis of fourteen questions, asking, for example, whether objectives were made clear, whether the professor encouraged student re-
action, and whether the student thought the professor graded fairly.
Question 13 asks, "Considering the previous 12 items, how would you
rate this teacher in comparison to all the others you have had in the
department?" and 14 asks, "In comparison to all others you have
had in the institution as a whole?"

It is an indication of the all-pervasive tolerance (or perhaps carelessness) on the campuses and the enduring prestige of professors that, except in the case of gross incompetence or sneering provocation from the lectern, the judgments by students of professors are usually so kindly and respectful, that student evaluations discriminate but little between a rather good teacher and a rather poor one.

Evaluation—which really implies, even if clumsily and inchoately, some sort of performance norms—is now beginning to be suggested for other areas of professorial endeavor. The vogue in the general society for seeking out objects worthy of blame and for muckraking and the stringency of public fiscs has inspired nightmares in professors who are unable to justify with hard evidence of accomplishment their $16,571 salaries[18] for a workyear of thirty nine-hour weeks. However, within the colleges and universities professors are agonizing or preparing reluctantly for performance criteria that may be more rigorously applied before there are raises, promotions, and, should it come to that, retention or its opposite. With stagnating enrollment and smaller budgets, who should be retrained, assigned heavier teaching loads, endure salary cuts, or (Jesus Christ! Could it really come to that?) "let go"?

Departmental promotion and tenure committees and university committees on forward planning and faculty welfare are now consumed with devising procedures for determining specific criteria for evaluating teaching, research, and service. They seek the impossible, which are criteria that will be just and that will still not frighten anyone unduly.[19] Many of these systems include weights to be assigned to various types of professorial work. It is the weight given to work under the heading of "research" that is most frightening. For here the product is most easily examined and, as it turns out, is most conclusively found wanting. As was observed earlier, fewer than 5 per cent of the professors—and these are heavily concentrated (though still a minority by far) in the classy, big places—are consistent, productive researchers.[20] About three quarters of the professors in the course of their lives have published little or nothing.

Those who devise and seek to apply performance criteria to all professors propose to do so in order to be fair—fair to those who pay their salaries, fair to the youths who, it is claimed, apply to them for instruction, fair to ancient ideas of scholarly or scientific usefulness, and, most especially, fair to those professors on the campuses in question who do indeed devotedly labor for the above-named groups.[21] The previous chapter claimed that often in the

North American colleges and universities the teaching is ineffective, the research paltry and the service trivial. Few professors can admit to themselves or to others that they are substandard in any of the areas named. On the other hand, the rare professorial bird who believes that he is a paragon in all of these areas is likely to be, in addition, an insufferable rate-buster whose *hubris* could very likely bring in its train the disingenuous application of evaluation criteria by other vengeful professors determined to get him out of the way.

Declining enrollments, constricted financing, competition for ever fewer goodies, and discussions of performance criteria have increased the demand for a new kind of administrator to replace the "excellence" developers and brick-and-mortar men of the sixties. The most successful swashbuckler on our campuses now is the Hard Man.

H.M. is usually "brought in from the outside" (that is, he is hired away from another institution) and imposed as a chairman on a frightened, reluctant department after he has assured the academic vice-president and deans that he is indeed capable of shrinking the old fief and lightening the campus of its "deadwood" in order to improve faculty "quality." Once installed, he uses the word "quality" a great deal in the departmental meetings. He stacks the departmental Promotions and Tenure Committee with yes-men, and warns, "If we don't make the tough decisions, they [the administrators further up the line] will." If H.M. does indeed manage in two or three years of his incumbency to "let go" a few languishing untenured professors or (more remarkable yet) a couple of *fainéant* tenured ones, he could be a choice candidate for a deanship—usually elsewhere. For the havoc his standards and methods cause in terms of roused paranoia and assembled enmities make the atmosphere in his disrupted department one of resentment seeking vengeance. Worse yet, when H.M. departs, he often leaves the "producers" who he arranged to be brought in to replace the deadwood (almost all of which remains in place) to face the music of those who long for and who will scheme for their carelessly constructed version of the good old days.

Of course, the peculiar institution of tenure is an obstacle that is difficult for the "Hard Man" or any other reformer to get past. Even when drunks, schizophrenics, or disruptive fools who happen to be tenured have abandoned the classroom, colleges have customarily kept incompetents on rather than face the trial of the offender by his peers. Harassment can take the forms of frozen wages, the assignment of take-it-or-leave-it "research" jobs that must be done away from the department in little offices, in "institutes," or in the recesses of the library, and the obliteration of the loser's name from official communications. But even harassment has been rare in the recent past. Loose academic accounting and the customary absence of any performance criteria kept the screw-up, if he chose to stay on, hidden until his retirement.

Most academic administrators know now that a slipshod error of the boom years was the all-too-ready award of tenure. If one projects a no-growth model on the American academic plant, as indeed one must, the conclusion is inescapable that only a small proportion of those few who will get professorial jobs in the future can expect to enjoy that privileged condition.[22] Of course, few of those aware of what has taken place since 1970 assume that tenure will endure in its present form. Alternative forms of protection for academic freedom and the long gestation period that major research projects may require—for example, five- to seven-year contracts or sharply lowered retirement ages—would still leave the job of distributing or removing job protection to the professors' peers, which means that professors would, as they have in the past, protect those who are likable and nonthreatening.

The infrequent removals of professors for "adequate cause" have almost always been justified by the phrase in the AAUP's 1940 "Statement of Principles on Academic Freedom and Tenure" that permits the discharge of tenured faculty "under extraordinary circumstances due to financial exigencies."[23] Our professors know very well that "financial exigencies" are now with us and will intensify in the years ahead. The interpretation of "extraordinary" is likely in the future to fall to administrators whose ability to hold their own jobs will be based on their willingness to make tough decisions.

One often-posed defensive strategy for frightened professors is unionization. It is a fact that the higher up on the prestige rankings the professors are, the more likely they are to consider themselves self-regulating professionals. Prestigious professors compare themselves to the physicians or lawyers who set standards of admission and performance by means of their organizations such as the American Medical Association or the American Bar Association. There has been noteworthy progress toward the recognition of college-level teachers' rights to organize, to bargain collectively, and to strike over certain issues.[24] With a few exceptions—notably in New York City,

Florida, and Massachusetts—organizers of the American Federation of Teachers or the National Education Association are most successful in geographical areas where unionization is well advanced in other occupations and where working conditions and the images the professors have of themselves are closest to those of the teacher-workers in the high school. In other words, unionization moves forward mostly in urban four-year or in two-year "community colleges." A lot of economic deterioration and a transformation in professional attitudes will have to take place before one is likely to see a strike for better working conditions by the faculty of Davidson College in North Carolina or of the University of Houston or Montana State University. And one wonders whether many boards of trustees and the education committees of state legislatures will accept closed shops on the campuses along with the occupationally specific privilege of tenure.[25]

Despite the alterations or expectations described above in the atmosphere on the college campus, these changes have still not affected in many concrete ways the lives of the several hundred thousand college and university teachers now on the job. Efficiency snoops are not taping for evidence professors who lecture too simply, too abstractly, or too briefly. Uniform grading curves for certain departments are being only discussed, not imposed. Though teaching loads are no longer decreasing, only in a few places have they started to increase again. Young men or women who failed to publish largely and prominently in the course of their initial five-year appointments at Columbia University or at Yale are still being cut, but now are unlikely to find decent jobs only one tier down. Excepting areas such as the big public institutions in Wisconsin, New Jersey, and, most especially, New York, which have severe financial troubles, few professors who publish a little solid stuff or a lot of trash now fail to get tenure. It is more likely now than in the past that those who publish absolutely nothing at a respectable school may lose their jobs after five years. The actual requirements to hold a job once obtained remain modest. In most places staff reductions are being arranged by not replacing retirees or those lost through other kinds of attrition.

Serious losers in the constricted job market have been those college teachers (so often women) with part-time, "temporary," or "visiting" contracts, which are not being renewed yearly as they were in the past.[26] Almost everywhere some "adjunct" professors, who worked on a year-to-year basis, are notified in March that their contracts are not renewed for the next September. There are as yet no serious attacks on the committee-led concept of self-governance. Evaluation procedures and performance criteria are evolving (only evolving, let it be noted) for teaching and publication, but not yet for service. As things are now, presidents or other administrators who actually try to run their institutions decisively on the basis of some sort of declared program will call forth furies of all sorts. The drift continues.

Earnings remain good, though since 1972 faculty salaries have not kept pace with inflation. Several states, among them Florida, Georgia, Texas, and Rhode Island, have frozen academic wages. But the sniping at the well-being of the academics has not yet produced much serious economic discomfort among faculty members with jobs.[27] In 1975–76 the average salary for all ranks, both sexes, at all institutions, of $15,571 does not include summer-school teaching, the income of working wives, and other bits and pieces that boosted median *family* income to a figure in excess of $23,000. In 1974–75 one tenth of all academic families took in more than $40,000 from all sources.[28] Most full professors can still afford a nice house, two cars, expensive college educations for their bright children, and the regular placing of what is left over in growth mutual funds.

In terms of family income for the academic year 1974–75, the average academic was far better off than the average family ($12,836) or the average college graduate ($20,124). Indeed, it appears that the professors are doing all right.

That is, until one looks rather deep beneath the surface. The professors are planning. That same capacity of the good pupil and student who is not yet a professor to measure the prospects before him and to get large assignments in punctually compels the professors to look ahead. The auguries are grim. The occupationally specific crystal ball that academics all peer into reveals no more "education" presidents or governors as in the past, but in their places, cost accountants and performance judges with stopwatches and tally sheets. The students of the future appear to be sparser on the campuses and seem especially fuzzily outlined about their pretty heads.

What the peerers into the future perceive in raspingly sharp detail and in threatening colors is thousands of hungry, grasping men and women in their late twenties who are thin and have hooked noses. They have smooth, sunken cheeks, and "Ph.D." is stamped on their foreheads just over the deep, vertical wrinkles separating their eyes.

The dark eyes dazzle with good health and ambition. The figures look like they could work like oxen and they clearly all want professorial jobs. Professors now uneasily on the job foresee a "lifeboat" or *tirage* period ahead.

The three playlets below have recently taken place in good American academic departments which, until about four years ago, prided themselves on harmony. A diligent collector of tales could record hundreds more that would all make the same point—morale is bad and decorum is declining. The names have been changed in order not to single out a few of the many, many professors who are frightened and are therefore behaving badly.

I. For two days now everyone in the English department at one SUNY campus has been whispering about the "two-megaton" meeting in which Oliver Bork, the new chairman, only suggested mandatory classroom visitations. Old Bill Phant, his fine orator's voice trembling and then breaking at the end, should have asked for a few clarifications before he shouted at Bork:

"I have taught my classes here for ten years, and you, especially, will not come into my class unless I want you to. And I, by God! don't want you to."

Bork should not have tried to qualify gently, because he stammered too much and thus roused his Sancho Panzas, Archie Florin and Alex Drachman, who also erred in shouting, almost in unison:

"If we don't set standards for raises in the years ahead, the goddamn deans and the trustees will."

This made Maxine Deeping and Eddie Kirchner cry. Right then Bork should have dismissed the whole pack rather than clumsily (everything he does is clumsy) trying to restore order—all the while rousing more people to shout insults or murmur, "Disgraceful! Disgraceful!". Bob Bernberg then poked his long-nailed index finger into the chest of sweet old, pudgy Freddie Cranston, who never hurt anyone in his life. Really the solid people in the department should have demanded an immediate adjournment rather than merely sitting there rocking with their heads in their hands as the scenes went on.

II. The Katzes of Columbia, Missouri, will have no more of their big faculty parties. Last weekend their guests drank almost twice as much hard stuff as they ever did before. Debbie Parson broke two pieces of mother's Haviland and laughed shrilly as she apologized. That shit Lundberg, whom Hal Katz had always defended despite his rudeness, ground out a cigarette on the second-best Chinese rug.

In years past, Sherry Katz would end the party by yawning frankly as she looked at the last few guests and saying loudly, "Hal, darling, let's go to bed, so these poor people can go home." Exit laughing.

But this time Phil Brazely gave his wicked imitations of each and every dean or chairman of other departments immediately after these personages left and in front of those still on hand while they looked unsmilingly on. Barbara Hobbing remarked too loudly that Georgie Lanten's latest sport jacket (Who cares what the guy does in the privacy of his own apartment or when he's in St. Louis?), which had an art-nouveau pastel print, made her think at once of tutti frutti. The old enmity of Korn and Park finally reached the point where they shouted and actually jostled each other in the backyard. Next time those two might start slugging by the Tiffany lamp.

And what kind of "clarifications" (almost the only word that Hal Katz could understand in the slurred monologue) did Harvey Altberg want of some remark Hal purportedly had made about Harvey to Ernie Blassingame in the corridor by the drinking fountain April before last? And then for a whole hour and very late, Harvey slurred New Jersey English to Reggie Sleigh, who slurred back in Oxford English. The Katzes could not tell what they were complaining about, could not interrupt them, and finally ordered both just to "Get out!" at 2:25 A.M.

By then it was far too late to clean up the place before hitting the sack. Sherry and Hal Katz had to face it all the next morning. Upon comparing notes, they concluded once again that the biggest eaters and drinkers were those who do not ever invite the Katzes back.

Nope, no more big parties. From now on it's only dinners of a baked salmon or onion pies for "a few nice people we really like."

III. Herm Peikko is one of those known to be wavering on the critical tenure decision for Steve Kehr, who has nothing of substance to recommend him as a professor except for his restrained, quiet behavior. The new dean has told the chairman that he will hold the department responsible for maintaining "quality" at this second-rank state university in Virginia. What this means is that the department that hired Steve and kept him on these seven years must now let him go and not place the onus for the atrocity on the administrators. If the department does not fire Steve, there will be almost no chance of getting any new positions and damn few promotions of any sort for years ahead.

Steve's students complain about his monotonous voice. Herm does not doubt that Steve's backaches, which serve as excuses for him to cancel so many classes, are psychosomatic and that Steve really hates teaching. His messy desk is piled high with what looks like the materials someone in his field would use to do research. The piles change in appearance but no publishable research has ever appeared. Steve Kehr has been seen cultivating his roses, which he enters in the state fair, just after he called to say that due to a sinus infection he could not make the universitywide Discipline Committee's meeting.

Steve has good manners. It takes him a long time to do so, but he reads lots of his colleagues' manuscripts to cleanse them of grammatical and spelling mistakes. In happier times—that is, about five years ago—Steve helped Herm build the Peikko's rock garden. Sylvia Kehr took Alice Peikko's kids into the Kehr's house both times Alice went to Esalen. Steve and Sylvia are trusting souls who just put an addition on their neat little house in order to accommodate their third child.

The "hard noses" say, "Everybody can't be promoted." The softies, who are only a little less lazy than Steve, say, "He could never get another job in this market." Or, "It would be a death sentence to shove him out of the nest now." The softies are a majority.

In the old days most people minded their own business and, though feelings were hurt in hundreds of little encounters, nobody got fired. Now Herm, who has a most unfortunate compulsion to agonize aloud, has made enemies of the hard noses, whom he has called "executioners," as well as of the softies, whom he has called "self-seeking chickens." Most of all, Herm Peikko is angry at the old chairman for not firing or at least sternly warning Steve years ago. He is also furious at Steve Kehr for putting him in this dreadful position. Herm turns pale and looks away when he encounters Steve, and they no longer speak.

Brooding about this matter has taken over a large part of Herm's life. His new lectures have been badly prepared, and he is unable to work determinedly on his second book. He has eczema on his wrists. Should he start taking Valium?

As was mentioned earlier, the cause, at once hidden and portentously looming, for the pessimistic discounting of the future and the decline in morale is the products of the graduate schools, those great flagships of academic expansion in the sixties.

We have already noted the enormous increases in financing from all sources for all sorts of higher education following Sputnik. The expansion in facilities was most dramatic for the graduate schools, which were the particular objects of federal largesse. The effect of the improved, expanded, and newly founded graduate schools can be seen in the increases in doctorates awarded by American universities. There were 3,290 doctorates awarded in 1939–40; 6,420 in 1949–50; 9,829 in 1959–60; 29,866 in 1969–70. Most forecasters expect that our annual output of doctorates will stabilize at between 30,000 and 35,000.

There was only a brief period in the middle 1960s when there were a few more academic jobs than there were people ready to fill them. The present oversupply of people ready, competent, and eager for professorial work is going to become ever larger. Allan M. Cartter, the academic demographer who in 1969 was one of the first to perceive that the graduate schools had indeed overexpanded (see note 4 to Chapter II), has projected that as few as 3,000 to 5,000 new Ph.D.'s may find faculty employment per year in the 1980s.[29]

These aggregate or gross statistics have already been made vivid in the individual universities. Members of the "search committees" of those few departments with a position or two to fill get far too many applications. An advertisement for a tenure-track (that is, a permanent position with the fifth year being the "review" or up-or-out year) appointment for a biologist at a four-year (that is, no graduate teaching) college in Louisiana brings forth 237 vitas. A one-year appointment at the University of Dayton to replace a geographer away on a Fulbright in Morocco flushes out only a few less. A famous linguist whose arrogance and opportunism has made him vigilant, intrepid enemies at the University of Texas and who used to move around a lot can no longer find a job opening elsewhere and must face harsh music for the remaining fifteen years of his career. Tenured professors no longer even seek other positions. Distinguished professors at Harvard and Berkeley have favored and perfectly credentialed students who must abandon the prospect of finding teaching jobs. There is scarcely an academic marketplace at all.

Allan Cartter has estimated that the median age of faculty members was thirty-nine in 1970. Due to tenure and the paucity of young people entering the professoriat, this means that the under-35 group will virtually disappear. A no-growth professoriat will lead to a median age of forty-eight by 1990. The professors of the universi-

ties are ever more becoming a conservative, unproductive geron-
tocracy. The professors of the 1980s will surely be more out of touch
with their students than those of the present. Everett Ladd and
Seymour Lipset have suggested:

> Other occupations more open to youth may come to the fore as
> sources of ideas and leadership for reform. There may also be an op-
> portunity for non-academic centers of research to take the lead in
> scholarly innovation, much as has occurred in other societies when
> universities have become stagnant.[30]

The only people who still are able to move from campus to campus now are business-wise, "tough" administrators. They know that
out there, clawing at the gates of the respectable and worse colleges
and universities, obsequious to the point of being prostrate, are
young people who not only are tough but who would consider
professorial jobs exceedingly desirable if the working conditions were
a great deal less comfy than they are for the incumbents. These potential rate-busters are far from being as casual about researching as
those who confidently began professorial work in the sixties. Grateful, with their eyes on the main chance, the new professors would
suck up to the hardheaded administrators, and after their installation, the featherbedding, make-work committees on the campus
would be yet more superfluous than they have been in the past.

Besides, the well-trained, eager-to-please young professor-aspirants probably have a great deal more in common with the students now occupying the campuses. The new Ph.D.'s are rock-music
wise, movie wise, and dope wise. Many would leap at the chance to
sign a contract for a twelve-hour teaching load promising a $10,000
salary after three years of hard work. The new Ph.D.'s would probably be gratified by assurances of successive, five-year contracts (assuming satisfactory performance at the end of each review period) in
the place of tenure. Even if professorial work loads, real wages, and
the perquisites were to revert back to what they were in 1959 (and
we recall that in 1959, working conditions for university professors
were not much different than before the First World War), much of
the psychic income would remain. The professorial job package
would still be preferable to high-school teaching, commission selling,
or penurious idleness—which are the alternatives facing thousands
of products of the great graduate schools who are more fit for the
jobs now in the grip of most college and university professors.

The old techniques for culling the numbers of job seekers have not worked and will not work nicely in the years ahead. Some professors in the graduate schools are attempting to set up additional qualificatory hurdles which might be summed up under the heading "higher standards." However, higher standards only increase the attractiveness to some people of the new Ph.D. who meets these standards compared to the lazy professor he or she would eagerly unseat. The lack of professional or scientific alternative employment has led, even in these uncertain times, to increases rather than decreases in graduate-school enrollments—for graduate school is an attractive haven for the intelligent unemployed. Few graduate deans or graduate professors will cut back. They want all the *other* graduate programs in their areas to decrease admissions by two thirds.

A department in a college or university that has a slot for a new Ph.D. may indeed set high standards for the professor for whom the administration gives them a "line." However, what happens far too often is that, if a dazzlingly intelligent, rapaciously ambitious, and subtly obsequious candidate were actually to be hired, the new employee would expose, terrify, and therefore unify to opposition the incumbents, who will compromise any professorial responsibility in order not to endanger their perquisites and comforts. It is most sad that what often happens is that a department replacing someone or even adding a position may actually hire a candidate who promises nothing distinguished whatever and so does not threaten the pathetic norms of those on the job. Hiring, even in view of the superior candidates available, can, especially in inferior places, go more easily to a loser than to a potential winner. We have no good reasons to assume that the readily available supply of well-trained, energetic young people ready for work is going to result in a more meritorious professoriat.

Underlying all the anxieties disclosed in this chapter are the weaknesses and uncertainties in the outside economy as well as a certain lassitude or even despair in the larger society. Inflation, overexpansion, stagnation in other areas of endeavor, and several varieties of social pathology have all intruded into the campuses as well. One can take fuel or energy costs as examples. A certain "Energy Task Force" in Washington announced late in 1975:

> As a rule of thumb in planning for 1976 energy costs, institutions which have relied on petroleum products or natural gas as primary energy sources should quadruple the unit price paid in 1969–70—the last year of stable national energy prices.[31]

The efforts of Kansas State University to employ new windmills or those of the University of Kansas to use heat from its burned trash are not going to help much. A "Higher Education Price Index" developed by the Department of Health, Education and Welfare recently showed that campus costs were rising only a little less rapidly than the consumer price index and several other indexes such as those for capital equipment costs and construction.[32]

These last two items were larger proportions of total college and university outlay than they are now. And campus costs would be rising very much faster if professional wages were to keep pace with the consumer price index. Well into the seventies, due to heavy financing, higher education bore up well under what the economists call the "cost disease"—that is, a progressive hemorrhaging of the exchequer caused by the utilization of a constant complement of workers to produce a constant product for which they get constantly better paid.[33] In other industries one expects entrepreneurs to raise productivity by substituting capital for labor. Professors now on the scene have resisted larger classes or the replacement of their live lectures by filmed or recorded performances of another specialist or even taped performances of themselves. Professors continue to demand complete control of their classes and object that teaching machines or films or TV hookups might make teaching impersonal and (worse) professors superfluous.[34] Everyone expects that higher education will remain unchanged, labor-intensive, and therefore very expensive.

As instructional costs remain high, energy costs, maintenance, and other fixed costs will demand larger wedges of the pie. Campuses are becoming more expensive for students and for national, state, and local fiscs just as the general society is becoming skeptical about the worth of a college degree in particular and the worth of universities in general.[35] Generous financing, particularly from some states, was still being forwarded in the mid-seventies. However, almost no one expects this to go on much longer.

The sharp increases in enrollments in 1975 and 1976 were widely believed to be temporary and a reflection of the shrunken job market —particularly for young people. These recent increases confirm that the campuses are ever more frankly being used as refuges for those unable to find satisfactory positions in the open economy.[36] The pool of available eighteen-to-twenty-two-year-olds will increase little if at all in the 1980s and 1990s. The colleges have already crowded in far more so-called "students" than they can possibly "educate" in any traditional way. Politicians in tune with their constituencies and their own consciences already encounter more urgent demands for revenues. Something will have to give on the campuses. It will probably be the professors.

Most of the campuses still look lovely. The signs of decay do not present themselves emphatically to the untrained, unseeking eye. Few professors or trustees worry at all about organized student radicalism now. The campus police have come to recognize that effective narcotics suppression is quite beyond their power and that the campus drug problem may never have been serious anyway. On the open campuses, thefts of bicycles and cars are common. Professors' offices are rarely vandalized as they occasionally were in the wild sixties, but they are often quietly relieved of their $500 electric typewriters and $750 desk computers by students possessing stolen master keys.[37] The University of Vermont abandoned intercollegiate football, but only occasionally does one hear that the trustees of a small institution are permitting their athletic programs to perish with dignity due to honest accounting. However, just as the pressure for evidence of scholarly or scientific research on the part of the professors is increasing, the financial position of the subsidized presses is becoming precarious. The University of Miami, facing a $3.3-million deficit, phased out its twenty-eight-year-old press. Others will follow.

Few professors support their own professional organizations—possibly because membership is considered expensive. It costs thirty dollars per year for someone earning $15,000–$19,999 to be a member of the American Historical Association, forty-seven dollars per year for membership in the American Psychological Association, twenty dollars for the American Society of Biological Chemists; thirty-five dollars for the American Chemical Society. Professors have not been paying these membership fees in sufficient numbers, and some of their blanket scholarly or scientific organizations are sickly. In order to keep functioning the Modern Language Association and the American Historical Association are cutting their services and dipping into their small endowments. The AAUP (the cost of membership for a professor earning more than $15,000 per year is thirty-six dollars) is facing a "difficult period" because memberships, which peaked in 1971 at 91,000 have been falling. Membership fell 6,000 in 1972 and 10,000 in 1973, and it has continued falling at a slower rate since then.[38]

All these things are indicative. Professors are only exceptionally motivated to such forceful activities as the writing of checks that would serve to raise the respectability and solidarity of their occupation. They are still unable to specify what the product is that they offer and, even if it were to be specifiable, whether it might be worth the cost. We have already returned to the old and normal condition of academic life, where there are not enough students and too many professors.

VIII

Reform?

Almost every conceivable scheme for reform in American higher education would result in fewer professors. This chapter will discuss some suggested changes in our colleges and universities likely to affect professors now on the job or of interest to people considering professorial employment.

There are already available discussions of American higher education that claim and probably demonstrate that our colleges and universities are not now imparting much of what one might broadly call traditional education. Most of our institutions of higher learning are rather in the business of conferring degrees which are indeed obtained by large numbers of American youths after the application of vastly varying amounts of preparation, devotion, and money. Among others, Caroline Bird in *The Case Against College* claims that most American students do not want either the education available or, for that matter, the degrees that mark the conclusion of the time put in. Bird also believes that, even where the education offered is very good and where the students work to acquire it, the degree celebrating the accomplishment of that education is still outrageously expensive and therefore is a "dumb investment."[1] Bird, I believe, coarsely attributes much of the expense and the claimed irrelevance of college to the professors, whom she views as the keepers of the gates that allow access to respectable positions in society. The blame for irrelevance and expense is more diffuse and lies deep in the American past and with the larger society. Americans have scarcely even looked for better ways to occupy the time, energy and imagination of youths aged eighteen to twenty-two. Admittedly, the ones on the campuses are better off than those (overwhelmingly of poor families) unable to find jobs of any sort or any acceptable formal programs to guide their growth and to channel their aggressions. In any case, nearly half of the age group from which the youths on the campuses come are the essential raw material that permits the professors to hold on to and to enjoy their jobs. Present student-faculty ratios considered, any alternative use of these middle-class young adults would reduce the number of college and university students and would therefore require a corresponding reduction in the number of professors.

We come back to a painful matter. Stated essentially and brutally, the great and enduring danger to the professors, and most especially just now, is the very attractiveness of their jobs to others. There simply are no occupations which combine such high prestige, low demands for measurable accomplishment, looseness of supervision, remarkable job security, and flexibility of working conditions in such extremely pleasant surroundings. Significantly, in studies of professional satisfaction, college professors always rank highest. Aside from a vague skepticism which may, in fact, be growing less vague, the most vital and perhaps ineradicable dangers to professorial incumbents are the many advanced students recently graduated or still working in the overexpanded graduate schools. Thousands of these well-trained and impeccably credentialed and recommended professor-aspirants would accept a great deal less than the perquisites of those middle-aged men who are still enjoying, if uneasily, rather soft and constantly interesting jobs. They would also be more docile when threatened by trustees with ideas or by cost accountants ordered to impose some performance criteria or other. What these hungry job seekers thus have brought about for the profession as a whole is the specter of a return to the employment conditions of 1959—or the normal condition in American colleges and universities in which there are far fewer jobs than there are competent people to fill them. If normal conditions prevail a few years longer (and this does seem likely), the Great Campus Craze of the sixties will become a subject for wistful nostalgia.

A strategy to lessen the deepening fears of the professors on the job might be deliberately to lessen the attractiveness of their employment. As Willard Quine, a professor of philosophy at Harvard, has observed:

> Vocation and amenity vary inversely. When academic life is hard, only the dedicated will put up with it. Allay the rigors and you draw men away from other occupations. The academic life, when eased of hardship, has other attractions besides pursuit of truth. It is clean and

somewhat prestigious work in pleasant surroundings, and the vacations are long. It is a continuation, even, of one's glorious collegiate youth.

Affluence was in some paradoxical ways counter productive, and, as we mourn its passing, we may console ourselves with that reflection.[2]

It would, of course, be sadistic to lessen the appeal of professorial jobs by requiring employed intellectuals to wear hair shirts or to put in an annual month or more (as has occurred from time to time in Red China) doing agricultural stoop labor. If rigors are to be imposed on the professors, they should be reforms of the sort that, while lessening the threats to them from potential rate-busters outside, would also increase the work accomplished by our academic intellectuals. Reform should also bring greater benefits to the students, the intellectual community, and the society at large. However, unless higher education were to take on entirely new tasks or to be radically restructured, all the usually suggested reforms would bring with them reductions in the numbers of professors needed for the job at hand.

If we were to increase teaching loads by one third, we would decrease the number of professors required (as well as the required offices and parking spaces) accordingly. Even if work loads were not increased so much for those few (mostly in two-year colleges) who already teach fifteen hours a week or for those very few (see Chapter VI) who are heavily engaged in productive research, a statutory minimum of twelve hours of teaching per week would probably render redundant at least 20 per cent of the present number of professors.

Similar observations and conclusions might be made for other proposals to use professors better, to make them do more work. Using campuses (and the professors on them) the year round or even lengthening the academic year to, say, ten months would bring either or both of two unappetizing alternatives: Students would graduate sooner (thus decreasing the quantity on hand at any time of the industry's principal material—students), or the course requirements for degrees (already assumed by most to be onerous already) would have to be increased.

Though not immediately apparent, other reforms that are occasionally proposed would also lead to decreases in the number of professors. At present the laziest 33 per cent of the professors now drawing regular checks are protected by confusion as to what the socially constructive tasks of the colleges and universities should be. They are also shielded by obfuscation as to what professional work is, and how that work is to be demonstrated, and by the institution of peer review (that is, judgment by other professors, usually within academic departments) as the basis and system for hiring, promotion, and tenure.

The official claim at colleges and universities is, as we have said, that professors work at educating, researching, and performing service for their various public constituencies. The case has already been made in this book and elsewhere that, on the whole, American colleges and universities work together to maintain existing class distinctions, to keep young people of the middle classes off the job market during their difficult years, and to give these young people degrees. In most of our institutions of higher learning, an elaborate and effective charade is enacted on the campuses across the country with "education" being directed at people who do not want it but who go through the motions of acquiring evidence for that education in order to qualify for degrees that are essential to obtain jobs for which those degrees are unnecessary.

It is likely that, provided alternatives and possibly more useful employment were found for the least educable third of American college students, education, research, and service at American colleges and universities would gain rather than otherwise by their departure. But, of course, smaller enrollments would require fewer professors.

We would hope that a weakening of departmental responsibility for hiring, supervision, and rewarding would, if reform were our object, necessarily have to be accompanied by job descriptions and performance criteria objectively and successfully applied. It is nearly always the case that departments actually hire, retain, and reward those who are comfortable and discreet and who do not threaten existing (and usually vague and minimal) levels of teaching, research and service.[3] Therefore, the assignment of specific tasks and the establishing of criteria by careful, fair, and responsible outsiders would necessarily result in the expulsion of a number of professors we can easily assume to be at least one third of the present work force.

Tenure has long been under attack. The removal of this guarantee would cause psychological carnage, if not sudden penury, and might be a draconic imposition on many persons unable readily to find similar employment or possibly employment of any sort. Another peril of the elimination or even effective weakening of tenure might be just the sort of crimes that some defenders of tenure fear. Who would fire whom when job protection was removed? Many crotchety, energetic, and noble men and women fear ideological firings by presidents, trustees, and crusading newspaper editors. If majorities were to rule in many departments, the best and therefore most threatening would go first. There are doubtless hundreds of chairmen and deans who would relish the elimination of tenure in order to heal quickly some festering old sores. Most professors are grudge carriers. Feuds whose origins are petty (the usual academic case) ought not to be settled by calamitous economic means. There do indeed exist some fine professors whose teaching is not readily evaluated or whose original and beneficial research is very slow to be born. Very good teaching and research potential are easier to denigrate or ignore than to prove.

A usual proposed alternative to tenure is renewable five- to seven-year contracts with a year or more of notice if, after a review, one's performance is found wanting. This would still offer greater job security than that in any other occupation. However, the uncertainty and livelier competition for five- or seven-year contracts would surely increase devotion to their tasks by the professors with jobs. Such a change would lessen the total number needed and so set gently adrift those who were unfit. Therefore, fewer professors.

There are alternatives or solutions to the present impasse of American higher education which propose maintaining or even increasing the number of professors. We might decrease the size of classes and thus increase the total number of classes—perhaps by a third or more. Or one could so structure degree requirements that students would be required to work more closely under professorial supervision and thus approximate the teaching atmosphere and the student-faculty ratios and cost per contact hour at the best (and presently most expensive) good little colleges. Or one could increase substantially the number of government-subsidized programs for poor children so that they too can have four years off to get "educated," to find themselves, and to cap it all off with a degree.

Alas, all of the above contain the assumption that large numbers of prepared and eager eighteen-to-twenty-year-olds are now being deprived of personalized education that they could use to better themselves and us. The contrary is true. Almost all of the American students now on the campuses or likely to be there in the years immediately ahead would like most to be left alone or, if forced to endure some degree-oriented class attendance, passively entertained at the level of a slick television offering.

Students might be less reluctant to submit themselves to higher education in its still dominant forms if that education were energetically and skillfully presented. As mentioned earlier, a part of the blame for the unappetizing nature of much college teaching (still overwhelmingly by means of lectures) is that the system that turns out apprentice professors provides at no stage in their preparation instruction in how to teach. There are available some rather detailed and reasonable suggestions for improving college teaching.[4] All sensible projects for improving college teaching demand that the professor think about what he is trying to do, that he consider the relevance of what he teaches, and, of course, that he work rather harder than is his custom. This might be a good partial solution.

Better teaching accompanied by harder work could also lessen the attractiveness of the jobs. Unfortunately, almost all of the workable suggestions for teaching come from the colleges of education, against whom the mandarins of the usual academic disciplines enforce a quarantine. Professors at the graduate schools who have turned out the great majority of the professors now on the job, and those now eager to take new jobs, should new jobs appear, are not going to permit educationalists to weaken their insistence on research—however irrelevant that research may be to the college student or however much of that "research" remains embryonic or only claimed.[5] Requiring that the professors now on the job begin the necessary introspection and self-discipline to improve their teaching is almost too visionary to consider. An enduring fault of our colleges and universities is that just what has been accomplished in the classrooms has not been subject to any kind of dependable scrutiny. Unless there is ahead of us a shakeup too thorough to imagine at present, the continued prestige of their calling is likely to permit the professors to continue to pretend that their advanced degrees and the fact that they have salaried positions certify that the service they provide in their classrooms, whatever that might be, is worth the very high price paid for it.

As an interim summary here: It seems now that the great campus boom of the previous fifteen years was in many ways an expensive mistake. A search for the villains is idle, for the great doubling in size was the product of something in the air around us. The cause was a regnant and unchallenged social and political ideology which positioned marvelous benefits for ever more higher education—benefits that could not possibly have been realized. It is possible to be more generous and claim that, even if the accomplishments in teaching, research, and service on the part of the newer and bigger and costlier universities have been disappointing—before, during, and after the boom the professors began their careers as men and women honestly devoted to the tasks of discovering, preserving, and advancing knowledge. While they enjoyed their perquisites, the professors did little harm to others and no harm to themselves. Perhaps the splendid facilities and their pampered staffs might be acknowledged as a worthy and conceivably even noble indulgence for an overrich and overoptimistic society. Throughout the period 1960–75, the universities altogether cost less than the quixotic space program. None of the magnificent new campuses of the State University of New York cost as much to build or to operate as one aircraft carrier.[6]

My purpose in this book has been honestly and vividly to inform. Since I have not been able to accept or to devise any reasonable schemes of reform that would preserve for the professorial occupation anything like its present amenities, prosperity, or numerical strength, in desperation I offer the following sketch for an overhaul of American higher education. My plan would preserve the number of professors, but, alas, not their present working conditions.

We could assemble an independent commission of public-spirited men, none of whom were at present college professors, who would consider the following proposals and the means slowly to put them into action:

I. Select about ten large universities and about fifty four-year colleges with incontrovertible records of excellent teaching and research and require that they function in the future almost exactly as they have in the past.

However, an important change in these institutions would be that one half of the students in these elite colleges and universities *not* be males from Protestant and Jewish families earning more than $25,000 a year. Students outside of these categories would have their education subsidized much as the present cadets at Annapolis and West Point.

II. Expand the junior- and community-college systems yet more, but raise the students' performance norms and severely limit the traditional academic or liberal-arts courses at these institutions, which would therefore be more honestly technical schools. Tuition at these places would be free, but the programs would become more rigid and practical.

III. Change the names of the other institutions—which are now called "colleges" and "universities" to "resorts." For example: The Resort of Indiana, East Tennessee State Resort, Morgan State Resort, Resort of St. Catherine, or Slippery Rock State Resort. The trained attendants at these thoroughly reorganized institutions might still be called "professors," but their work would be much altered. Their wages would remain high—just as they are at present, but they would have to be on the job eleven months a year and thirty hours a week.

The professors would lecture or otherwise teach nine hours a week. Before their series of lectures, which would be very much like the lectures customarily given at colleges and universities at present, the professors would publish their topics and course objectives and append to them suggested reading, practices, and experiments. However, traditional liberal-arts or professional education at the resorts would be solely on a take-it-or-leave-it basis; the professors would not be required to demonstrate any enrollments at all. For the students there would be no attendance requirements or credit awarded. The professors would, however, have to *offer* courses.

Professors would get ribbons, medals, and trophies awarded in public ceremonies upon publication of their research results, but the research would be done entirely on their own time, though at facilities provided by the resorts. In addition professors would be regularly examined to determine if they were abreast of their declared areas of scholarly or scientific competence in two languages besides English. Professors would be viewed somewhat more as a public resource than at present and would be on call to talk or to listen (expenses, but no honoraria) as a service to any public agency.

Professors at the resorts would assume many additional obligations. They would usher and punch tickets at a greatly increased number and range of movies, rock concerts, public lectures, plays, dances, happenings, and athletic events. All professors would undergo extra training in clinical psychology and be ready to counsel individuals or groups of troubled students. Professors would be on call for 2:00 A.M. bull sessions in the dormitories—but for these extraordinary duties they would get a double-time allowance. Professors would man (and woman) hot lines for the drug addicts, the alcoholics, the raped, the gays, the obese, the blacks, or any other group of youths that wanted a hot line or a drop-in center. Professors would also run the babysitting co-op, the speed-reading clinics, and the fitness programs.

Tenure would be available to those accepting a one-third cut in salary. Otherwise the faculty would be awarded successive three-year contracts, renewable a year before expiration.

The academic resorts would necessarily require large, well-trained, and well-rewarded security and maintenance forces, because like national and state parks, they would be declared and even advertised as open to the comings and goings and heavy use of all taxpayers whatever their age or social condition might be. However, only youths aged eighteen to twenty-five would be provided a total of thirty-two months (that is, the equivalent of our present four eight-month academic years) of room and board and pocket money for two hundred dollars a month while in residence at the resorts. Any youth of any social background could distribute his or her thirty-two months of subsidized residence any way he or she wished over the eight years allowed for those months of honest fun to be used up.

IV. The professional schools of medicine, dentistry, pharmacy, undertaking, engineering, education, and others would be halved in size or enrollments determined on basis of national needs. They would be separated from the resorts and attached administratively to the nearest community college, after which they would continue to function very much as they do at present. Each professor declared redundant at a professional school (perhaps from a table of random numbers suitable for application to the last digits of social security numbers) would be humanely retrained for employment at the resorts.

What I propose would make professors more useful and lessen the attractiveness of their employment, while still keeping professorial work more appealing than alternative careers outside the resorts. These proposals might even provide for steady increases in employment for the new type of useful academic attendants, who could still enjoy the psychic income from their privileged positions, the parklike work site, the constant presence of voluptuously appealing youths, and the reassurance of being addressed as "Doctor" or "Professor."

Whatever happens, it would be an act of gross barbarism to allow the splendid academic plants now in existence to deteriorate. And it would be unfair for the professors now trembling in their chairs to assume the bulk of the guilt for a *démodé* faith in higher education that was the natural consequence of a *démodé* social ideology and the public affluence that gave the faith institutional form. However soiled a lot of professors may have been pictured in this book, the entire group of more than a third of a million are the inheritors of an ancient and honorable calling devoted to the communication, discovery, and preservation of truth. Many thousands of professors now working in pleasant or not so pleasant circumstances do indeed perform their functions well. They teach, research, and serve energetically, devotedly, and successfully. The professorial class, more than any other, buys and reads books, defends and ennobles literacy, talks and listens, and, perhaps most importantly, fends off the rampant cultural cancer that is mass-market television. Turned loose too quickly into the hard, make-a-buck-or-perish world, many of the incumbents would be incapable of sweeping streets or selling shoes. Perhaps some of the unfit ones are a bulwark that should be maintained at some cost against the media-mush-mediocrity that could conceivably envelop us all.

For ecological reasons alone a lot of the professors—like the whooping crane, the alligator, and the adorable panda—none of which accomplishes a hell of a lot—should be preserved. Despite what was included in the jaundiced or skeptical parts of the book, professors are kindly—particularly to people who are not professors. Most seek to recognize and reward distinguished accomplishment by their students. They still stand for the maintenance and advancement of high culture as venerably conceived. The fact that on their committees it is more important to talk about a problem than to solve it is not without some redeeming value. We treasure some rare birds for the songs they sing.

However, the professors cannot remain as isolated as they have been from criteria of public responsibility. It is worth asking if there are special reasons to exempt professors from the market pressures that are a rod and a stimulant everywhere. Taxpayers, legislators, and trustees should be able to ask just what they have been getting for such staggering outlays. Students ought to ask more questions regarding the purposes their present courses or degrees serve. Professors might be expected to declare what they are supposed to be doing and how they are trying to do it.

Notes

I

1. Frederick Rudolph, *The American College and University* (New York: Knopf, 1962), pp. 193–200.

2. Ibid., pp. 47–48.

3. Laurence R. Veysey in his *The Emergence of the American University* (Chicago: University of Chicago Press, 1965), pp. 125–33, makes clear that most of the returning travelers exaggerated the extent to which the research was pure, the professors were free, and the teaching standards were high in the German universities.

4. Henry Adams, *The Education of Henry Adams* (Boston, 1906).

5. However, see the sections in Ernest Earnest, *Academic Procession* (Indianapolis: Bobbs-Merrill, 1953), pp. 220–29, and in Rudolph, pp. 373–93.

6. See Veysey, pp. 418–28.

7. Rudolph (pp. 207–12) stresses the importance of the decision in the Dartmouth College case in 1819 in assuring the independence of college governing boards from other public bodies.

8. For more on this, see Walter P. Metzger, "Academic Tenure in America: A Historical Essay," in *Faculty Tenure* (San Francisco: Jossey-Bass, 1973), pp. 93–159.

9. Theodore Caplow and Reece J. McGee, *The Academic Marketplace* (New York: Basic Books, 1958). The book is gripping not only because of its ironical style and sage recommendations, but because, though drawn from data more than twenty years old, the discussions of prestige and inefficiency are strikingly accurate for occupational conditions today.

II

1. See Seymour E. Harris, *A Statistical Portrait of Higher Education* (New York: McGraw-Hill, 1972), 435–43. Most comparative figures in higher education are comparisons of somewhat different quantities. Students in American and Soviet universities study subjects that are not considered university subjects in France or Great Britain. The figures

contain no allowances for the intensity or quality of higher education. In Canada and Germany, academic standards are high in almost all universities. In Brazil and in India there are scarcely any standards at all. Italy and Great Britain have institutions of varying quality. The United States has some of the best and some of the worst.

2. Ruml's influential writings on higher education began in 1955 and ended with his death at sixty-six years of age in 1960. His views are best summarized in his *Memo to a College Trustee* (New York: McGraw-Hill, 1959, 94 pp.).

3. Daniel P. Moynihan, "The Politics of Higher Education," *American Higher Education: Toward an Uncertain Future,* vol. II (*Daedalus,* Winter 1975), p. 131.

4. This campaign is an outstanding example of the maxim that one can prove anything with statistics. I am much indebted in the following discussion to the excellent article by Allan M. Cartter and Robert L. Farrell, "Academic Labor Market Projections and the Draft," in *The Economics and Financing of Higher Education in the United States: A Compendium of Papers Submitted to the Joint Economic Committee, Congress of the United States* (Washington, D.C., 1969), pp. 35–74.

5. *Teacher Supply and Demand at Universities, Colleges and Junior Colleges 1961–1962 and 1962–1963,* Higher Education Research Report, 1963-R3 (Washington, D.C.: National Education Association, Research Association, 1963, 86 pp.).

6. Cartter and Farrell, op. cit., p. 365.

7. Walter P. Metzger, "The American Academic Profession in 'Hard Times,'" *American Higher Education: Toward an Uncertain Future,* vol. II p. 37. Metzger adds, "A profession may fatten in a sickly way."

8. This is the thesis of Alain Touraine in his *The Academic System in American Society* (New York: McGraw-Hill, 1974). Touraine is a French sociologist.

9. Taken from Moynihan, op. cit., p. 129, who observes in an accompanying note (p. 146), "Federal outlays for higher education have been about proportional to the general increase in the Department of Health, Education and Welfare. From just over $20 billion fiscal 1964, it rose to just under $50 billion in fiscal 1969 to an estimated $110 billion for fiscal 1975."

10. Ibid., p. 130.

11. Quoted in ibid., p. 137.

12. *The Chronicle of Higher Education,* February 10, 1969.

13. Charles H. Anderson and John D. Murray, eds., *The Professors: Work and Life Styles Among the Academicians* (Cambridge, Mass.: Schenkman, 1971), p. 5.

14. (New York: Basic Books). Some qualifications are necessary. The

system held in the most prestigious universities and was slowly established again even in the newer places after 1972 or so.

15. One chronicler of the academic profession was quite dazzled and in 1967 gushed that in the previous five years, "Academic salaries skyrocketed [*sic!*] 21 percent, compared with only 13 percent increase in the manufacturing wage level." See David G. Brown, *The Mobile Professors* (Washington, D.C.: American Council on Education), p. 12.

16. Of course, Erich Segal, author of *Love Story*, went much too far and was effectively fired by Yale. However, several hundred lesser institutions would have forgiven anything for such extraordinary visibility.

17. *The Leaning Ivory Tower* (San Francisco: Jossey-Bass, 1973), p. 113.

18. "Life in a Yellow Submarine," *Harper's Magazine*, October 1968, 97–98.

19. *The Chronicle of Higher Education*, April 6, 1970.

20. Table in *The Chronicle of Higher Education*, October 27, 1969.

III

1. A good book on Parsons that reveals a great deal about lower-echelon academia as well is James D. Koerner, *The Parsons College Bubble* (New York: Basic Books, 1970).

2. "Temporary" quarters tend to remain in use. One cost-conscious administrator has claimed, "The only difference between 'temporary' and permanent buildings is that the 'temporary' ones are more expensive to maintain."

3. Pierre van den Berghe, *Academic Gamesmanship* (New York: Abelard-Schuman, 1970), p. 12.

4. Ben Morreale, *Down and Out in Academia* (New York: Pitman, 1972).

5. Kenneth E. Eble, *The Profane Comedy* (New York: Macmillan, 1962).

IV

1. Quoted in Allan Mazur, "The Socialization of Jews into the Academic Subculture," in Charles H. Anderson and John D. Murray, eds., *The Professors* (Cambridge, Mass.: Schenkman, 1971), p. 278.

2. For a rare and rather pensive view differently stated, but agreeing in essentials with what follows, see Aristides (pseud.), "Sex and the Professors," *American Scholar*, Summer 1975, pp. 357–63.

3. David P. Gardner, *The California Oath Controversy* (Berkeley: University of California Press, 1967), p. 248.

V

1. Theodore Caplow and Reece J. McGee, *The Academic Marketplace* (New York: Basic Books, 1958).

2. I must refer the reader again to Caplow and McGee's classic.

3. The University of Hawaii quit all visits to their campus when too many candidates were discovered to have faked interest in order to get a free trip.

4. Robin Higham, *The Compleat Academic: An Informal Guide to the Ivory Tower* (New York: St. Martin's, 1974), p. 22.

5. See "Who is the Fairest?" in Caplow and McGee, pp. 159–66.

6. Pierre van den Berghe, *Academic Gamesmanship* (New York: Abelard-Schuman, 1970), p. 74.

7. A visiting French professor once told the American who took him to lunch that at his home university in Clermont-Ferand the administration building was called *"le pannier des crabbes,"* "the crab basket."

8. The remarks of Slaunwhit, Blanchard, and Lilly (my creations) are lifted from Herbert B. Livesey, *The Professors* (New York: Charterhouse, 1975), p. 318.

9. New York *Times,* February 29, 1972.

10. Actually Yale only "suspended" him for a year. The whole Mills case surfaced just as Yale was being criticized for permitting the extramural, publicistic activities and substantial earnings of professors Erich Segal (*Love Story*) and Charles Reich (*The Greening of America*).

11. For these percentages I thank Professor Marcia Synott.

12. And at the major universities the proportion of Jewish faculty is highest. See Everett Carll Ladd, Jr., and Seymour Martin Lipset, *The Chronicle of Higher Education,* September 22, 1975, p. 2.

13. "About one quarter of the general population are Catholics, but they make up a little less than one-fifth of all faculty members and just over one-tenth of the faculty members at major research institutions." Ibid.

14. See Allan Mazur, "The Socialization of Jews into the Academic Subculture," in *The Professors,* ed. Anderson and Murray (Cambridge, Mass.: Schenkman, 1971), pp. 265–87.

15. *Academic Marketplace,* p. 111.

16. "The Second Sex in Academe," *AAUP Bulletin,* LVI, no. 3 (September 1970), p. 285.

17. "Women, presumably through some mix of discrimination and cultural imperatives, go against the grain. They start out from a higher socio-economic position and end up at less prestigious places." Ladd and Lipset, loc. cit.

18. "Women as a group occupy very much the same status as they did in 1967." *Chronicle of Higher Education,* September 29, 1975.

VI

1. Robin Higham, *The Compleat Academic: An Informal Guide to the Ivory Tower* (New York: St. Martins, 1974), p. 155. Richard Miller in his *Evaluating Faculty Performance* (San Francisco: Jossey-Bass, 1972) suggests nine categories for judging the quality of a professor's labor: teaching, advising, faculty service and relations, management (administration), performing and visual arts, professional status and activities, publications, public service, and research.

2. I should have stated much earlier, perhaps, that this has been the author's working assumption throughout. Hazardous perhaps, but I will stick with it. I am criticizing dimensions, performance, honesty. —R.D.M.

3. However, a "star" can be as threatening a rate-breaker as the man who publishes too much and may, for comparable reasons, be stabbed in the back by colleagues who resent him for "showing off."

4. Course titles taken from the 1975–76 catalog of Middle Tennessee State University, Murfreesboro, Tennessee.

5. J. H. Hexter, "Publish or Perish—A Defence," in *The Professors*, ed. Anderson and Murray (Cambridge, Mass.: Schenkman, 1971), p. 134. Italics in the original.

6. I might add Oscar Wilde's observation: "Education may be an admirable thing, but it is well to remember that nothing worth knowing can be taught."

7. Pierre van den Berghe, in his *Academic Gamesmanship* (New York: Abelard-Schuman, 1970), p. 89, remarks to a hypothetical beginner, "Your first book, even if it does not sell, probably adds $50,000 to your life income." He also adds, "Once you have attained the status of a full professor on the strength of a sizable bibliography, the marginal utility of further publications is minimal."

8. A ten-page article and a two-hundred-page book are both respectable even in "book fields."

9. Actually, the scare phrase "publish or perish" obscures the paucity of work accomplished in big research institutions as well. In a survey of how professors spend their time, the sociologists Everett Carll Ladd, Jr., and Seymour Lipset concluded that in "major" (which they left undefined) institutions 42 per cent of the professors had never published a book, 11 per cent had never published an article, and another 10 per cent had published nothing in the previous two years. "How Professors Spend Their Time," *The Chronicle of Higher Education*, October 14, 1975.

10. A term of denigration among the few "big producers" is "one-book-man," which describes in a nutshell someone who publishes his dissertation, gets tenure on the basis of it, and stops research or inquiry

thereafter. I cannot resist the temptation to add here the apocryphal story that at Union Theological Seminary the scare phrase is "Publish or Perish."

11. See Lionel S. Lewis, *Scaling the Ivory Tower* (Baltimore: Johns Hopkins University Press, 1975).

12. Others have remarked on the perils of distinction in the academic community. Higham (p. 252) warns the dramatizing teacher, "Become too successful in this respect and your colleagues will knife you in the back." Van den Berghe (p. 89) warns the untenured faculty member against "excessive" publication that may require "a special toned-down *vita* for internal use."

13. My thanks to "Professor X," *This Beats Working for a Living* (New York: Manor Books, 1974), p. 58.

14. See, for example, Jacques Barzun and Harry F. Graff's *The Modern Researcher* (New York: Harcourt, 1956) for the social sciences.

15. In some fields, such as engineering or other technical fields, the loss is costly due to undiscovered, duplicated work.

16. "Our survey confirms that American academics constitute a teaching profession, not a scholarly one." Ladd and Lipset, op. cit., p. 2.

17. This is the central theme of the articles assembled by Charles H. Anderson and John D. Murray in *The Professors: Work and Life Styles Among the Academicians* (Cambridge, Mass.: Schenkman, 1971).

VII

1. *The Chronicle of Higher Education,* November 10, 1975.

2. *The Chronicle of Higher Education,* February 9, 1976, p. 11.

3. Ibid.

4. See "Panel to Probe Decline in College Board Scores," *The Chronicle of Higher Education,* November 3, 1975, p. 10.

5. See "Drop in Aptitude Test Scores Largest on Record," *The Chronicle of Higher Education,* September 15, 1975, pp. 18–19. The same article notes that high-school grades for seniors have been steadily rising.

6. Characteristically, Spanish, the supposedly easiest modern language, declined little. Latin and ancient Greek actually increased—but from tiny enrollments to figures that were only a little less so.

7. *The Chronicle of Higher Education,* March 1976.

8. Caroline Bird, in *The Case Against College* (New York: David McKay, 1975), suggests that 75 per cent of the college students are either uninterested or incapable of college work as traditionally conceived. She distinguishes little between the ranks or selectivity of the colleges and universities.

9. Lionel S. Lewis, in *Scaling the Ivory Tower* (Baltimore: Johns

Hopkins University Press, 1975), says that, aside from enrollment figures, "there is evidence that what is known about someone's classroom performance is fabricated from gossip, rumor, ex parte evidence and other random and unreliable means of intelligence," p. 23.

10. See "University Courses in Learning to Read," *The Chronicle of Higher Education,* October 14, 1975, p. 7.

11. The "life experiences" listed helped one Roy Wagner get 30 of the 128 credits needed for the B.A. (which he got *summa cum laude*) at Fordham University. See "College Credits for Real Life," New York *Times,* August 3, 1975.

12. The University of Virginia still maintains its system, which was established in 1842. The only penalty is expulsion, and about ten students a year are expelled. See *The Chronicle of Higher Education,* September 2, 1975, p. 14.

13. See "Is a Crime Against the Mind No Crime at All? Undergraduate Plagiarists Are Heirs to the Now Sleazy and Dilapidated Romantic Ideal of Creativity," by Judith Plotz of the English department of George Washington University in *The Chronicle of Higher Education,* February 2, 1976, p. 32.

14. *The Chronicle of Higher Education,* April 26, 1976, p. 2.

15. For more on this, see Aristides (pseud.), "Sex and the Professors," *The American Scholar,* Summer 1975, pp. 357–63.

16. See "The Explosive Growth of 'Faculty Development,'" *The Chronicle of Higher Education,* November 3, 1975, p. 3.

17. A staff member of Kansas State's I.D.E.A. ("Instructional Development and Effectiveness Assessment") program said that much of his success in getting faculty co-operation was due to assurances that evaluation would not be used *against* a professor. "We no longer have calls from administrators saying, 'Can I get the poop on this guy?' because we don't give it out." Ibid.

18. Average for both sexes, all ranks, at all institutions for the academic year 1975–76. *The Chronicle of Higher Education,* February 9, 1976, p. 5. The average for male full professors at public universities was $25,403; the average for female instructors at public two-year colleges was $9,227.

19. A book being waved about by chairmen and academic administrators lately is Richard I. Miller's *Evaluating Faculty Performance* (San Francisco: Jossey-Bass, 1972). Miller includes an annotated bibliography on pp. 97–140.

20. "Only 4 percent indicate their interests lie heavily in research," Everett Carll Ladd, Jr., and Seymour Martin Lipset, "How Professors Spend Their Time," *The Chronicle of Higher Education,* October 14, 1975, p. 2. See also the evidence assembled by Lionel S. Lewis, op. cit.,

pp. 30–36, to suggest that less than 5 per cent of the academics are "highly prolific, major producers."

21. A detailed attempt at assigning "points" for a large range of legitimate sorts of professorial work can be found in Robin Higham's *Compleat Academic* (New York: St. Martin's, 1974), p. 272. Higham allows five points for each course taught each semester, twenty points for a book, two for each year of service on a committee or the faculty senate, and values of from one to ten for each of thirteen other professorial activities.

22. See John G. Kemeny, "The University in a Steady State," *American Higher Education Toward an Uncertain Future*, vol. II (*Daedalus*, Winter 1975), pp. 87–96. For more on tenure see *Faculty Tenure* (San Francisco: Jossey-Bass, 1973); a good bibliography is on pp. 259–69.

23. Statement given in full in *Faculty Tenure*, pp. 249–53.

24. See "Two Courts Limit Topics That Must Be Bargained," *The Chronicle of Higher Education*, February 17, 1976, p. 8.

25. There are several direct or implied attacks on unions for college faculties by the academic mandarins who contributed to the two volumes of *American Higher Education: Toward an Uncertain Future* (*Daedalus*, Fall 1974 and Winter 1975). See also the somber appraisal of the likely consequences of unionization on faculty quality by Lewis, op. cit., pp. 173–80.

26. Salary gains by women lagged behind those of men in the academic year 1975–76. See *The Chronicle of Higher Education*, February 9, 1976, p. 5.

27. Ladd and Lipset, "Faculty Income Favorably Compared," *The Chronicle of Higher Education*, October 6, 1975, p. 2.

28. We can assume that the 1975–76 figure would be higher. See ibid.

29. See the discussions in *Outlook and Opportunities for Graduate Education*, Board Report No. 6, 1975 (Washington, D.C.: National Board on Graduate Education), pp. 29–37.

30. *The Chronicle of Higher Education*, May 24, 1976, p. 16.

31. "Energy Costs Bleak for 1976," *The Chronicle of Higher Education*, November 3, 1975, p. 8.

32. For the fiscal year 1973–74, campus costs rose 8.6 per cent; consumer prices 8.9 per cent. "Unprecedented Price Pinch," *The Chronicle of Higher Education*, October 6, 1975, p. 1.

33. Walter P. Metzger, "The American Academic Profession in 'Hard Times,'" *American Higher Education: Toward an Uncertain Future*, vol. II, p. 30.

34. Ibid.

35. Caroline Bird in her *The Case Against College* may offer some shaky conclusions, but the statistical evidence she presents along the way

is convincing and frightening. College may have "paid" those who invested in college in the fifties and early sixties. It certainly does not "pay" now.

36. See "They're Putting Lids on Enrollments," *The Chronicle of Higher Education*, November 3, 1975, p. 1.

37. "Growing Crime Rate Worries Campus Police," *The Chronicle of Higher Education*, August 18, 1975, p. 8.

38. *The Chronicle of Higher Education*, January 27, 1975, p. 3.

VIII

1. See her Chapter IV, "The Dumbest Investment You Can Make." (New York: David McKay, 1975).

2. "Paradoxes of Plenty," *American Higher Education: Toward an Uncertain Future*, vol. I (*Daedalus*, Fall 1974), pp. 39–40.

3. This is the theme of Lionel S. Lewis in his *Scaling the Ivory Tower: Merit and Its Limits in Academic Careers* (Baltimore: Johns Hopkins, 1976).

4. See, for example, Kenneth E. Eble, *Professors as Teachers* (San Francisco: Jossey-Bass, 1972); Richard D. Mann et al., eds., *The College Classroom: Conflict, Change and Learning* (New York: John Wiley, 1970); William H. Morris, ed., *Effective College Teaching: The Quest for Relevance* (Washington, D.C.: American Association for Higher Education, 1970). All of these include bibliographies.

5. Kenneth Boulding, a distinguished economist now at the University of Colorado has noted that one reason for the low status of the educationalists and their projects is

> unquestionably the almost forced collegiality which the low status of schools of education imposes on them. This is perhaps the collegiality of the ghetto or the excluded community, but it operates nonetheless to reinforce existing mediocrities and to ensure that any distinguished achievement is ruled out and any distinguished achiever is chased out. One of the great tragedies of the university campus is that there is so little communication between the other disciplines and the schools of education.

"Quality versus Equality," *American Higher Education: Toward an Uncertain Future*, vol. II (*Daedalus*, Winter 1975), p. 301.

6. When I offered this observation to a retired admiral, he dismissed my argument with the remark: "Everything costs less than an aircraft carrier." —R.D.M.

Acknowledgments

In writing this book I used the work of many previous writers on American academic life. I also depended heavily on the compilations of the National Center for Education Statistics in Washington, D.C. One must give credit where credit is due. Therefore, all the footnotes.

The notes should lead the aroused reader to a lot of additional literature on American colleges and universities. There were four sources for the book that were especially rich and emboldening. The cold analysis of the French sociologist Alain Touraine in his book *The Academic System in American Society* (New York: McGraw-Hill, 1974) strongly buttressed my assumption throughout that our colleges and universities have always served to maintain the existing class structure. Caroline Bird's book *The Case Against College* may contain some sensational conclusions, but it establishes her claims that, for most students now on the scene, the American curriculum is irrelevant and unwanted and that, even in the case of a good match of student and the college, education is usually far too costly for the student and for those who do the subsidizing. *The Chronicle of Higher Education,* a newsletter published some forty times a year and intended mostly to inform academic administrators, is consistently informative and coolly objective. It is worth noting well that Touraine, Bird, and the editors of the *Chronicle* are not American professors. Lionel S. Lewis's *Scaling the Ivory Tower: Merit and Its Limits in Academic Careers* (Baltimore: Johns Hopkins, 1975) came to me too late to be incorporated adequately into my text. I claim that many professors are lazy, self-seeking, and frightened of an examination of what they do to deserve their pleasant working conditions and good salaries. I could do so more confidently with Lewis's book in hand.

I have used fellowships and grants to great advantage in my earlier publications—and I remain grateful. However, I wrote this one with the help of advances from my publisher. It was always useful to confer with my agent, Peter Matson, and my editors, Betty Prashker and Hugh O'Neill. Their suggestions for strengthening the book were helpful. My careful and constructive copy editor was James Ricketson.

I have been an assiduous collector of academic tales. Over the years many professors and students have offered me sincere and honest views about themselves, the profession, and the milieu. Since many of them unknowingly provided me with material that could be damaging to themselves or to particular third parties whom I have no wish to hurt directly, I have preserved their anonymity. Similarly, many administrators, professors, and students read all or parts of the book as it was being written. Many were distressed. Some objected to the jaundiced presentation. Almost all admitted the aptness of what I have declared or described, but told me that the preservation of their academic reputations required that their names be disassociated from my text. I can safely thank Helen K. Billings, Doris K. Holmes, Temple Ligon, Mike Lagrone, and Janet Parrish.